BEOWULF AND EPIC TRADITION

BEOWULF
AND EPIC TRADITION

BY

WILLIAM WITHERLE LAWRENCE

PROFESSOR OF ENGLISH IN COLUMBIA UNIVERSITY

HAFNER PUBLISHING COMPANY
NEW YORK
1961

PUBLISHED BY
HAFNER PUBLISHING, INC.
31 EAST 10TH STREET
NEW YORK 3, N. Y.

Library of Congress Catalog Card Number 61-8941

Printed in the U.S.A.
———
NOBLE OFFSET PRINTERS, INC.
NEW YORK 3, N. Y.

TO

GEORGE LYMAN KITTREDGE

Preface

BEOWULF occupies a unique position in the literature of Western Europe as the earliest poem of importance in any vernacular after the collapse of Roman civilization. It is the herald of modern letters, as the *Iliad* and the *Odyssey* are of classical letters, and it is not unworthy of comparison with those earlier and greater epics. Like them, it reflects the manners and ideals of an age which may with some propriety be called "heroic." Its chief adventures are as fantastic as any in the wanderings of Ulysses, yet its historical background affords an unrivalled picture of the early life of our pagan ancestors. Political and social conditions are as vividly and as truthfully set forth as if there were no demons lurking in the mists at nightfall, no dragon watching on the windy heights. But the main importance of a great poem must lie in its poetry. As to this, no apologies for *Beowulf* are necessary. The tale itself and the traditions encircling it have all the authority of centuries of story-telling over ale-cups and by winter firesides. Then, in a happy hour, it became the theme of a gifted poet, and received its final epic form. Although it deals with the exploits of Scandinavian heroes, it is a thoroughly English poem, written in the English language, in a verse and style characteristically English, and infused with the spirit and ideals of English folk. There is every reason why we of to-day who have inherited those traditions should know *Beowulf*, and appreciate it as a work of art.

Unfortunately, an understanding of it is difficult, even for the cultivated reader, without some special guidance. I am not one of those who think that appreciation of poetry comes alone through sensuous absorption in the impressions which it creates. I believe, on the contrary, that enjoyment of it is heightened as well as rectified by acquaintance with its literary antecedents and with the conditions that produced it. This is peculiarly the case with poetry so remote from modern life as Anglo-Saxon. But it is not easy to gain such special knowledge. A translation, however excellent, is not sufficient. Even for the practised mediævalist, *Beowulf* requires long and arduous study. The results of such study have hitherto been made very little available to the general reader. Admirable histories of early literature and excellent books of reference have often failed to do the poem justice, or even to state facts about it correctly. Many people, otherwise well informed about English literature, think of *Beowulf* as the crude expression of a barbaric age, not comprehending its beauty

and its artistry, its significance as an expression of
the first great age of English letters and as a picture of European life in the early Middle Ages. The
poem has seemed doomed to remain to a large
extent the possession of scholars, a sealed book excepting to the initiated.

With this situation in mind, I undertook the
present volume, about ten years ago. I have been
constantly occupied with *Beowulf*, in teaching
and investigation, for some twenty-five years, and
I have published a considerable number of studies
intended only for specialists. Yet I have always
been allured by the prospect of writing a book for
those interested in the poem as literature. I believe that this is quite as much needed at the present time as further detailed investigation of un-
solved problems. It is far easier to write a book for
scholars, buttressed with sapient and lengthy notes,
than it is to present highly technical and disputed
matters in readable fashion. But it is through such
synthesis that research gains final justification.

My task has been greatly simplified by the appearance of *Beowulf, an Introduction to the Study
of the Poem*, by Professor R. W. Chambers of the
University of London, one of the most learned,
exhaustive, and judicious contributions ever made
to the study of early poetry. Disputed questions
are analyzed, theories summarized, documents reprinted, and elaborate bibliographical apparatus

provided. Like an older warrior, Professor Chambers has offered complete equipment and sage advice to those about to make their maiden venture into the perilous lists of *Beowulf* criticism.

It would be worse than fruitless to attempt a second time what has already been accomplished with so much distinction, and a poor return for the honor which Professor Chambers has done me in his dedication. But the main object of my book is quite different. His *Introduction* is addressed primarily to the scholar and the student; in the phrase of a discriminating reviewer, it is "prolegomena for an expert." This volume, on the other hand, makes its appeal to those who wish to gain a sound knowledge of *Beowulf* so far as it may be done without an understanding of Anglo-Saxon, and to those who are just beginning a reading of the poem in that language. It is concerned with the fruits of research, rather than with the processes by which those fruits have been ripened and gathered. It presupposes no knowledge of the Middle Ages. It does take for granted, however, a willingness to read the epic itself with care, and to spend considerable time and thought in endeavoring to comprehend its peculiarities and the remote and unfamiliar civilization which it reflects.

Moreover, I have restricted myself, in the main, to a single avenue of approach. What, after all, is the greatest difficulty experienced by the modern reader of *Beowulf?* It is, I think, — apart from the language, which is cared for by translation, — the lack of acquaintance with the great traditional stories which men of early days knew by heart; with the contents of those stories, the ways in which they were perpetuated from generation to generation, and the customs and ideals which informed them. My aim in the following pages, then, is to review the subject-matter of the poem, both the main plot and the chief subsidiary material, and to show how this appears to have been gradually combined into an epic, giving due attention to the social and political background. I have called the book *Beowulf and Epic Tradition*, but I have aimed, not at the separate treatment of a specialized subject, but at that information which the reader most needs.

The difficulties in writing this volume have been far greater than I anticipated. Many important questions are still unsettled, and the steering of a safe course between rival theories is always hazardous. My decisions will naturally not always command assent. But my general aim has been conservative: to utilize the results of the best and latest research without admitting doubtful or hypothetical conclusions. Outworn and discarded views have received scant attention, or none at all. Conjectures, however brilliant, which lack reasonable proof have been omitted. I have not hesitated to repeat much that is familiar to every specialist, but this has often cost much labor in clearness of statement. A good deal of chapters IV, V, VI, and VII is based upon my own published researches, and chapter VIII reviews afresh the whole development of the material from its origins to its final epic form. I have tried to be as severe with myself as with others, and not to allow my own published conclusions a place unless they have stood the test of criticism. Moreover, I have refrained from advancing any new theories of my own. I have, of course, not traced the transmutations of epic narratives in detail; this would be of little interest save to the specialist, and would require far more space than the present volume affords. The temptation to illustrate by extracts from early literature has generally been resisted; the uninformed reader is not always enlightened by being confronted with unfamiliar material, and attention should be concentrated upon the poem itself. Quotations have been sparingly introduced, in order to save space, but frequent references to line-numbers have been added. I assume that the reader will always have the original or a translation at hand, and that what is said here will be subordinated to careful reading. I have used the second edition of the Wyatt–Chambers text (1920), indicating the places where I have departed from the decisions of those editors. The quantities of vowels have not been marked, excepting in quotations or titles. Some information in regard to editions, translations, and the soundest and most helpful commentaries has been added. This bibliography might of course be indefinitely extended. The notes, which will be of service to the more advanced reader, consist of brief comments on points not fully developed in the body of the book, and references to special discussions elsewhere. It should be understood that these notes are merely suggestive, and that much which would be in place in a monograph has been omitted. Genealogical tables, and an outline of the whole poem, will be found in appendices.

Finally, I hope that this volume may be of use to advanced students, even if that is not its main object. The danger in technical investigation is that one gets to see details rather than the picture as a whole. Those engaged in research may gain something from a statement of ultimate results, if only by way of comparison with their own conclusions.

I am indebted to several friends. The late Professor William Henry Schofield first suggested that I write this book, and criticized a portion of an early draft of it. Dr. Henry Goddard Leach has given me information in regard to the *Saga of Samson the Fair*. I have been assisted in various ways by my colleagues, Professor Brander Matthews, Professor George C. D. Odell, and Professor Dino

Bigongiari, and especially by Professor George Philip Krapp and Professor Harry Morgan Ayres. I owe much to the unwearied interest and the illuminating suggestions of Professor George Lyman Kittredge. My greatest obligation, which cannot be stated in detail, is to the multitude of scholars whose patient labor has made such a book as this possible.

A few minor alterations have been made in printing the second impression. These concern details which were overlooked in the proof-reading, and statements which may be made with greater caution. I must repeat that I have been obliged to decide according to my best judgment many points a discussion of which the scope of the present book does not permit.

W. W. L.

January, 1930

Contents

Contents

BEOWULF

1

INTRODUCTION

SIR WILLIAM TEMPLE, in his essay, *Of Poetry*, expressed the opinion that "Gothick" verse "was of a raving or rambling sort of Wit or Invention, loose and flowing, with little Art or Confinement to any certain Measures or Rules," though with "a sort of Gingle that pleased the ruder Ears of that People." We may smile at this, and forgive Sir William, when we reflect how little his contemporaries understood such matters; but we ourselves sometimes underestimate the highly conscious and formal artistry of mediæval vernacular poetry. The conception of the earlier Middle Ages as a barbarous era, with learning dead, and literature moribund, was so long accepted that some vestiges of it have survived even to the present day. In the very beginning, then, we must agree to judge *Beowulf*, the first great poem in a vulgar tongue in the "Gothick" period, not as the improvisation of an untutored minstrel, but as a well-considered work of art, composed according to strict rules by a well-trained poet.[1]

Anglo-Saxon verse was, of course, as much confined by "measures and rules" as that of Dryden or of Pope, and it was deeply rooted in the traditions of professional singers, the main features of whose craft were shared by the poets of the other peoples of Germanic stock. The details of its metrical system are imperfectly understood; its rhetorical features are easier to grasp. Clearly, so far from being in any way primitive, it was over-elaborate, on its way to decadence. Variation and repetition were too freely and too mechanically employed; set epic phraseology too often took the place of inspiration. The art of the singer was coming to resemble that of a worker in mosaic, placing in new combinations pieces ready to his hand. "Love of style," says Dr. Ryder, in commenting on *The Little Clay Cart*, "slowly strangled originality and enterprise in Indian poets, and ultimately proved the death of Sanskrit literature." [2] A similar fate, aided by other causes, was in store for Anglo-Saxon. *Beowulf*, the finest extant example of this poetry, shows less exaggeration in rhetorical artifices, but enough to bear witness to their dangers. Although derived to a large extent from popular sources, as were the lays of the *Poetic Edda* or the lyrics of the troubadours, it is, like them, extremely conventional, the product of an *ars poetica* of settled principles and careful development.

Moreover, it is highly sophisticated and aristocratic, essentially a courtly epic. It was no wild outpouring of adventure for the ears of the vulgar, but an elegant entertainment for a royal circle.

The conjecture has been made, on the basis of its didactic quality, that it approaches a "mirror for princes," giving instruction in the virtues that should distinguish royalty.[3] This, I think, is a mistake; Anglo-Saxon poets, like those of Germanic stock generally, were incurably hortatory; they looked upon the pointing of a moral as one of the best adornments of a tale. There can be no doubt, however, of the aristocratic temper of *Beowulf*. In the seventh and eighth centuries the English people were divided, as their ancestors on the Continent had been, into petty "kingdoms," sometimes coalescing into larger units, but chiefly occupied in fighting native tribes and quarrelling among themselves. The great common disaster of the Viking ravages had not yet come to solidify them into a nation. This essentially tribal society, like that of many a people in a much more primitive stage of culture, was highly formal. It was hedged about by rigid taboos and conventions. Its insistence upon etiquette was as great as that at the court of Queen Elizabeth; its conceptions of duty as rigid as those of the Puritans. Although the historical characters in the epic flourished some two hundred years earlier, they are represented according to the manners of the seventh or eighth century. It is really not a picture of the ruder life on the Continent, but of the more civilized courts in the north of England. The fundamental basis of the

social order was, however, the same. In his attitude toward all this the poet is not in the least
naïve. His feeling for the historic past is, in its
way, as sophisticated as that of Gibbon for the
Roman Empire. His main plot was taken from old
tales about demons and a dragon. But these have
assumed epic dignity by virtue of their setting;
they do not appear incongruous with historical
heroes. The whole must be taken, if the parallel is
not too far pressed, in the same way as the poems
of Chaucer more than six centuries later, as the
work of a man familiar with courts, and writing for
a courtly audience.

The subject-matter of the epic, like its metre and
its rhetoric, was traditional, the stock-in-trade of
the professional poet, which had been handed
down from generation to generation. The unknown author was, to the best of our knowledge, a
contemporary of the Venerable Bede, who died in
735. Some two centuries had passed since an age
of warlike achievement which had crystallized
into legend, into tales which had become, with the
passage of time, the common heritage of singers
and audiences alike. These had been brought to
England, where they appear to have been perpetuated by oral transmission in the form of epic
lays. Out of this pagan material the poet of *Beowulf* constructed his epic, and this remains the
backbone of his work, along with the folk-tale plot.

But new influences in England were affecting him deeply, and giving to his poetry a new coloring. These influences, it is to be observed, were themselves in the direction of formal artistry, of literary models rather than of oral tradition, so that his poem is an even more conscious and cultured production than it would have been had it followed the fashions of earlier story-telling alone.

This change was, of course, the introduction of Christianity among the Anglo-Saxons, upon which followed a remarkable interest in letters. In the seventh century the Irish monks were active in the north, and their preaching was fortified by that of the celebrated mission of Augustine, which in the same century extended its efforts effectively from its headquarters in the south to the Anglian kingdoms in the north. The Irish monks were scholars as well as missionaries; their schools were famous, and they taught their converts the best that had remained of classical letters. The Roman churchmen, too, brought with them a knowledge of Latin and Greek, a love of books and learning, not only establishing ecclesiastical foundations noted for scholarship, but keeping closely in touch with the best that the Continent had to give. The result was that England came to lead the world in humane letters. When Charlemagne looked about for a scholar to direct his palace school and combat heresy, he chose, not a Continental scholar, but the celebrated Alcuin, a product of the Cathedral school at York. It was not a day when barbaric verse, pure and simple, commanded such enthusiastic hearing as that touched with the spirit of the new learning. But the technique of pagan poetry survived, as the normal means of expression in the vernacular. The church naturally discouraged heathen traditions, and supplied its converts with themes drawn from Christian and classical letters. Tales of strange adventures and fierce contests in the dim past were too well loved to be lost, however, and *Beowulf* is the great example of how such tales continued, with such alterations as would make them acceptable to the Church. The most striking of these alterations, which we shall consider in a moment, was the avoidance of all references to heathen deities, and the envelopment of the whole in an atmosphere of Christian piety. How far the new acquaintance with classical literature affected the poet of *Beowulf* is more difficult to estimate with certainty. The verse-men of the seventh and eighth centuries who turned to Biblical and classical themes were influenced by the style of their models; it seems unlikely that the poet of *Beowulf* could have remained unaffected by the new learning which was all about him. Did he imitate the *Æneid*, consciously or unconsciously, or are the resemblances between this and his work accidental? These are questions that must be discussed later.[4] The main point to keep in mind is that the natural tendency of the time was to add to pagan artistry a new element of sophistication from learned sources.

Had Christianity not come to Britain and controlled the activity of its poets, we might have had a *Beowulf* with a heathen mythology, like the lays of the *Poetic Edda*. The art of the Germanic professional poet, which we can study from the precepts of the *Prose Edda*, consisted not only in memorizing great traditional stories and controlling a variety of metres and rhetorical expressions, but in an intimate knowledge of the gods and goddesses, great and small. It is a blemish on the Anglo-Saxon epic that the newly learned Christian piety crowded this out, not only because of the incongruity of representing the wilder heroes of the Migration Period as swayed by the gentle precepts of the Church, but because this is on the whole so awkwardly done. The religion of the characters seems imposed upon them rather than natural to them. The poorest and weakest parts of the poem are to be found among the definitely Christian passages. The only thing that is naïve about the poem is its theology. Here is untried material, and a childlike attitude toward a new faith. Tradition had not yet taught the poet how to treat it with technical assurance. But, though ever present, the Christianity is all on the surface. The real vitality of the epic lies in its paganism.

It appears altogether probable that *Beowulf* was composed pen in hand, or written from the poet's dictation. Undoubtedly the traditions of the professional poet, as these had been handed down through the centuries, were largely concerned with verse unwritten and perpetuated orally. Improvisation was not an accomplishment but a requirement; the well-trained singer was expected to lift up his voice at short notice whenever he was requested to do so. All the indications seem to point to the transmission of historic and legendary material from the Continent to Britain in memory, in rhymed form. But our poet was living in a very different time from his predecessors. The new and convenient art of writing introduced by the Christian missionaries, and the constant study of written texts, would certainly have made it easy and natural to transfer composition in the vernacular to the written page. Such must have been the case with the Biblical paraphrases belonging roughly in the era of our poet, which, though associated with the name of the rustic Cædmon, are the work of different clerics, and with the legends and lives of saints versified according to the old rules of pagan poetry by Cynewulf and his contemporaries in the later eighth century. We do not know whether any Germanic poem of the epic amplitude of *Beowulf* existed before the introduction of Christianity. It is quite possible that none did exist, and that the plan and general execution of the whole was suggested by Vergil or other classical models, — in short, that *Beowulf*, like the *Æneid*, is a book-epic. Decision in regard to these matters is difficult; dogmatic statements are impossible. No one familiar with the ability of primitive peoples to compose and retain in memory long epic narratives will deny the possibility of this for Anglo-Saxon; but it does not seem probable for *Beowulf*, composed in the golden age of Anglo-Saxon learning, and stylistically far removed from communal verse.[5]

We first reach certainties with the tenth century, in which, for palæographical reasons, the extant and unique manuscript of *Beowulf* may be placed. The usual "round date" given is the year 1000. The whole codex consists of two separate sections bound together; and our epic is only one of the pieces in the second section; it is preceded by a fragment of a life of St. Christopher, an account of the *Wonders of the East*, and a version of the *Letter of Alexander the Great to Aristotle*, all in prose, while a part of a metrical version of the apocryphal *Book of Judith* follows it. The three pieces preceding, and the first 1939 lines of the epic, are in the writing of one scribe, and the remainder of *Beowulf* and *Judith* in that of another. This shows us immediately, what we should infer for many other reasons, that the extant version is only a copy. The language is, in the main, West Saxon, but the presence of many Anglian forms indicates that, like almost all extant Anglo-Saxon verse, the epic was originally composed in a northern dialect. The great poetical period of Anglo-Saxon letters, the eighth century, was rudely terminated by the Viking invasions; but the best productions of the north were preserved by being transcribed into the West Saxon dialect in the south, after Alfred and his successors had freed that part of the island from the mounting tide of Scandinavian occupancy. One likes to associate the copying of *Beowulf* with the brief revival of letters in the days of Dunstan and Æthelwold, when native culture was revived for a brief time before becoming completely submerged. The linguistic evidence in the manuscript is not sufficient to indicate the exact district or kingdom in which the poem was first composed. The varied dialectical forms may be due in part to the individual peculiarities of scribes. Some extreme southern — Kentish — forms are observable. There may, indeed, have been several copyings before the poem reached its present form in the extant manuscript. Evidence in regard to the original date of composition is equally unsatisfactory. Linguistic, grammatical, and metrical tests must be taken with great reserve, but so far as they go, they support the evidence of the style and treatment of the subject-matter in pointing to North-

umbria or Mercia in the late seventh or early
eighth century.

It is to be noted that the epic is substantially
complete; out of a total of 3182 lines only about a
dozen are hopelessly damaged (2215–2220; 2227–
2230; 3151–3155). The opening and closing lines,
which in early manuscripts are often missing or imperfect, are in excellent shape. This is of course
due to the fact that *Beowulf* is protected by the
pieces preceding and following in the codex. The
scribes were careless, and made many mistakes.
Obvious errors abound; letters, words, and sometimes whole half-lines are missing. Corrections
have occasionally been made, and letters freshened
up, not always happily. Punctuation, spacing,
syllabic arrangement, and the marking of vowel-
length are all provokingly inconsistent. The whole
is of course written as prose, for economy of space,
but there is no difficulty in rearrangement in lines
of alliterative verse. The division of the whole into
an introduction and forty-three sections of unequal
length, indicated in the manuscript by Roman
numerals in the margin, is puzzling, since the arrangement is not always in accord with canto division as we understand it. An ingenious theory [6] has
been advanced to account for this numbering, but
the older explanation still seems most probable,
that it really does represent a division into cantos,
perhaps with some inaccuracies in copying. The

matter is of no great consequence; the divisions may well be merely the work of some scribe, and they may safely be neglected by the modern reader.

Beowulf was perhaps esteemed and recopied in the Anglo-Saxon period for quite other reasons than those for which we prize it to-day. The material with which it is associated in the codex may give us a hint of those reasons. The *Wonders of the East* and the *Letter of Alexander the Great to Aristotle* describe marvels fitly to be grouped with Grendel and his dam, with the dragon and water-monsters of *Beowulf*. Alexander was especially interested in informing his tutor Aristotle about strange beasts and dragons in the East. It may seem odd to think of *Beowulf* as having been valued for its information about natural history, but there would have been nothing strange about such an attitude of mind in the tenth century. The Church abhorred monsters, but lost no chances to learn more about them. Possibly, too, Beowulf may have seemed, to those who copied his adventures, like the hero of a pious tale or a saint's legend. The slaying of Grendel, an evil spirit descended from Cain, and of the dragon, gives him somewhat the character of·St. George, whose dragon contests in Libya were so alluring to the English that they made him their patron saint. In the story of Judith, freeing her people from the menace of Holofernes, told in the fragments following *Beowulf* in the codex, we may see a parallel to the exploits of Beowulf, freeing his own people from a dragon, and the Danes from their resident demons. Beowulf's piety, and the favor shown him by the Lord, are constantly stressed as in the typical saint's legend. Although the Christian veneer seems the least admirable part of the poem, from the literary point of view, it may, by a curious irony, have saved the whole from destruction, in days when many a bonfire of old manuscripts was lit for the faith.

An interesting autograph, "Lawrence Nowell," written at the top of the first page of the codex, shows that this must have belonged to the scholarly Dean of Litchfield, who died in 1576, the author of an Anglo-Saxon dictionary, and the writer of various studies on early literature. Nowell left no evidence, however, that he realized the value of his possession. The manuscript later passed into the hands of Sir Robert Cotton, the celebrated antiquary of the days of Queen Elizabeth. His library was a favorite resort of literary men; Ben Jonson was a frequent visitor, and Bacon gained from it much of the material for his *History of Henry the Seventh*. No stretch of probability is required to imagine Shakespeare looking curiously at the volume. Sir Robert kept his books duly lettered and numbered, in a series of cases surmounted by busts of Roman emperors, with Cleopatra and Faustina on the distaff side; so the manuscript is still known, from the bust of the Emperor Vitellius on the bookcase, as "Cotton Vitellius A xv." After the death of Sir Robert Cotton in 1631, his magnificent library was moved about London, first to Essex House in the Strand, then to Little Dean's Yard, Westminster, where, a hundred years later (1731), it was badly damaged by fire. Fortunately the *Beowulf* codex escaped with a scorching. On the foundation of the British Museum in 1753, it found at last a safe and permanent resting-place.

The late recognition of the importance of *Beowulf* as a piece of literature may have been due in part to its position in the codex, virtually buried in less important material. Carelessness and imperfect knowledge were also partly responsible. When the antiquary Humfry Wanley published a summary of the subject-matter, with a transcript of the opening lines, in the celebrated *Thesaurus* of Dr. Hickes, in 1705, he got things very wrong indeed. Neither Wanley nor Hickes seems to have had any idea of the importance of the poem. The honor of printing the first edition (1815) and of making the epic known to the world belongs to a Dane, Grim Thorkelin, who journeyed to England, copied the manuscript, and employed a transcriber to make a second copy. He thought mistakenly that *Beowulf* was a Danish poem which had been translated into English, and he took pride in the conviction that he was restoring to Denmark (though he had himself been born in Iceland), after a lapse of more than a thousand years, a genuine native epic. Despite inaccuracies, his work was of great value. It made the poem accessible to scholars, and preserved a record of the manuscript at a time when it was in far better shape than it is to-day. With the work of the first English editor, Kemble (1833, 1835), the poem was fairly started on its modern career. Only through a series of happy accidents has it survived at all, which suggests that unhappy accidents may have destroyed much other early verse that would give us equal delight to-day.

It is convenient to call the man who composed the epic, essentially as we have it, the *Beowulf* poet. In using this term we shall not forget that additions and alterations may have been made in his work, in the course of later copyings and transference to another dialect, and that, in a sense, the multitude of men who shaped and reshaped, through succeeding generations, the old tales that he utilized, also have a claim to authorship. The immediate sources from which he drew have of course perished, but there can be no doubt, as already suggested, that he was only giving final form to extant narrative material. He was no more original in subject-matter than Shakespeare or Molière. Just how he worked, on the basis of current songs or lays, what form these had assumed, and whether they were circulating in Britain in oral or written form, or both, cannot be determined. It seems clear, however, that such epic lays existed. The *Fight at Finnsburg*, which forms so interesting a supplement to *Beowulf*, appears to belong in that category, despite the fact that its beginning and end are missing. But the epic is no mere patchwork, nor is it possible to isolate older lays in it. Many critics of the later nineteenth century thought otherwise, following the prevailing theory that popular epics could by careful scrutiny be resolved into their component parts. The apparent success of this theory as applied to Homer and the *Nibelungenlied* led to its application to *Beowulf*, and to daring and positive results. In a modified form belief in the possibility of demonstrating multiple authorship has continued down to the present day. Such analyses often throw light on the structure of the poem, but their chief service has been to show its unity. The results reached by different scholars do not agree, nor do their "lays" square with what we know of early popular poetry. The fashion of the epic song is one thing; that of the leisurely and extended epic, another. Tests of language, style, and metre fail to show differences between parts of the poem supposedly from the hands of separate composers. Inconsistencies and repetitions are found in most long poems, and repetition, in particular, is an ingrained stylistic characteristic of Anglo-Saxon verse. Sometimes the poet has even introduced varying and irreconcilable accounts of the same event, as in the descriptions of the burying of the dragon's treasure in the final adventure. But this does not mean that we can segregate two separate songs on the subject. The voice of Kyd sounds now and again from the lines of *Hamlet,* but no one can distinguish accurately the lines written by the elder dramatist. Much more weight is attached by modern critics to the individual plan and execution of the *Beowulf* poet, who subdued existing narrative material to a controlling artistic purpose of his own. The creation of any work of art defies exact analysis of the elements that compose it.[7]

The "plot" of the epic, stated briefly, reads like a wonder-tale. Beowulf, prince of the Geatas, puts an end to the ravages of the demon Grendel, who for twelve years has nightly haunted the hall of Hrothgar, king of Denmark, killing and eating Hrothgar's warriors. In a second combat, Beowulf kills the demon's dam in her abode beneath the waters. In his old age, he fights against a dragon that has attacked his people, and dies in delivering them from the scourge. A more elaborate outline of the epic quickly assumes a very different character, however; it becomes historical and realistic, with long episodes, shorter digressions, passing allusions to legend, scenes of court life, and genealogizing. The opening passage sets the keynote; first of all, instead of a description of the demon, or of the hero, or even of the haunted hall, the ancestors of the Danish monarchs are enumerated, with particular emphasis upon the coming and the funeral of Scyld, the founder of the Scylding line. Or, for another test, observe the way that the dragon episode is told, with the accounts of how men of early days first gathered the hoard, and the long digressions setting forth, in detailed fashion, the feuds of Geatas and Swedes through three generations. Meanwhile, as so often, the main action of the poem waits, cap in hand, until the historical reminiscences are over.

A sharp separation of these two main currents of interest, the supernatural and the realistic, which naturally suggests itself, and which has long been traditional, is justified by all we can learn of the actual growth of the epic. By one of the accidents of story-telling, and long before the composition of our poem, a Jack-and-the-Beanstalk hero, Beowulf, the "bee-wolf" (that is, "bear"), — a boy with an animal strain in his parentage or rearing, like so many early champions, — was elevated, with his double exploit of killing two trolls, one in a hall and the other under water (a narrative which forms the substance of a widespread folk-tale), into a circle of dignified historical personages. Either before or after this combination, he was also made a dragon-

slayer. Both popular tale and historical setting retained their individuality. Many traces survive of
the hero's primitive character, after he has been
made over into a Germanic prince. Supernatural
strength in wrestling and swimming, and supernatural ability to exist under water, are still his
own. The story of his slothful and ignominious
boyhood, known to folk-lorists as "the male Cinderella" theme, was not discarded. The bright and
beautiful prince "was for a long time in no estima-
tion, the warriors of the Geatas did not account
him good for anything, nor was the lord of the
Wederas minded to assign him an honorable place
on the mead-bench; they were convinced that he
was sluggish, an unwarlike ætheling" (2183-2188).
On the other hand, the historical material is no
mere background. It is vital to the story, and must
have been so in earlier versions of more popular
character. It lends to the rather childish contests
with monsters a plausibility not found in folk-
tales, and provides an interest which, if secondary,
is hardly less absorbing than the main plot. In the
final epic version the champion of fireside yarns has
become a model hero, versed in etiquette, eloquent
in speech, a wise and temperate ruler. It increases
the dignity of the demons and the dragon that so
admirable a prince should condescend to slay them.
The amalgamation of folk-tale and historical tradition, then, while not absolutely complete, has pro-

duced a species of narrative distinct from either, but possessing, in large degree, the charm of both.[8]

All this is familiar enough, yet we are in danger of underestimating the importance of the historical elements, and of misconceiving the peculiar nature of their appeal. We may grant freely that the backbone of the epic is the supernatural plot. Men of Anglo-Saxon blood have always loved good contests and good sportsmanship. Beowulf fights fair in long and dangerous struggles, carefully described, against demon adversaries, who are not made too definite. The poet is wise enough to rely upon imagination to do its work, though he kindles imagination by occasional descriptions, — the uncanny abode of the Grendel tribe, in the dark forest, where hoar-frosted trees overshadow stagnant waters; the grave mound filled with antique treasures, where the dragon watches on the windy heights. There is plenty of stirring action, the proper business of epic. But the audience obviously waited with no less eagerness for reminiscences of old historic tradition. Almost every page of *Beowulf* gives evidence of how completely this filled their minds. The poet had only to suggest, in order to evoke vivid recollections. He could take for granted acquaintance with long and complicated feuds, touching only upon such moments as seemed to him effective; or he could trace, with fresh detail, a long sequence of events which had crystallized into heroic story. His digressions often seem to us to clog the action, and distract attention from it. But there was little suspense in the plot; the story was familiar, what was important was detail. And no part of this detail, in days when there were few ways of learning about the past, was more absorbing than history, or what passed for history. Tastes have changed since then. One sometimes wonders at the fascination exercised by long genealogies. In the Icelandic sagas the luxuriant family trees, with every bough and twig duly pictured forth, seem to us to darken high adventure with their spreading branches. The same is true of Irish and Welsh. As for *Beowulf*, a modern story-teller would hardly have thought it worth while to give the entire royal lines of both the sovereigns at whose courts the action takes place. But the earlier habit of mind is of great significance. If we are to read the epic as it was meant to be understood, we must endeavor to recapture, so far as we may, its intense interest in early heroic tradition, and to gain familiarity with its complexities.

The historical portion of *Beowulf* is remarkable for its fidelity to fact. With all its elaborations, it preserves a certain restraint. This is particularly striking when it is compared with later versions of the same material. Contrast, for example, its account of the feuds of Danes and Heathobards with the same events in the pages of Saxo Grammaticus, five centuries later. Although *Beowulf* stresses the personal elements, — the ill-starred love of the Danish princess and the Heathobard prince, the vengeance slumbering in the heart of a Heathobard warrior for a sire once killed by the Danes, — it obviously presents with some clearness the earlier outlines of the tale. The long speech of the old fighter who kindles the feud anew (2047–2056) is of course pure fiction, but it enriches the tragedy, it does not disturb it. How different is the situation in the pages of the Danish monk! The very foundations of the story are shattered — the Heathobards, traditional enemies of the Danes, have themselves become Danish. So in Icelandic, although the story develops along other lines. The further events recede into the past, of course, the greater the departure from fact. But this is not all; there is in *Beowulf* a sobriety of temper in dealing with history which is quite its own. The point of view of the poet is, in general, as impartial as that of a modern historian. He has a hero, and his work involves glorification of that hero and the hero's people, but he gives due tribute to the greatness of other folk. This was the usual procedure of a minstrel of the Heroic Age, who knew of all notable men about the circle of the seas. Since the first two adventures lie at the court of the Danes, it is natural that their greatness and their traditions should

occupy the earlier portion of the poem. The episodes deal chiefly with them; the longest digression,
the tale of Finnsburg, is a story of Danish heroism.
But as soon as the second adventure is over, and
Beowulf and his men sail back to their native land,
the Danes are quite forgotten, and the new setting
brings up the richest reminiscences of the Geatas
and the Swedes. Meanwhile, throughout the entire
epic, the poet has not forgotten other great heroes
and peoples than those with whom he is directly
concerned; they might be the subjects for more
long tales for winter evenings, did time but serve.

Folk-tale and history are so closely interwoven,
however, that we must be constantly on the alert
for distortion of fact. And *Beowulf* is, after all, a
story, in which the imaginative effect is of supreme
importance. Fortunately, a certain amount of
documentary evidence is available by which the
veracity of the poem may be tested, and it is frequently possible, where this evidence does not
exist, to make fairly safe guesses as to what is
elaboration of actual occurrences, and what is invention pure and simple. Thus the death of Hygelac, the sovereign of Beowulf, at the hands of the
Franks and their allies, is confirmed by Frankish
historians, and the accession of Hygelac's son,
Heardred, has antecedent probability in its favor.
But the connection of Beowulf with the noble
house of the Wægmundingas and his activity as

king of the Geatas is probably wholly fictitious, not merely because of his folk-tale origin, but also because of the lack of events which the poet can remember, too few for the long reign of so illustrious a king. A stout fighter would surely not have played a passive rôle in the long contests with the Swedes, the hereditary foes of his people. In dealing with the realistic background, then, it is frequently wisest to take refuge in the phrase "historical or legendary." Early poetry was not concerned to separate fact from fiction. Complete accuracy of historical detail would not increase the realism or the charm of the picture of early Germanic life in *Beowulf*. The story-teller betters things for the business of poetry, and his canvas is veracious in a different way,— in its fidelity to the spirit of the age, and to manners and customs, forms of government and conceptions of duty, as they actually existed.

Moreover, if the poet was impartial in his outlook, he was in no wise cold-blooded; he felt with extraordinary poignancy the underlying tragedy of the events which he was recording. When history is retold as epic, the human element becomes all-important. Political development means little; passion and emotion, much. Events of great ultimate historical significance are forgotten, and details, by their peculiar appeal to the imagination, become the springs of action. The further actual occurrences recede into the past, the more marked is the tendency to motivate them in terms of human emotion. This dramatic element in the historic background is of great consequence for the artistic effect of the epic. Royal greatness is but the prelude to tragedy; sufferings more poignant than those inflicted by demons arise from ambition and greed. An atmosphere of impending fate envelops the courts of the Northland, brilliant though they be. The poet constantly glances into the future, emphasizing the tragic irony of human life, in particular the life of those upon whose brows a crown is set. But, as is his habit, he suggests rather than describes. Since the fortunes of his heroes and heroines are already well known, he indulges in no long explanations. A word or two evokes vivid memories; a phrase strikes the heart of tragedy. Against the main themes of the epic there run, contrapuntally, minor themes, and the effect is missed, as in an elaborate piece of polyphonic music, when the attention is centred wholly upon the outstanding melodies. To be specific, the adventures with Grendel and his dam are the main theme of the first part of the epic; and the tragedies of the Danish house of the Scyldings, the chief of the secondary themes. In the latter part of the poem, the main secondary theme is the long tragic feud of the Geatas and Swedes, set against the contest of Beowulf with a fire-spewing dragon. Allusion and reminis-

cence, leading themes and minor themes, are interwoven with bewildering variety. This literary
method presents great difficulties to the modern
reader. Subtle and elusive intimations are effective only for him who fully understands their significance.

Next to an acquaintance with heroic story, a
comprehension of early social conventions is necessary to an intelligent reading of the poem. What
were the warrior's obligations to his king and to
his kinsmen? These were defined with the utmost
strictness, and were not lightly to be transgressed.
Highly organized rules of conduct, as has already
been observed, often exist in a simple and even
primitive community. The great social principles
of the Migration Period were, in the England of
Bede, after the lapse of some two centuries, still
the governing force in the Anglo-Saxon state.
Upon these the whole motivation of the poem de-
pends. Their main outlines are easy to grasp,
partly because of their essential simplicity, and
partly because of their complete unlikeness to the
social conventions of modern times. They undergo
no essential modifications in being turned to the
uses of poetry. The clash of conflicting duties with
each other, and with the elemental passions of love
and hatred and ambition, supplies the poet with
his richest themes. Tribal law and tribal custom
are the rocks against which the lives of men and

women are shattered, like surf on a storm-bound shore. We can as little understand the tragic elements in *Beowulf* without comprehending the social laws underlying them as we can read aright the *Œdipus Rex* or the *Electra* without knowing the Greek ideas of destiny and fate.

In a word, then, "he who would bring back the wealth of the Indies must take out the wealth of the Indies." He who would understand truly the artistic effect of *Beowulf* must study the pageant of Germanic heroic life, and the conventions which governed it. The chapters that follow are designed to make this clear.

First of all, it is necessary to comprehend the story and structure of the poem, and the family relationships of the principal personages. A reading of the text or of a translation will be assisted by an outline of the action, and by genealogical tables (Appendix A and Appendix B). Some idea should meanwhile be gained of the great peoples in the circle of heroic story, and of their common social ideals and social organization (chapter II). This is concretely and vividly illustrated by detailed analysis of the tragic histories of the two great royal houses against which the main action of the epic is projected (chapter III). Realistic historical material furnishing the subject-matter of a highly dramatic tale is provided by the *Finnsburg Fragment* and *Episode* (chapter IV). In sharp contrast stand the supernatural narratives of the epic. An introductory study of the imaginative processes that underlie such narratives will deal with the figures of Scyld and Breca (chapter V). This will lead to consideration of the supernatural adventures of the hero with Grendel and Grendel's dam (chapter VI), and with the dragon (chapter VII). Finally, the whole history of the epic material will be reviewed, so far as it is possible to follow it, from the beginning, and the circumstances of the composition of the present poem in England will be discussed (chapter VIII). Throughout the whole book the chief emphasis will be laid upon the different forms and permutations of epic tradition.

II

PEOPLES AND SOCIAL ORGANIZATION

THE classification of the peoples mentioned in *Beowulf* according to their proper geographical and linguistic relationships forms a sound basis for the comprehension of the background of the story; yet such a classification presents many difficulties, even with all the resources of modern investigation at command. Our knowledge of the sixth century is imperfect; the most careful sifting of the available evidence yields incomplete results. Moreover, it was an era of confusion and transition. Political boundaries were shifting and ill defined, as was naturally the case with peoples in a migratory stage. And even if an exact reconstruction of historical conditions were possible, it would, of course, not be in harmony with the epic. Imagination has modified fact; history has become poetry. We have to reckon, too, with the ignorance of the poet, which critics do not always take sufficiently into consideration. How could any man in northern England in the seventh or in the eighth century have accurate knowledge of political and geographical conditions on the Continent, particularly in the outlying regions of the north, some two centuries earlier? Such knowledge as he had must have reached him through oral tradition in the main, — the least safe and constant of guides.

In all probability the *Beowulf* poet had no clear idea of the relative positions of the tribes in his tale, though he could distinguish these tribes clearly and name eminent rulers and heroes identified with them. His chief business was to recall and to elaborate their epic traditions. Geography in the earlier Middle Ages was a rudimentary affair. Directions were reckoned chiefly by east and west, rather than by north and south. Epic descriptions of such places as can be identified rarely agree with the actual features of the landscape. For example, the chief city of the Danes, where the hall Heorot stood, has generally been identified with the ancient Lethra on the island of Zealand, now the small village Leire, near Roskilde.[1] But the traveller who visits this quiet hamlet, with its swampy meadows pierced by arms of the sea, will find little to recall the rugged landscape in *Beowulf*, — the beetling cliffs on which the coast guard watches, or the high, rocky forest land, where the mountain stream breaks into a pool beneath. The reason is simple. The domains of Hrothgar were pictured in the epic by a man who knew the sea-cliffs of northern England, but he was, as we shall see, telling a tale of waterfall-trolls, which had derived its characteristic scenery from Norway. He probably had no idea at all what mountainous country or the coast of Denmark really looked like. Similarly, efforts to show, on the basis of descriptions in the epic, that the residence of King Hygelac of the Geatas was located near modern Göteborg in Sweden are totally unconvincing.[2] To argue that this must have been near rocky land because the dragon lived on a cliff near the sea, or because a beacon was erected on a headland in memory of the hero, is to confuse romance with reality. A safer guide to geography is the evidence of place-names. On this basis it seems fairly safe to locate Hrothgar's residence at Leire (Lethra) in Zealand, though the identification has been doubted. Efforts to determine the site of the hall Heorot are fruitless. The exact position is, indeed, of no special consequence for an understanding of the epic. It must also be remembered that place-names are sometimes used with seeming definiteness in obviously fictitious parts of the poem. Beowulf, an imaginary person, swimming with Breca, an imaginary prince of an imaginary people, the Brondingas, lands among the Finns, while Breca comes to land among the Heatho-Ræmas. Had the poet any clear notion of the location of these peoples? It is in the highest degree doubtful. The geography of a supernatural feat of endurance in swimming need not be exact. But the poet's instinct was correct; he knew enough to appear to be precise and matter-of-fact.

The aid that sober realistic detail gives to a marvellous story was not discovered by Defoe.

A great people like the Danes consisted of an
amalgamation of many individual tribes, recognizing one king as their leader. Their wide distribution is emphasized by calling them East-Danes,
West-Danes, South-Danes, and North-Danes, each
term standing by metonymy for the people as
a whole. Similarly, the poet refers within eight
lines (2913–2921) to the armed forces that opposed
Hygelac in the Low Countries as Frisians, Hugas,
Hetware, and Merewioingas (Merovingians). When
we are told that Hygelac attacked the Hugas
(a poetic appellation for the Franks) and was defeated by the Hetware, we are not to take either
statement with entire literalness; each name does
duty for the entire combined force. Again, poetic
terms give color and variety; the Danes are not
only Scyldingas (shield-men), but Ar-Scyldingas
(Honor-Scyldings), Sige-Scyldingas (Victorious
Scyldings), Here-Scyldingas (Army Scyldings).
Such variants served another useful purpose: they
assisted in the composition of alliterative verse.
The metre required at least one alliteration, linking
the two half-lines of verse, and two alliterating
stressed syllables were very common in the first
half-line. The choice of words was thus considerably restricted, and it was convenient, if not
necessary, to have poetic variants, beginning with

different consonants or with a vowel, to use in referring to a people who, like the Danes, must of necessity be frequently mentioned. We must be careful not to draw conclusions in regard to ethnography from the conventions and necessities of poetic style.

The epic is concerned mainly with two great Scandinavian peoples, and most, though not all, of the episodic material deals with Scandinavian heroes and tribes. The historic setting is well confined to the sixth century; only rarely is reference made to events lying outside that period. This was near the end of the era known as the Age of the Great Migrations, a term which may be somewhat misleading. There were, indeed, through the fourth, fifth, and sixth centuries, many conflicts for the possession of territory, and frequent marches and resettlements. But the peoples were not constantly on the move; their existence was not nomadic. The occasional long journeys were brief as compared with the periods of colonization. For many years before the Age of the Migrations began, the "barbarian" peoples had manifested symptoms of the great awakening which was later to make them supreme in Europe; but the actual beginning of the movement is rightly reckoned from the clash between the Romans and the Goths in the fourth century, in consequence of the pressure of the Huns from the north and east. A faint and much-altered reminiscence of this early time appears in *Beowulf* (1201), in the reference to Ermanric, king of the East-Goths, who committed suicide about 375 at the approach of the Huns, but who was remembered in epic story as a cruel tyrant. A fine example of the complete transformation of history by imagination is the pathetic legend, best read in Icelandic sources, which grew up about him: the love of his son Randver for the lovely Swanhild, whom Randver had to escort as a bride for his own father, — a love recalling that of Tristram for Isolt, the wife of his uncle Mark.[3] The terrible punishment which followed, according to the story, was long a favorite theme of singers. The poet of *Beowulf* apparently remembered the death of Randver on the gallows (2444 ff.), and he mentions Ermanric by name (1201), though he makes no mention of the bright-eyed Swanhild, trampled to death beneath the hoofs of wild horses.

The general outlines of the migrations of the Vandals, the Goths, the Franks, and the Anglo-Saxons, in the fifth and sixth centuries, may be traced with some clearness, but relatively little is known of the Scandinavians at this time. Being so far away from contact with Rome, they probably remained more static, though inter-tribal warfare obviously caused occasional redistribution of territory. The true Migration Period of the Scandinavians belongs in the so-called Viking Age, which, whatever its limits, did not begin until long after *Beowulf* was composed.

The term "Germanic" has been so universally adopted for that subdivision of the great Aryan or Indo-European family of languages with which we are here concerned that no other term can conveniently be substituted for it. Yet it requires some explanation; it appears to emphasize unduly the importance of the ancestry of those German scholars who gave the word its currency. The Germanic peoples were of course in no way particularly identified with the territory covered by modern Germany; they stretched from southern Russia, where the Goths were settled in the fourth century, when they first came to grips with Roman power, to Iceland, which was settled mainly by Norwegians in the ninth century. The usual subdivisions are: North-Germanic, comprising the Danes, Swedes, Norwegians, and Icelanders; West-Germanic, mainly English (Anglo-Saxon), Dutch, and German; East-Germanic, Goths, Vandals, and Burgundians. These subdivisions have been established rather on the basis of language than of geographical location, yet, roughly speaking, the results of the two classifications coincide.

The Danes come first to notice about 500; before that time nothing is known of them. It would appear that they conquered and absorbed the Heruli, a people frequently mentioned by Roman historians,

and it has been suggested that the legends of
their great Scylding dynasty are really, in historic
basis, Herulian. Their relations with neighboring
tribes, as the Heathobards and the Frisians, are obscure and perplexing. We shall have occasion later
to notice their feuds with these tribes, as reflected
in *Beowulf*, but heroic story cannot be relied upon
to guide us safely to historical relationships.[4] How
far the boundaries of the Danes extended in the
sixth century cannot be determined with certainty.
The centre of their power appears to have been the
island of Zealand, as in modern Denmark. Scandia
(modern Skåne), the southern end of the great
northern peninsula, was included in the kingdom,
and the terms "Scede-land" and "Sceden-ig"
appear to have been used by metonymy for the
whole Danish realm. Certainly we are not to conceive of the Danes as forming one unified "nation,"
but, as already suggested, as a collection of tribes,
each with its own prince, rendering homage to a
sovereign whose chief function was to assume
leadership in time of war. These tribes must have
felt a certain solidarity, however, from common
speech and customs, and they may well have recognized the practical benefits of union in days of violence and change. They were obviously no mean
folk, though the epic glorification of them must not
be taken too literally.

The relations between Danes and Angles are interesting. The Danes clearly occupied, to a considerable extent, the lands left vacant by the Angles when the latter migrated to Britain. They particularly venerated the old deity or hero, Ing, whose name appears in the term "Ingævones," that division of the Germanic peoples who dwelt, according to Tacitus, "nearest to the sea." The Angles are mentioned by Tacitus as belonging to the Ingævones, and there is some evidence that they shared early religious cults with the Danes. The Anglo-Saxon kings included Scyld (Skjold), the eponymous ancestor of the Danish Scylding dynasty, and other Danish figures, in their royal genealogies. It has even been conjectured that the Anglian part of the English stock was of common blood with the Danes. If the Angles in their new homes in Britain felt a close kinship with the Danes, they might all the more readily listen to tales of Danish kings. But the praises of the Danish dynasty, and the intense interest in their fortunes which *Beowulf* displays, are sufficiently explained by the impartial enthusiasm of the poet for great figures of heroic story. In early days historic legend often found its warmest welcome, and its most brilliant transformations, in lands far from its own home.[5]

The Geatas, the people of Beowulf, claim equal attention. Unfortunately, little is known of them.

They are particularly prominent in the later part of the epic, through the detailed accounts of their prolonged hostilities with the Swedes. The best critical opinion places the Geatas in what is now Sweden, south of Lakes Wener and Wetter, and locates the "Swedes" of the poem to the north of them. The identification of the Geatas with the Jutes of Jutland, which rests upon arguments too elaborate to be discussed here, does not appear convincing.[6] It is worth noting that words like *sæ* and *heafo* (2394, 2477), used in describing the waters separating Geatas and Swedes, need not necessarily denote the ocean. Such terms are very loosely used in the epic, partly in consequence of the demands of alliteration. They may well refer to the great Swedish lakes. Indeed, one late Swedish source describes a battle between the two peoples as having been fought on Lake Wener, on the ice. Such reminiscences of actual combats are far more trustworthy evidence than descriptions connected with fictitious portions of the epic. The capital of Hygelac may even have been near the southern shore of one of the great lakes, where defence against northern enemies could be quickly undertaken. The Geatas (Gautar) are placed by Procopius, writing in the middle of the sixth century, in Scandia, and appear to have been a powerful people; but it seems probable that not long after the death of Hygelac they were defeated by the

Swedes, and absorbed by them. Dire forebodings of this misfortune are heard near the close of the epic. The vanished glories of this people gave to the exploits of their heroes, and to their own checkered fortunes, a melancholy fascination. We shall have occasion later to observe how deeply this affected the Anglo-Saxon poet.

The Norwegians do not appear in *Beowulf*, and the Icelanders, chiefly men of Norwegian stock, did not settle on their barren island until the second half of the ninth century, more than one hundred years after the composition of the poem. Nor do the eastern group of the Germanic peoples, the Goths, Vandals, and Burgundians, require notice here. The fourth-century translation of the Bible into Gothic by Ulfilas is a precious document for the student of language, but none of the fine old legends which show faintly beneath the Latin of the chronicles of the Goths has survived in the Gothic tongue. This is a great pity, since Gothic story deeply affected later epic. Nor is anything extant of vernacular Burgundian tradition, which played so large a part in the formation of the Sigurd–Siegfried material. Traces of Vandal story are wholly absent in the Germanic dialects.

Peoples and sovereigns of the West-Germanic branch are of some consequence in a study of *Beowulf*, though these lie outside the main concerns of the story. A very considerable settlement of

Saxons remained in the old homes on the Continent after the migration to Britain, and probably maintained relations with their kinsmen in England. Valuable evidence in regard to Germanic conditions is afforded by the Old Saxon epic, *Heliand*. Though treating of the life of Christ, and composed a century or more after *Beowulf*, it presents pagan poetic technique and pagan social institutions practically unchanged. Similarly, the primitive conceptions of the relations between retainers and over-lord appear in the fine passage in the Cædmonian *Genesis* translated from the Old Saxon. No similar Continental survivals of Old Anglian remain. The Angles, who had dwelt to the north of the Saxons, in the narrow part of the Jutic peninsula and the islands to the east, must nearly all have migrated to Britain. Bede says that their land "which is called Angulus . . . is said to have remained uninhabited from that time to the present day." This is perhaps exaggerated, but there can be little doubt that such of the Angles as remained were soon absorbed by neighboring tribes. The Jutes, who probably dwelt to the north, in the point of the peninsula, were apparently racially less akin to either Angles or Saxons than these were to each other. It is possible that some of the Frisians took part in the conquest of Britain. They were an important people in early times; their homes along the coast of modern Holland and

northwestern Germany, about the mouth of the
Ems, gave great opportunities for trading and
raiding. But they early disappeared from the
theatre of European affairs, absorbed by their
powerful neighbors, the Franks. In the time of
Charlemagne they no longer had an independent
existence. The most important of all the episodes
in *Beowulf*, the tale of Finnsburg, which reflects
Danish–Frisian feuds, mentions a tribe subordinate to the Frisians, the Eotens, probably to be
identified with the Jutes, and, as already suggested,
used by metonymy for the group of peoples opposed to the Danes in the story. *Beowulf* has nothing at all to say of the Saxons, and refers to the
Angles only in a single passage, which may be interpolated (1925–1962).[7] Does this indicate connection of the poem with an Anglian court in the
north of England? This will be discussed in the
closing chapter; for the moment we may note that
the tale of Thryth, the shrewish queen of the old
Anglian king Offa, who is remembered in *Widsith*
as a stout fighter on the Continent, is of high interest as preserving recollections of old traditions
overseas, and of early popular story.

It has sometimes been asserted that the Anglo-
Saxons did not possess a rich fund of native stories,
since traces of these in early English literature are
few and unimportant, and since the *Beowulf* poet,
writing in English for English people, incorpo-

rated so little native tradition into his poem. But that poems and tales on native subjects are not extant does not prove that such never existed, and *Beowulf*, written at a time when the English had not developed a national consciousness, and were deeply interested in the deeds of other peoples, professedly takes as its theme Danish and Geatic heroes, and could bring in native material only episodically. A somewhat more convincing argument is the absence of Anglo-Saxon traditions from Scandinavian story-telling. The Scandinavians, like the Anglo-Saxons, were very deeply interested in the deeds of foreigners. Their greatest tale, the Volsung–Nibelung narrative, is based mainly on materials from other lands. But in all the wealth of epic material in Old Norse there is little about heroes of Anglian or Saxon stock. This silence is not proof that such warriors were not remembered abroad, but it seems to indicate that they attained no wide celebrity in the noble company of Germanic champions.

An excellent idea of the heroic world of the *Beowulf* poet and of his audience may be gained from the little Anglo-Saxon poem, only a hundred and forty-three lines long, known as *Widsith*, "the Far-Wanderer." [8] This should beyond question be read by every student of *Beowulf*. It consists mainly of an enumeration of the princes and peoples whom a minstrel, speaking in the first person, asserts that he has visited. But it is all fiction; Widsith and his travels are quite imaginary. No human being could possibly have seen Ermanric, who died in 375, and Alboin, king of the Lombards, who flourished in the latter half of the sixth century. Such pleasant deceptions are common in early story. So Taliesin, "primary chief bard to Elphin" in the Welsh *Mabinogion*, informs us that he was present at the Fall of Lucifer, the campaigns of Alexander the Great, the sailing of the Ark of Noah, and the nativity of Christ. But the fictitious setting of the Anglo-Saxon poem serves a useful purpose: what might otherwise be a bald collocation of names gains vividness and interest through the assurance that a singer personally visited them in his wanderings.

Widsith, in its present form, is a mosaic of "information-verses" dating from different periods. A part of it, a mnemonic jingle beginning

> Attila ruled the Huns, Ermanric the Goths,
> Becca the Banings, the Burgundians Gifica,

— of no greater literary merit than "thirty days hath September," — is perhaps the earliest Anglo-Saxon verse extant. Other passages give priceless glimpses of the Migration Period, illuminated by flashes of genuine poetry, supplementing other epic tradition. The pretty picture of Widsith celebrating the queen of Ermanric, Ealhhild, in song, in company with his brother minstrel, Scilling, though fictitious, is no doubt true to early custom. How far the piece is from a genuine autobiographical account of the journey of a Germanic minstrel to the Gothic or Lombard court is shown by its geography, which, as Professor Chambers has pointed out, is "such as might have been made by a gleeman who drew his lore from the traditions of the ancient Angel. . . . Out of thirty-one tribes and places which we can identify all but two are connected with either the North Sea or the Baltic: and these two exceptions are not far remote." [9] The poem thus becomes of great importance in supplementing and confirming statements in *Beowulf*. Possibly the poet of *Beowulf* may have known a part or parts of *Widsith*. The little framework which encloses the piece — the lines at the beginning introducing the minstrel, and those at the end glorifying his profession — is late, probably of the eighth century, and perhaps not far from the time of the composition of *Beowulf*. The whole, though a patchwork, and though archaic and stiff in places, has a charm and dignity which are quite its own.

The pleasant picture afforded by the travels of the fictitious Widsith may well give a somewhat rose-colored view of tribal relationships, although even here strife looms up darkly in the background. The natural attitude toward neighbors, in those wild days, was one of hostility and suspicion, of aggression to extend territory, and defence to protect it. War was the chief business of life. In *Beowulf* the underlying cause of international complications is unsettled and long-standing feud, reaching far into the past. Danes are arrayed against Heathobards and Frisians, Geatas against Swedes and Franks. Similar conditions existed in the poet's own day, in the rivalries of Bernicia, Deira, and Mercia. The friendly relations between Geatas and Danes, so much stressed in the epic, probably rest rather on fiction than on fact. Beowulf is moved to help Hrothgar by desire for glory in troll-killing, and in return for the assistance given to his father, Ecgtheow, by the Danish king, when Ecgtheow had been outlawed for slaying. There may be an actual basis for this episode (459–472), but not for the paternity of the folk-tale hero. And there is a clear indication (1857–1858) that even Geatas and Danes were once at war with each other. Violence and feud within the group of associated tribes, or within a tribe itself, were analogous in many ways to the quarrels between openly hostile neighboring peoples. Injury, retaliation, revenge for the retaliation or a settlement by payment of money,— such was the process whether within a kingdom or between kingdoms. Warfare between two peoples was often made vivid by being conceived as the individual hostility of their sovereigns, just as in later times.[10]

Authorities differ widely in regard to the organization of the early Germanic state,[11] and the relative importance of the different forms of allegiance. The earlier critics were inclined to draw conclusions rather from Roman writers and from the legal codes of Continental peoples than from traditions preserved in Anglo-Saxon, Old Saxon, and Scandinavian vernacular literature. The dangers of generalizing from the *Germania* of Tacitus, a work strongly colored by the writer's desire to point a moral to decadent Rome, have long been recognized. Professor Gummere put it well in saying that "our typical German, like Plato's ideal horse, is a very difficult matter to define and draw; and, indeed, he has been drawn in every shade from absolute savagery to a graceful and accomplished person, as unlimited in courtesy and intellect as in muscular development, who 'cultive ses jardins, les vertus, et les arts.'"[12] The *Beowulf* poet clearly felt the antiquity of the tales he retold, but he probably did not himself try to archaize in his representation of manners and customs, though he must have recognized that tradition gave a picture different from that of his own times. Mediæval writers were, of course, prone to show antiquity in contemporary guise. We may, I think, safely assume that the fundamental conceptions of society and politics in *Beowulf* were those of Anglo-Saxon England of the seventh century.

The political unit of the Germanic state in the sixth and seventh centuries was the kingdom. This term often means no more than "tribal group"; it must not be too magnificently conceived, any more than "town," which was generally nothing more than a collection of dwellings surrounding a central hall, and protected by a stockade. A natural result of constant warfare was the gradual amalgamation of smaller kingdoms into more powerful groups, with the warriors of one commanding tribe as leaders. The kingdom of Hrothgar the Dane was such a loose organization of scattered peoples. His ancestors had been victorious in war, and had forced surrounding peoples to pay tribute. By the sixth century this process of amalgamation had gone quite far, but the resulting associations of peoples were very far from being "nations," in the modern sense of the word. Epic poetry exaggerates their brilliance and solidity. The ties that bound them were quite easily broken, fresh combinations were readily made, and the settled central organization of later days was lacking. When there was no firm national structure there could be no patriotism.

The king was not a mere figurehead; he was leader in war and the administration of justice, and his office involved religious functions, the precise nature of which is not clear. It was the greatest of misfortunes for a people to lack a sovereign, as did the Danes before the coming of Scyld (14-16).

The royal power was hereditary, though succession might be violated in consequence of the weakness or wickedness of the legitimate heir. The leading chiefs could not allow the safety of the kingdom to be jeopardized, in days when might generally made right, by allowing an incompetent man to wear the crown. A late reflection of the importance of this elective power in Scandinavia appears in Shakespeare's *Hamlet:* Claudius "popped in" between the election and Hamlet's natural hope and expectation that he would wear the crown on his father's death. Though the king had religious duties, there was no sanctity about his person which forbade getting rid of him if he misbehaved himself, as did Heremod in *Beowulf* (901 ff.). At the same time, disturbance of the normal succession through personal ambition was, even in these early days, regarded as dangerous, as sowing the seeds of future trouble. There can be little doubt that the picture of the usurpations in the house of Hrothgar, considered in detail in the following chapter, was meant to point as clear a moral as the ambitions of the houses of York and Lancaster during the Wars of the Roses in Shakespeare's historical plays.

The king was expected to provide his followers with treasure and with land, according to their merits and rank, and — what was equally important — with plenty of chances for fighting. Stinginess and lack of martial ambition were the worst faults that he could possess. The more distinguished chiefs and the other members of the royal family shared with him the management of affairs. Nobility depended upon birth — a respectable family tree was as necessary to a warrior as his sword. The men of higher rank constituted the main fighting force. The tried retainers, the *duguð*, are sharply distinguished in *Beowulf* from the *geoguð*, the younger and less experienced warriors. A particularly important group of fighters constituted the king's *comitatus*. Strong bonds of personal loyalty bound them to the king; they were his chief supporters and advisers; they rendered him unquestioning allegiance; they were bound to avenge him if he were slain or injured, and even to perish themselves, if they could get themselves killed, in case the exacting of vengeance for him proved impossible. In later times in Britain a distinction appears between the *gesīþas* ("companions") and the *þegnas* ("servants") surrounding the king, though both were of noble blood, but this distinction is not observed in the epic. The constant use of synonyms imposed upon the poet by the demands of Anglo-Saxon poetic style resulted in frequent violation of the strict meaning of such terms. This is apparent when we consider the term *ceorlas*, sharply contrasted with the *eorlas* in Anglo-Saxon laws and documents, but in *Beowulf* applied regularly to royal warriors and advisers, and once (2972) to a king himself. The strong democratic feeling in early Germanic communities may have assisted such confusions. The freemen receive no attention in *Beowulf*, but they were not despised. They were tillers of the soil, and no doubt sturdy fighters in time of need, but they did not make heroism a profession. They were dependents; they received protection from their betters, and rendered them yeoman service. There is no justification in *Beowulf* for the idea that the whole body of freemen in arms constituted the fighting force. Only the professional warrior class receives mention. If the peasantry gave assistance, this was not held worthy of remembrance. Nor does there seem to have been, even in the early Anglo-Saxon kingdoms, a system of representative government in which all free men had a voice. The basis for the rigid caste-system of the later Middle Ages is clearly observable, but, as Professor Ker has remarked,

the nobles have not yet discovered for themselves any form of occupation or mode of thought in virtue of which they are widely severed from the commons, nor have they invented any such ideal of life or conventional system of conduct as involves an ignorance or depreciation of the common pursuits of those below them. . . . The arts and pursuits of a gentleman in the heroic age are different from those of the churl, but not so far different as to keep them in different spheres.

There is a community of prosaic interests. The great man is a good judge of cattle; he sails his own ship.[13]

Feudal conditions are, however, clearly fore-shadowed in the dependence of the laborers on the ruling class, and of the latter on the king. The exact conditions of land tenure are obscure and de-batable, but it is clear that the king was expected to reward his most distinguished retainers by land as well as gold. A certain reserve of land and treas-ure was kept — the latter partly for ransoms (73). The epic takes no account of serfs, who were, in the main, captives taken in war. The poem never mentions them, if we except a highly doubtful con-jectural emendation (*þēow*, 2223).

Germanic society is best analyzed on the basis of the two great principles of political allegiance and family allegiance.

One of the noticeable things about *Beowulf*, as contrasted, let us say, with the *Song of Roland*, is the small number of fighters. Poets of the earlier period preferred to celebrate a heroic little com-pany rather than a mighty multitude, like the hosts of Charlemagne. The individual warrior assumed great importance, and personal allegiance to the sovereign was the first of his duties. No dis-grace was deeper than disloyalty, or even failure to render the fullest meed of service. Conversely, no misfortune was greater than to be deprived of a protecting lord and the joys of the mead-hall, even though a man were innocent of blame. The charming Northumbrian lyric known as *The Wanderer*, probably written at about the same time as *Beowulf*, or a little later, gives a vivid picture of the warrior deprived of those privileges.[14] The solidarity of the *comitatus* foreshadowed that devotion to a cause and to a chosen leader which has been one of the sources of the greatness of the English stock in modern days. How deeply ingrained this feeling was is well illustrated in the Old Saxon *Heliand* and the Anglo-Saxon *Genesis*. Christian epic could not depict the devotion of the apostles to Christ more vividly than as that of thanes to their king; and the Biblical story of the revolt of the fallen angels derived its chief poignancy from the tragedy of violated allegiance, and of the miserable condition of warriors deprived of their protecting chief. But this rigid system was bound to encounter difficulties in actual practice. The history of the Danish and Swedish royal houses furnishes striking illustrations: ambition to become king prevails over allegiance to over-lord; the breaking of faith brings its punishment to men like Hrothulf and Eanmund. Temporary fealty to a foreign king runs counter to loyalty to a sovereign at home: Weohstan the Geat fights against his own people, yet slays a prince of the house that he is temporarily supporting, because that prince has allied himself with hereditary foes. An oath sworn under necessity, cementing allegiance to an enemy, conflicts with the duty of avenging a liege lord; and Hengest the Dane, in the tale of Finnsburg, is racked by conflicting emotions, and can make no decision until one is forced upon him. Such are the complications of divided allegiance.

Similar difficulties arise from the endeavor to be true to the second great principle, allegiance to kin. This obligation seems, on the whole, to have been somewhat less binding, and to have been the first to weaken with the passage of time. But it must not be underestimated. It is analogous in many ways to political allegiance. If the king or any member of the *comitatus* were slain or injured, the duty of vengeance fell upon the rest of the band. Similarly, revenge for injuries inflicted upon any member of the family or clan group was a sacred obligation resting upon all other members; until the injury had been wiped out, the honor of the clan was darkly tarnished. Since the reprisal often exceeded in severity the original offence, prolonged feuds were frequent. An eye could not always be exacted for an eye, or a tooth for a tooth. For good measure, more extensive mutilations were more satisfying. This sort of thing could not continue indefinitely in a civilized state, so settlements of injury by payment of money or its equivalent became increasingly common. One is struck by the prominence, in early legal codes, of the exact enumerations of amounts to be paid for specific injuries, — so much for killing a man, so much for striking off a hand, and so forth. In such settlements a king or chieftain was the natural mediator. Ecgtheow, the father of Beowulf, slew Heatholaf, the Wylfing, and had to flee from the Geatas. He then came to the court of the Danish king, Hrothgar, who helped him out of his difficulties by sending money to the Wylfings to atone for the crime, and binding Ecgtheow himself by oath to keep the peace (459-472). Similarly, in the final adventure of the poem, the hoard of the dragon was plundered by a man who wished to get treasure to buy off an injury, and Beowulf, then king of the Geatas, apparently acted as mediator in the affair, and, by himself receiving for his services a part of the gold, inherited the curse that lay upon it. Tribal organization had its courtesies as well as its penalties; one of the most distinguished inter-tribal honors was the adoption of a foreigner into a native clan, as Hrothgar received Beowulf (946 ff.). Just how binding this ceremony was felt to be is not clear; but it must have involved some acceptance on the part of the "son" of supporting by force, in case of need, the cause of the family that he was joining. As time went on, and organized justice became stronger, devotion to the family grew less intense; but clan hatreds and feuds were difficult to extinguish. Violence gave way only gradually before the orderly processes of justice. Tribal law was somewhat like international law at the present day, liable to ruthless violation in times of passion. The surest redress was too often the wild justice of revenge.[15]

Occasions were bound to arise when the conventions of family allegiance conflicted with those of political allegiance, or with each other. A royal prince kills his brother by accident; what is the king to do? He is bound to exact vengeance on the slayer, as head both of the state and of the family. But how can he kill his own son? Again, the usurpations in the Danish and Swedish royal houses are a menace at once to tribal and family solidarity. A favorite theme with poets is the dilemma of a princess married to a foreign prince, who, at the outbreak of hostilities with her own people, is forced to choose between kin by blood and kin by marriage. Such is the fate of Freawaru, daughter of Hrothgar, of Signy in the tale of the Volsungs, of Gudrun or Kriemhild in the story of the Nibelungs. Marriages with this danger in the future were common in the feud-ridden England of the seventh century; Cyneburh, the daughter of King Penda of Mercia, married the son of his rival, Oswy of Northumbria, while Oswy's daughter married Penda's eldest son.[16] Different versions of the same theme represent fate working out in different ways. In the Nibelung story the course of action pursued

by the heroine is conceived in one fashion in Icelandic and in another in German tradition. The
more hampered a society is by convention, the
more distressing become the cases where convention does not prove a safe guide, where the choice
must be made between conflicting duties.

The great fascination which these dilemmas exercised upon mediæval poets has hardly been ade-
quately realized. They begin with primitive customs. In Irish, the great hero Cuchullin meets his
death through a conflict of taboos: he must never
refuse food offered him by women, and he must
never eat the flesh of his *totem* (the hound: Cuchullin, "hound of Culann"). But as he is going to battle, women offer him dog's flesh "cooked with
poisons and spells," which he is obliged to eat, and
so his days are numbered.[17] The Viking Age offers
striking illustrations. In the story of Gisli the
outlaw, "Gisli suffered from the law because he
had acted according to the best dictates of his con-
science in a very complex situation: to avenge his
wife's brother he slew his sister's husband."[18] Chivalry brought new complications, with its elaborate
code of love-conventions. The lady in the *Yvain*
of Chrétien de Troyes, debating with herself
whether she may yield to the demands of love, and
marry the slayer of her husband, faced a situation
analogous to that of her distressed sisters of earlier
days.[19]

Tragic motives in Germanic life, as they appear in *Beowulf*, will be analyzed in some detail in the following chapter. We must first consider briefly the evidence for the interpretation of the poem afforded by Scandinavian literature of the Viking Age and later.

Although this literature is all far more modern than our epic, covering a period from the middle of the ninth century to the time of Chaucer, or even beyond, it affords, by reason of its richness and variety, and its essentially pagan character, most instructive parallels and illustrations. The Viking Age is reckoned as extending from the first raids on the coast of Northumbria in the late eighth century to the settlement of Normandy in 911, or to the establishment of the great Scandinavian kingdoms in the eleventh century, particularly the empire of Cnut in England and Denmark. The Vikings, perhaps "creek-men" (*vîk*, a bay or inlet, as in *Reykjavík*, the "bay of smoke," in allusion to the geysers), ran their small, swift boats into the estuaries of the North Sea, made swift attacks upon the dwellers near by, and often escaped before resistance could be organized. Commerce as well as raiding offered an incentive to Viking voyaging; it is probably no mere chance that the rise of Viking power in the ninth century is coincident with the extinction of the commercial prosperity of the Frisians. In the latter half of this century, dissatisfaction with the ambitions of the Norwegian king, Harold Fair-Hair, led a group of his chieftains to settle in Iceland, then inhabited only by a few shivering Irish hermits. In general, the Norwegians colonized the northern regions,—Iceland, the Scottish and Irish coasts, and the outlying islands; while the Danes preferred southern England and the Continent. But no sharp division of nationalities is possible. In 845 the doughty chief, Ragnar Lothbrok, sailed up the Seine to the site of modern Paris, burning and pillaging as he went; and in 911 Hrolf, or Rollo, made his famous settlement in France, in the territory still called Normandy. The activities of the Northmen were by no means confined to Western Europe, however. They penetrated into Spain, into Russia, — here the Swedes were of importance, — to Constantinople or "Micklegarth," and their voyages to Greenland and North America anticipated Columbus by about five centuries.[20]

The lateness of the conversion of Iceland to Christianity (the year 1000) is noteworthy. While the Anglo-Saxons were absorbing the best surviving traditions of late classical and Christian letters, Norwegians and Icelanders were still clinging to a highly developed pagan polytheism, and embodying this in their poetry. Contact with Irish and knowledge of Irish traditions probably modified Scandinavian beliefs, but did not destroy their es-

sentially pagan character. Even after the introduction of the new lore of Christ, the Icelanders
were singularly tenacious of older fashions. Consequently, their traditional heroic poetry, which
had assumed highly artistic and sophisticated form,
and their prose tales or sagas, most of them un-
touched or but lightly touched by piety, are of great
assistance in forming a correct estimate of the institutions, legends, and poetic technique of their
cousins, the English. Due allowance must be
made, in comparing this literature with *Beowulf*,
for changes wrought by time. Tribal culture took
on new coloring, and events and motivation in
story-telling were altered by the influence of Continental literature and by the natural instability of
tradition. Yet fundamentally the institutions and
spirit of the people remained unchanged.

The lays comprising the great collection of Icelandic heroic poetry known as the *Poetic Edda*, or
Elder Edda, date in their present form mainly from
the tenth and eleventh centuries, though some are
later. Nearly all of them, however, embody traditions of high antiquity. Arranged by a mediæval
compiler in rough sequence, and provided with
explanatory passages in prose, they present a complete picture of the gods and heroes of Scandinavian story. The lays of the gods are chiefly important for the student of Anglo-Saxon as showing
the general nature of the Germanic cults practised

in Britain before the introduction of Christianity by Augustine and the Irish. If we could recover the lays utilized by the poet of *Beowulf*, we should probably find Odin, Thor, and Frey looming up in the background. This earlier belief must have differed in important respects from that of the Scandinavians of the Viking Age. Few traces of the older pagan cults survive in extant Anglo-Saxon verse, however, so their nature remains obscure. The abundant gnomic and proverbial material of the earlier part of the *Edda* may be profitably studied by those who think *Beowulf* exceptional in its insistence upon propriety of conduct. The second section, which deals mainly with the great legend of the Nibelung Hoard, with Sigurd as its central figure, contains little that bears directly on *Beowulf*. The Anglo-Saxon poet refers in passing to Sigemund (884 ff.), to whom he credits the slaying of a dragon, probably the same exploit later attributed to his son Sigurd.[21]

A comparison of the style and emotional quality of *Beowulf* and the *Edda* is most illuminating. While analogous in verse-form, the Scandinavian lays differ strikingly from the Anglo-Saxon in their dramatic intensity and passionate fervor. Their strophic structure and narrative method suggest the ballad; they take much for granted, and often leap into the middle of a situation. Speeches often succeed one another without connecting narrative.

The tranquillity, leisurely movement, discursiveness, and care for detail so noticeable in *Beowulf*, with its long lines unbroken by stanzaic division, are quite lacking. The lays are art-poems, but much closer to popular literary forms. The lost Anglo-Saxon songs which furnished the *Beowulf* poet with his material were probably stylistically different, having been in the possession of West-Germanic peoples long enough to take on other characteristics than are observable in Scandinavian. But the exact nature of the material which preceded *Beowulf* must remain a matter for speculation.

Much of the subject-matter of the heroic lays of the *Edda* reappears, in different and altered form, in the Middle High German *Nibelungenlied* (*circa* 1205). This poem is, however, too late, too sophisticated, too much affected by courtly and chivalric conceptions and by the fashions of the newer romance, to form a true epic parallel to *Beowulf*. Older fashions of thought and action are clearly visible, particularly in the latter part of the story, but conclusions in regard to Germanic ideals must be drawn with caution. The version of the Sigurd–Siegfried legend in the thirteenth-century *Saga of the Volsungs and Niblungs*, as it is called in the charming translation by William Morris, is far more instructive. The earlier part of the saga, which tells the dramatic story of Signy and Siggeir, contains illuminating parallels to situations in *Beowulf*, and throws a vivid light on Northern conceptions of duty.[22]

The extraordinary vigor of pagan tradition in Iceland is well illustrated by the *Prose Edda* of Snorri Sturluson. Snorri, who was assassinated in a family feud in 1241, is the most distinguished figure in Old Norse literature, most of which is, of course, anonymous. The *Prose Edda*, like the *Mabinogion* in Welsh, was compiled to give instruction to poets, whose calling demanded acquaintance with the heroic and divine legends of the past. The opening section, "The Deception of Gylfi" (*Gylfaginning*), sets forth pagan mythology in the framework of a dialogue between Odin and a certain King Gylfi. The second section, "The Poetry of Skalds" (*Skáldskaparmál*), begins, in similar fashion, with the conversation between a man named Ægir, deeply versed in magic, who journeys to the dwelling of the gods, and Bragi, the god of poetry and eloquence. More and more, however, the framework of dialogue is dropped, and instruction is given in traditional stories, and in the meanings of poetical expressions. The use of *kennings*, or rhetorical periphrases, so noticeable in Anglo-Saxon (*homera láf*, "what is left by the hammers," that is, the sword; *heofones gim*, "the gem of heaven," that is, the sun), attained in the later skaldic verse of the Scandinavians such elaborateness and intricacy that careful explanation is frequently necessary to show what the object described really is, and what the mythological references signify. Hence the necessity for such instructions as Snorri provided. The skaldic verse itself is not of high literary value. Most of it is a kind of heroic *vers de société*. Nor is it of great consequence for the student of *Beowulf*. The chief value of the *Prose Edda* lies in the summaries of the great heroic and mythological traditions of the North in its first two sections. The third part, the "List of Metres" (*Hattatál*), is of interest only for the specialist in Icelandic metrics. It must not be forgotten that the skalds, who attached themselves to kings and chieftains, celebrating them in song, making lays of derision against their enemies, and fighting stoutly with weapons if need arose, played a great part in the preservation and dissemination of heroic legends. They were great travellers, the knights-errant of literature in the days before feudal chivalry.[23]

Perhaps, when all is considered, the prose sagas must rank as the most distinctive literary achievement in Old Norse. They embrace a wide variety of subject-matter: historical material relating to Iceland, Norway, Greenland, and the Scandinavian settlements around the British Isles; mythical stories, like the *Volsungasaga* just mentioned; and paraphrases of romantic material from Latin and

Old French. The best of them were written in the later twelfth and the thirteenth centuries, but they continued as late as the fifteenth century. The simplicity, clearness, and charm of the saga prose was quite unequalled in mediæval Europe; it suggests Addison or Defoe rather than Malory or Froissart. The narrative power and vividness of the sagas, despite digressions, genealogizing, and an occasionally wearisome elaborateness of plot, would be noteworthy in any age. The passages of skaldic verse, though in themselves frequently obscure, generally diversify the tales very happily. The most important of all the parallels to *Beowulf* is in the *Saga of Grettir the Strong*, in which the troll-legends appearing in the Anglo-Saxon epic are made to shed lustre upon an historical character of the eleventh century. Of high interest, also, is the *Saga of Hrolf Kraki*, which combines vague reminiscences of early historical tradition with the stuff of folk-tales. In this work, which dates from the fourteenth century, and in the later sagas generally, fantastic and childish elements are prominent, and the heroic spirit of earlier times is enfeebled. Episodes drawn from foreign countries were often quite unsuited to native settings. In the *Hrólfssaga* we can see clearly material found in more primitive form in *Beowulf*, but it is a matter of the greatest difficulty to separate this from the accretions that have grown up about it and altered the motivation of the tale. Trustworthy results are almost impossible of attainment. Assistance is sometimes afforded by the *rímur*, ballads dating in their present form from the end of the Middle Ages, and, like the English, Scottish, and Danish ballads, preserving early traditions in popular form, and greatly altered. The troll-fights of Beowulf appear to be reflected also in the late sagas of Orm Storolfsson and Samson the Fair. The first of these is of minor significance; the second — a very significant and little-known parallel — is presented in a later chapter for the first time in English. Quite as necessary, perhaps, for a comprehension of the spirit of *Beowulf* are the typical sagas of the earlier period, the *Laxdale Saga*, the *Saga of Burnt Njal*, the *Saga of Gunnar Snake-Tongue*, which present no analogous incidents, but give striking pictures of the life of the Viking Age, and of the customs and ideals of that period.[24]

The Danes and Swedes have left little that assists in gaining a knowledge of conditions in *Beowulf*. Their early traditions must be laboriously reconstructed from references in West-Scandinavian literature, and from late and altered narrative material in Latin. The most important document of the latter sort is the *History of the Danes* of Saxo Grammaticus, who was a contemporary of King John of England. It may be compared in some ways with Layamon's *Brut*. Written at about the same time, it is in effect a romance, preserving in chronicle form many old traditional tales. Saxo's bombastic Latin prose is, however, a far less admirable medium of expression than Layamon's sturdy English verse. Icelandic material, brought to Denmark by wandering minstrels, furnished Saxo with the bulk of his subject-matter; much else in the history is common European property, and only a minor part is specifically Danish. Christianity and the lapse of time have brought strange alterations. Odin, the majestic chief of the ancient Valhalla, is a terribly shabby and discredited figure in Saxo's pages. "There were of old," says the Danish monk, "certain men versed in sorcery, Thor, namely, and Odin, and many others, who were cunning in contriving marvellous sleights; and they, winning the minds of the simple, began to claim the rank of gods." No more than this one sentence is needed to show that great allowances must be made in reconstructing heroic legend from Saxo. Yet the feat may be accomplished, in one sense. The ingenuity of Axel Olrik rescued one of the finest and most popular songs of the North from Saxo's Latin paraphrase, the celebrated "Lay of Bjarki," a typical expression of the devotion of the retainer to his lord, and of reckless heroism on the field of battle. Genealogical relationships in *Beowulf* are illustrated by the *Skjoldungasaga*, preserved only in a Latin transcript, but containing

precious information about early Danish kings. A
similar service is done for the Swedish royal line by
the *Ynglingasaga*. No mediæval traditions of interest in the study of *Beowulf* have been preserved
from Swedish sources, either in Latin or in the
vernacular. The Swedes had less intercourse than
the Danes with Icelanders, Franks, English, and
Continental Saxons; and their early heroic traditions must be learned largely from other peoples.[25]

Minor sources may be quickly disposed of. Occasional assistance is given by genealogies, chronicles, and charters; by biographies in Latin and the
vernaculars; by fragments of pagan epic material,
as those dealing with Walter of Aquitaine and
Hildebrand; and by the paraphrases of the Bible,
the lives of saints, and the liturgy, associated with
the English poets, Cædmon and Cynewulf, and their
contemporaries. Of considerable importance is
the remarkable group of lyrics, chief of which are
The Wanderer, *The Seafarer*, *The Song of Deor*, *The
Lover's Message*, and *The Banished Wife's Lament*,
produced in the eighth century in Northumbria.
These illustrate vividly the Anglo-Saxon elegiac
temper, expressing itself in conventional themes:
the loneliness of the warrior surviving the extinction
of a glorious race, or lamenting the loss of a lord
and the joys of the mead-hall; the anguish of a
woman separated from her lover or her husband;
the contrasts between past prosperity and present

misery. So strongly marked are the characteristics of this elegiac poetry that it is frequently possible to recognize in *Beowulf* native Anglo-Saxon elaborations of specifically Scandinavian traditions. We shall have occasion later to observe this in some detail.

For a full understanding of *Beowulf*, which touches life at so many points, no reading in the early Middle Ages is without significance. Whoever would enter completely into the spirit of the poem must survey a wide range of literature, pagan, Christian, and post-classical. Much of this, as we have just seen, is later than the eighth century; some of the significant Scandinavian analogues are as late as Chaucer, or even later. One of the greatest difficulties in reading for a better understanding of *Beowulf* is the making of due allowances for time and place, from the *Germania* of Tacitus to the latest Icelandic sagas and ballads.

III

THE TRAGEDIES OF THE
ROYAL HOUSES

HOW history serves the purposes of epic and gives realism and dignity to popular story can best be comprehended by reviewing in some detail the fortunes of the great royal houses of the Danes and of the Geatas. Such detail may appear confusing, but it would give a false idea of the extraordinary richness and complexity of the picture if it were too far simplified. The main outlines are clear enough, and we shall take great pains to keep these outlines constantly in mind. The events are, in general, not set forth in the poem in connected sequence; this sequence has to be reconstructed from scattered passages, and from references in later Scandinavian literature.[1] No attempts will be made in this chapter to distinguish fact from elaboration, except where this can be done safely, and where it illustrates how imagination moves along the paths of realism, not depending for its effects upon the supernatural. Our main effort will be to gain such a knowledge of the old stories about the Danes and Geatas as the poet took for granted. And this must include events lying both before and after the action of the poem, since the fringes of tradition are often of high significance.

The first thing that strikes the reader, at the opening of the poem, is the emphasis upon the power and magnificence of the dynasty of the Scyldings. The Danes had once suffered a time of grievous distress, lacking a monarch. With the coming of the infant Scyld, who drifted to the shores of the country in an open boat, no man knew whence, a change came in their fortunes. Scyld became in due time a powerful monarch, striking terror to the hearts of neighboring peoples, and exacting forced tribute. The sovereigns succeeding him are rapidly reviewed. The beginning of the action is laid in the reign of Hrothgar, the fifth of his dynasty, who maintains its high traditions in superb fashion. As a symbol of his power, he builds a great hall, at once a banqueting house, a council chamber, a throne room, and sleeping-quarters, calling it Heorot, "the hart," perhaps after the beast symbolical of royalty.[2] Its radiance, like the fame of Hrothgar, shines "over many lands." Here in this stately building sits the king, victorious in war, mild in peace, dispensing justice equitably, and dealing out treasure with a lavish hand. His domain presents an idealized picture of royal splendor.

The main purpose of all this is obviously to give a proper setting to heroic narrative. The audience is assured that it is to hear of no mean folk, but a great people, renowned in story, with an illustrious royal line derived from a half-supernatural founder. Such full-throated trumpeting of Danish glories has sometimes been regarded as having sprung, in an earlier form of the story on Scandinavian soil, from national feeling. But, as has already been suggested, such feeling was hardly possible in the earlier Middle Ages, in society as it was then organized, and nothing is plainer than the readiness of singers and audiences to busy themselves with illustrious foreign heroes. There is a subtler purpose, too, in emphasizing Hrothgar's apparent prosperity; it contrasts sharply with impending tragedy. The immediate danger confronting the Danes is the incursions of the demon Grendel, who comes slinking under cover of night to devour the revellers in the hall, and mock their boasted power. But the king faces troubles more serious than this. His sovereignty, won by disregarding the legitimate successor, can hardly pass unchallenged to his sons. A scheming nephew, aided, it would appear, by a treacherous counsellor, is already plotting to seize his throne. An ancient feud with the neighboring Heathobards is only temporarily quieted by the betrothal of his daughter to the Heathobard prince. His great mead-hall itself is fated to go up in smoke and flames, with kin arrayed against kin beneath its walls. In a word, the house of the Scyldings, apparently so brilliant, is overshadowed by the darkest clouds of future calamity.

We are told that Hrothgar has ruled fifty years, that he is wise and venerated; but these are epic characteristics of the powerful king, like Charlemagne's *barbe fleurie* and Beowulf's reign of fifty years. Historically, he must have worn the crown a considerable length of time. Yet it rested uneasily on his head. The legitimate successor, after the death of his elder brother Heorogar, should have been Heorogar's son, Heoroweard. But for causes that are not clear this prince was passed over, and Hrothgar ascended the throne. This was not necessarily unlawful; the succession in Germanic kingdoms was, as we have seen, elective as well as hereditary, and Heoroweard may have been unfitted to rule because of his youth or for other reasons. A hint is dropped (2160) which indicates that he was, even in his father's lifetime, not treated with the consideration that he might have expected, but it is difficult to escape the conviction that Hrothgar's later troubles were due in part to his neglect of the rightful claims of his elder brother's son. It is certain that he shows him scant honor in the royal hall. Beowulf was wiser: when urged, after the death of Hygelac, by Hygelac's own widow, to assume the sovereignty, he refused, preferring to act as protector for the prince. It looks as if the temptation to be king had been too great for Hrothgar, and as if he feared the nephew who might have worn the crown. For he favors Hrothulf, the son of his younger brother, who has no prior claim to the throne, giving him the place of honor beside him on the high seat, and making him his partner in war as in peace. Heoroweard, on the other hand, has no share in the brilliant festivities in honor of Beowulf, and the armor of his own father is given to Beowulf (2155–2162), a great shame and humiliation for the son. In the background of this dazzling court, then, lurks the neglected and insulted Heoroweard, hating equally the uncle who has supplanted him, and the cousin who enjoys the royal favor.

Meanwhile Hrothulf, the favored nephew, cherishes his own designs. He bides his time, accepting the honors that Hrothgar heaps upon him. But he is obviously not quite trusted. At the ceremonial banquet given Beowulf after his victory, there is in the speech of Hrothgar's queen, Wealhtheow, a direct appeal to Hrothulf to support the succession of Hrothgar's sons, — and her sons as well, — the boys Hrethric and Hrothmund. After all that his uncle has done for him, says the queen, he can hardly act in any other way. And in the adoption of Beowulf as a son by Hrothgar we may see—though the event is of course fictitious —an indication that the poet means to represent Hrothgar as desirous to gain a powerful ally for his sons, or a place of refuge for them at the court of the Geatas if they should need it. The plans of the treacherous Hrothulf matured slowly; much later than the main adventures of the poem, he assisted Hrothgar in war with the Heathobards. But the final tragedy is foreshadowed in dark hints. The statement in *Widsith* that "uncle and nephew held peace together for a very long time" (45–46) points to a later quarrel. When Hrothgar's son came to the throne after his father's death, Hrothulf at last threw off the mask. Scandinavian sources are of considerable assistance at this point. It appears that Hrothulf attracted to his person a body of the doughtiest Danish warriors, and after exploits abroad, returned one day to Heorot, and demanded of young King Hrethric its surrender. Hrethric parleyed, offering rich treasure, but Hrothulf refused these overtures, attacked the hall, slew Hrethric, and himself ascended the throne. What became of the young prince, Hrothmund, the brother of Hrethric, we are not told; perhaps he fell in the fight, perhaps he went the way of so many royal youths who have stood between ambition and a crown.[3]

It seems probable that Unferth, the *þyle*, or "orator" of the Danish court, obviously a prominent counsellor, had some share in increasing the enmity between Hrothgar and Hrothulf. We are told — a suspicious circumstance — that he enjoyed the confidence of both. He was certainly a man with an evil temper and a bad reputation. His character is sufficiently revealed in the attack that he makes on Beowulf's courage at the ceremonial banquet. To accuse a guest of having failed to make good a boast was a deadly insult, to which Beowulf replied with great adroitness and dignity, mentioning in retaliation a shady page in Unferth's own history, — he had not treated his kinsmen honorably at the play of swords, an insult even more deadly than Unferth's, and met by no denial. Unferth does not appear in Scandinavian analogues of the story of Hrothulf; he may have been introduced into the tale by the Anglo-Saxons. We shall have occasion in the following chapter to examine in some detail the interlude in which he figures.

Perhaps one of the reasons why Hrothulf received much attention in *Beowulf* is that he became so famous a monarch, presiding, like Arthur or Charlemagne, over a court of distinguished warriors, and celebrated in song and story in Scandinavia under the name of Hrolf Kraki, — "Hrolf the tree-trunk," — possibly in allusion to his height, like that of a tree with the branches lopped off, or to the crookedness of his figure. One of his champions, Bothvar Bjarki, was especially famous.

The older part of his name, Bjarki, — "the little bear," — is strikingly similar in meaning to Beowulf, the "bee-wolf," that is, "bear." And it also seems likely that reminiscences of Beowulf's exploits with Grendel were transferred to Bjarki, who, according to the *Saga of Hrolf Kraki*, comes from the land of the Gautar (Geatas) to the court of the Danish king, and defends him from the nocturnal attacks of a troll. Some scholars have even assumed that the two heroes were identical; but there are great differences in their careers, and the resemblances are not strong or numerous enough to warrant such a conclusion. On the other hand, it is easy to understand that when Hrothulf supplanted Hrothgar in popularity, tales of Hrothulf's champion, Bjarki, might well be affected by reminiscences of the mighty deeds done at Heorot by Beowulf. In the saga and in Saxo, heroic legend is overgrown by a rank blossoming of the weeds of story-telling. The treachery by which Hrothulf won his throne was completely forgotten, and his honor, fortitude, and generosity were emphasized. At the time when *Beowulf* was composed, Hrothulf's renown must already have been considerable, even though he had not yet, as in later years, completely eclipsed the fame of his uncle.[4]

Ambition and crime had made Hrothulf king of the Danes, but he was not to go unpunished. The rightful heir to the throne, according to strict succession, the neglected Heoroweard, came at last into his own. Like Hamlet, he delayed long in his revenge, not venturing to attack Hrothgar, and even swearing fealty to Hrothulf, when the latter became king. He had been so long inactive that he was perhaps not regarded as dangerous. But his hour came; he took advantage of Hrothulf's foreign feuds to enlist for his fortunes a party of Swedes, with some followers of his own from Denmark, and struck to win the crown, slaying Hrothulf in his own hall. The courageous defence of Hrothulf, and especially the bravery of his champion, Bjarki, in the smoke and tumult of the burning hall, were long celebrated in Northern poetry, particularly in the famous *Lay of Bjarki*. But the triumph of Heoroweard was short-lived. He had won his throne at last, and was sitting as sovereign near the blazing ruins of his hall, and receiving homage. Suddenly he espied a single survivor of Hrothulf's men, and promised him protection if he would enter his service. The retainer agreed, but in the very act of swearing loyalty, stabbed Heoroweard to the heart. Thus was Hrothulf avenged, and thus the House of the Scyldings came to an end.

Contrasting with these dark figures stands the bright form of Freawaru, the lovely daughter of Hrothgar, equally entangled in the web of fate, but through no fault of her own. When the poem opens, she is betrothed to Ingeld, prince of the neighboring Heathobards, — a match of love as well as of political necessity. Beowulf sees her on his visit to the Danish court, and, on returning home and relating his adventures to his sovereign Hygelac, prophesies that evil will come of her marriage. The old feud that her betrothal is designed to end goes back, as Scandinavian sources suggest, to the time of Hrothgar's father, Healfdene. Apparently Froda, king of the Heathobards, slew Healfdene, and the duty of revenge fell upon the latter's sons. If the *Saga of Hrolf Kraki* may be trusted, this duty was accomplished, and Froda died in the cinders of his own hall. Vengeance then passed to the Heathobards, but before they could attack the Danes, Hrothgar proposed that Freawaru and her dowry should end the feud, and so it was arranged. But the best part of the story was still to come, and the poet of *Beowulf*, anxious that his hearers should enjoy the tragic climax, adopted the bold device of making his hero *prophesy* to Hygelac the future course of events.[5] Probability is here sacrificed; Beowulf might have felt that no good would come of the match, but he could hardly have foreseen the course of future events in so detailed and accurate a way. The point is worth noting, as an example of how far the poet was willing to go for the sake of emphasizing the tragedy of history. When the bride and her retinue shall have arrived in the halls of the Heathobards, one of the Danish thanes who are accompanying her will have the imprudence and tactlessness to wear the sword and armor of a Heathobard warrior, slain in past feuds. This will be no very pleasant sight for the Heathobards, and least of all for the son of the dead man, bound by custom to take blood-revenge. Then an old Heathobard warrior will egg on the youth to action, setting the ancient feud abroach, while the ale-beakers go round the hall. So vengeance will assert itself, the bride's thane will be murdered, and the slayer will make his escape, since he knows the country better than the Danes who would fain pursue him. Thus the old hatred between the two peoples will awake, the love of Ingeld for his young wife will cool, the oaths of peace and promises of friendship will be broken, and war will ensue.

That Beowulf prophesied truly, we know from *Widsith*, which relates that Hrothgar and Hrothulf "beat down the attack of Ingeld, hewed down at Heorot the host of the Heathobards" (45–49). It would appear, then, that the episode culminated in an invasion of Denmark by the Heathobards, that Ingeld attacked Hrothgar in his own hall, but was defeated and slain, though he succeeded in burning Heorot. The exact course of the story is not quite clear, and has been variously reconstructed. The unhappy Freawaru vanishes from the picture;

what became of her can only be imagined. Hrothgar, though victorious in the end, was humiliated
by the failure of his diplomacy and the destruction
of his royal residence.

The poet of *Beowulf*, it will be observed, emphasizes one particular scene in the story. Not the
historical relationships. He makes small account
of these; and as time went on, his own conception
of them was completely blurred, Froda and Ingeld
even coming to be regarded as Danish kings. Not
the fate of the unhappy princess, or the sufferings
of her husband or father. The one episode that
poets most loved was the speech of the "old warrior," urging the son to blood-revenge. It had, no
doubt, become one of the stock pieces of their rep-
ertory long before *Beowulf* was written, and it certainly continued as such for centuries, the very
scene, perhaps, of the Anglo-Saxon lay that the
pious Alcuin had in mind when he reproved monks
for diverting themselves at table with songs of
Ingeld rather than with praises of Christ, and put
down "that damned heathen" where he belonged:
ille perditus paganus plangit in inferno. We shall
have occasion to notice this later in another connection.

Then at the ale-drinking an aged warrior speaks . . .
who bears in mind all the deadly slaughter of men [in
days gone by]. Bitter of heart and grim of purpose, he
tries the temper of a young warrior, wakens war-enmity:

"Canst thou, my friend, see the sword, the dear weapon, which thy father bore to battle on his last fight, wearing his visored helmet, when the Danes slew him, when the bold Scyldings gained possession of the battle-ground, at the time when Withergyld fell, after the passing of heroes? Now the heir of one of those slayers, insolent in his armor, moveth about the hall, boasting of the deed, and wearing the sword which thou by right shouldst wield." So he urges on the youth again and again with bitter words, until the time comes when the thane of the queen sleeps in death, stained with blood from the bite of the sword, for the deeds of his father, having forfeited his life. The murderer escapes, for he knows the country well. (2041–2062.)

Heremod, a Danish sovereign not included in the Scylding genealogy in the poem, is nevertheless mentioned in a way that piques our curiosity. Violence and stinginess were his chief characteristics. He is twice contrasted with Beowulf: once by a warrior improvising a lay in the hero's honor (901 ff.), and once in a speech by Hrothgar (1709 ff.). The epic leaves us in the dark as to the full story, but later documents are of some assistance in reconstructing it. In the *Anglo-Saxon Chronicle*, and in certain of the Scandinavian royal genealogies, Heremod immediately precedes Scyld, as his father. But in *Beowulf* Scyld is founder of the royal Scylding dynasty. In Saxo's history the father of Scyld is named Lotherus, and his career presents striking similarities to that of Heremod. It may thus be possible to fill out the outline of

Heremod's career, which is only hinted at in *Beowulf*. Very great allowances must be made for alterations and discrepancies; it must always be remembered that Saxo wrote some five hundred years later than the poet of the Anglo-Saxon epic. Putting all the evidence together, however, it appears that Heremod, a younger son, went into exile when his elder brother ascended the throne. But this brother was incompetent, and the Danes longed for the return of the younger son. Their hopes were gratified; Heremod came out of exile, deposed his brother, and seized the crown. His evil nature soon manifested itself. He slew his companions in his drink, and, what was almost as bad, he failed to reward his followers with royal liberality. So his people had to get rid of him. Exalted at one time over all men, and then deposed, and sent into exile in misery and disgrace, he afforded moralists like Hrothgar an alluring theme. It seems likely that he may really belong in the Scylding genealogy historically. His name alliterates with the names of the members of that royal line, Healfdene, Heorogar, Hrothgar, and the rest, and the little story just reconstructed has an air of realism about it which may indicate a basis in actual fact. It seems improbable that the poet would have selected this example of royal depravity from the Danish house unless there had been some real foundation for it. Heremod may have been dropped from the illustrious Scylding line in song and story, in consequence of his sins. Perhaps he preceded it, and poets took his expulsion from the kingdom, after which time the Danes suffered for lack of a leader (15), as a convenient opportunity for giving the rulers of the shieldmen a new and glorious progenitor in the mythical Scyld, whose whole figure may be only a personification of the protecting shield of warfare.[6] We are, however, dealing with a baffling mixture of fact and fiction, in which guesswork has to be our guide. Decision is difficult, and perhaps of no great consequence. But Heremod must always be of interest to the student of Germanic conceptions of kingship.

After the pompous account of Danish glories at the opening of the epic, the picture of the royal court to which Beowulf belongs may seem a trifle colorless. The Geatas are indeed represented as a great people, and their sovereign, Hygelac, as a mighty monarch. But there are no loud trumpet-calls proclaiming the power of their ancestors, and court ceremonials are far more quickly disposed of. When Hygelac is first introduced we are told that "the building was splendid, the king was valiant, in his lofty hall" (1925-1926); then, after a somewhat elaborate compliment to his queen, the action begins forthwith. Similarly, at the opening of the final adventure, the poet wastes no time on descriptions. "Then unto Beowulf's possession did the broad kingdom pass; well did he rule it fifty winters, aged king, old guardian of the realm, until, on murky nights, a dragon's ravages began" (2207–2211), and the tale of the dragon and his gold is fairly started. Information about the Geatas is brought in more episodically than in the case of the Danes, and not given prominence as a setting for the story. Yet, when this information is pieced together, the historical canvas is even more crowded with figures, and the action more complex.

Tragedy is again heavy in the air, as is natural in the closing adventure, which ends with the death of the hero and the extinction of his people. The fate overshadowing the Danes in the earlier part of the poem is far more subtly suggested. Each people suffered for the ambitions of its sovereign: Hrothgar deprived the rightful heir of his crown, and sowed the seeds of domestic calamity; Hygelac wantonly attacked a distant people, and drew hostility upon his folk in days when they needed all their strength to protect themselves against their neighbors the Swedes. For the student of heroic legend and early custom the tale of the Swedish wars is extremely important. A remarkable picture of inter-tribal warfare extending through three generations may be reconstructed, reflecting with great vividness actual conditions of Germanic life, and probably actual events. Historic fact, while frequently subordinated to human interest, is apparently little distorted. There is no great amount of external evidence to support this conclusion, but much in the character of the narrative itself.[7]

The two most prominent figures in the Geat royal family are Hygelac and Beowulf. They are, however, very differently depicted. Beowulf constantly betrays his origin as a folk-tale hero. A certain unreality surrounds him as king; he is more at his ease as a slayer of monsters. Hygelac, an authentic historical figure, is convincing enough as king, but he is less individualized than Hrothgar, and hardly more than the typical sovereign. He has little to do in the action of the poem save to receive the conquering hero, and afford him an opportunity to recount his adventures. But he serves as a convenient central person about whom the other kings of his house may be grouped. It will be clearest, in reviewing these kings and princes and their fortunes, to examine, first, traditions which appear to be founded mainly on fact, and then the processes by which Beowulf has been fitted into this historic setting.

Hygelac's father, Hrethel, was the *nefa* of Swerting (1203), of whom nothing is known. The word *nefa* may mean "nephew," "grandson," or merely "descendant." Swerting may have been an imaginary or collateral ancestor; a name alliterating

with "H" would be expected. One incident in
Hrethel's life is remembered, mainly for its poetic
value, though it may well be founded on fact. He
had two sons, Herebeald and Hæthcyn. Herebeald was accidentally killed by an arrow from his
brother's bow. This tragedy, as already pointed
out, had an especial poignancy on account of the
conflict of duties which it involved. Hrethel was
bound to take vengeance on the slayer of his son,
but, on the other hand, could not do violence to a
kinsman. His sufferings are emphasized by the
poet, who had in mind, apparently, the tragedy of
Ermanric, the Gothic king who, according to
Northern tradition, hanged his son Randver on the
gallows because of Randver's guilty love for his
father's bride.

Sad it is for an aged warrior to see his young heir riding
the gallows; well may he then fashion a lay, a song of
lamentation, when his son hangeth, food for the raven,
and naught he can do will avail, old and wise though he
be. . . . He looks with aching heart on the bower of his
boy, on the wine-hall deserted, a resting-place for the
winds, bereft of its joys. The horsemen sleep, the heroes
in the grave; there is no sound of the harp, no cheerful
clamor in the courts, as in days gone by. (2444–2459.)

This passage impressed Longfellow so much that
he quoted it in *Hyperion* — though he identified
the sorrowing father with "the old Danish hero
Beowulf"!

Hrethel died of a broken heart. At no great time thereafter began the long and devastating wars with the Swedes.

This extremely complicated story involves the same motives which have been traced in traditions centring about the royal house of the Danes — long-standing enmity between neighbors, jealousies and rivalries at home, conflicts between family and political loyalty. Vague and distorted reminiscences of the tale are found in later Swedish, Danish, and Icelandic sources. Clearly, it was one of the great feuds of early story, the memory of which lingered long after it had lost the clear outlines recognizable in *Beowulf*.

The whole falls into two parts, according as the events lie before or after the reign of Hygelac. Underlying it all is the prolonged and bitter hostility which seems to have been the rule between neighboring tribal groups. The ultimate causes that produced this hostility between the Geat and the Swedish people are obscure. The first trouble of which the poem informs us occurred in the reign of Hæthcyn, the luckless king who had accidentally slain his brother. Savage raids were made into Hæthcyn's territory by Onela and Ohthere, sons of the Swedish king, Ongentheow. The name of the locality where these attacks centred is preserved, —Hreosnabeorh (2477), — perhaps a fortification, perhaps a height used as a

natural defence (*beorh*, "hill," "mound"). In retaliation Hæthcyn then led an expedition against
the Swedes. This is told in circumstantial and apparently truthful fashion, in one of the most vivid
passages in the poem, to which rather too little
attention has been given (2922–2998; cf. 2479–
2489). The Geatas were at first successful, and
captured Ongentheow's queen; but a reverse
quickly followed. Ongentheow, the aged Swedish
king, slew Hæthcyn, and rescued his queen. After
a hand-to-hand encounter, he and his men drove
the Geatas to take refuge in the forest of Ravenswood, leaderless. Here the wearied warriors, surrounded by their enemies, were taunted through
the night by the Swedish king, who swore that in
the morning they should lose their lives, and some
should hang on the gallows. But at daybreak the
horn and trumpet of Hygelac, coming with rein-
forcements, were heard in the distance, whereupon
Ongentheow and his men retreated to a fortified
place. The fort was stormed by the triumphant
Geatas; Ongentheow was attacked and wounded
by Wulf, "so that the blood sprang out beneath
his hair." But Ongentheow fought on undaunted,
until his helmet was cloven by Eofor, the brother
of Wulf, and he fell mortally wounded. Eofor
despoiled him of his helmet, his coat of mail, and
his sword, and carried them in triumph to Hygelac, who rewarded both brothers richly with land

and treasure, and gave to Eofor his only daughter as a bride.

Thus the first stage of the feud ended, and a new sovereign ruled each people — Onela the Swedes, and Hygelac the Geatas. Onela was probably married to a sister of Hrothgar the Dane (62), though the evidence for this is not conclusive. A time of peace succeeded; perhaps the Swedes did not care to attack the Geatas again, since the death of Ongentheow had been balanced by that of Hæthcyn, or perhaps they were afraid of Hygelac, who was no mean enemy. Nor do the Geatas seem to have been inclined to initiate fresh hostilities; it is significant that when Hygelac's restless ambition led him to foreign conquest, he turned his attention to the Franks and their allies in the Low Countries. But this expedition bore bitter fruit. After the defeat of Hygelac and his army, a fresh opportunity was given the Swedes to attack their weakened and humbled adversaries. Historically, this may well have been the sequel, though it is complicated, as we shall see, by other matters.

Before tracing the later struggles, which led to the annihilation of the Geat kingdom, we must look with some care at the accounts of Hygelac's ill-starred raid, as preserved in the poem and in Frankish sources. It is a twice-told tale, but it must be repeated, since a comparison with the

chronicles illustrates the methods of epic so strikingly. The deep impression that this historical
event made upon popular imagination is shown by
the frequent references in the poem (1202–1214;
2354–2366; 2501–2508; 2913–2921).

The chief testimony is in the celebrated *History
of the Franks*, by Gregory, Bishop of Tours, who
died in 594, only some seventy years later than
Hygelac himself. Gregory began his book with
the Creation, but fortunately was able, as some
mediæval historians were not, to reach events in
his own century. This gives his work especial
value. At the beginning of his third book he tells
how the kingdom of Clovis was equally divided
between his four sons, one of whom, Theuderic,
"had a handsome and able son named Theudebert." A little further on he describes Theudebert's successful defence against Hygelac and his
marauding party. This probably lies in the latter
part of the first quarter of the sixth century, about
516 to 520, though possibly later.[8]

After these events, the Danes with their king Chlochi-
laicus made for Gaul by sea with a naval expedition.
After disembarking, they devastated one district of the
kingdom of Theuderic and took prisoners, and having
loaded the ships with captives and other spoils, were of
a mind to return home to their own country. Their
king remained on shore, intending himself to follow
when the ships should have reached the open sea.
When the news was brought to Theuderic that his terri-

tory had been laid waste by foreigners, he sent his son
Theudebert into those regions with a strong army and
great supply of war-gear. After killing the king, he defeated the enemy in a naval battle, and recovered all the
booty stolen from the land.

The same tale is told in the *Liber Historiae Fran-
corum*, a work of the eighth century, in part based
on Gregory, with the addition of one interesting
detail, that the attack was made on the "*Atto-
arios vel alios*." These are clearly the "Hetware"
of *Beowulf* (2363, 2916). The nationality of the
invaders is here, as in Gregory, understood to
be Danish — a mistake natural enough from the
point of view of Frankish historians, who would
not distinguish clearly between different tribes of
Scandinavian raiders.

Obviously, this engagement was long remembered, and there is evidence that Hygelac came to
be conceived as a kind of Gargantua or Pantagruel.
A passage in a Latin treatise, *On Monsters and
Prodigies*, written probably in England at about
the same time as *Beowulf*, represents him as a
giant, *quem equus a duodecimo anno portare non
potuit*, whose bones, as they lay on an island at the
mouth of the Rhine after his death, were so large
as to strike beholders with amazement. But curiously enough this account gets his nationality
right, *rex Huiglaucus qui imperavit Getis*, and may
also preserve correctly the general locality of his

defeat and death. Attention has recently been called to a manuscript in Leyden, which shows the forms "Hyglaco," "Higlacus," which are closer to the forms in the Anglo-Saxon epic than those in the other manuscripts. The Leyden writing is that of an Irish or Anglo-Saxon scribe. The inclusion of Hygelac in a collection of classical "monsters" suggests that the compiler was acquainted with the personages in *Beowulf*, and, with the evidence of the handwriting, points to composition in the British Isles. But the fact that Hygelac is made a kind of giant suggests familiarity rather with current oral traditions than with the epic.[9]

This episode furnishes an unusually significant test of the treatment of history in *Beowulf*. On the one hand, the epic, especially in one passage, parallels the documentary accounts quite closely. A loquacious Messenger prophesies trouble for the Geatas after the death of Beowulf.

Now must the people expect a time of war, after the death of the king is widely bruited afar unto Franks and Frisians. Strife was started fiercely against the Hugas, when Hygelac came faring with a fleet to the Frisian land, when the Hetware hewed him down in battle, conquered him by greater force, so that the mail-clad warrior fell, gave up his life amid his troop; in no wise did the prince give treasure to his men. Never since that time have the Merovingians been friendly to us. (2910–2921.)

The Franks (Hugas) held lordship over other tribes, even after their chief power was transferred to the south, into modern France, and of these tribes the Hetware (Hattuarii) dwelling along the lower Rhine, and the Frisians along the coast, were prominent. On the other hand, the whole point of view of the epic is different. To Gregory of Tours Hygelac was a pirate; to the poet he was a hero, whose defeat had to be portrayed as sympathetically as possible. The sting of this defeat is therefore softened by fictitious elaborations. Beowulf crushed the life out of Dæghrefn, the Frankish warrior who had slain Hygelac, and escaped by swimming, carrying thirty suits of armor back home. The Hetware could not boast of victory; "few escaped the warrior to see their homes again." Much is also made of the fate of the marvellous golden collar given Beowulf as a reward for slaying Grendel, and by him presented to Hygelac.

After Hygelac's death the throne passed to Heardred, his son. The epic states circumstantially that Hygd, queen of Hygelac, offered Beowulf "the hoard and kingdom, rings and the royal throne; she did not feel that the child [Heardred] could defend the ancestral seats of the kingdom against the peoples of other lands after the death of Hygelac" (2369–2372). Such an offer would have meant her own hand as well. Possibly tradition told of her marriage to Beowulf, and she may

be the widow who laments him (3150), if we read
the passage aright. The epic states positively that
her offer was refused; that Beowulf preferred to act
as protector of Heardred during his minority. It
is tempting to regard this as a special invention of
the *Beowulf* poet, emphasizing his hero's generosity
in not interfering with the legitimate succession,
and contrasting him with the Danish and Swedish
princes who caused great trouble by so doing. Beowulf's whole connection with political events must
be fictitious, unless we regard him as having supplanted some other person, and for this there is
no evidence.

Queen Hygd, daughter of Hæreth, may well be
historical. She is described as "very young";
perhaps she was Hygelac's second wife. He had
earlier given a daughter in marriage to Eofor. Yet
he is himself described as "young" (1831). We
must not take these epic descriptions of historical
characters—even when they involve no element of
the marvellous — too literally, or regard them as
necessarily reflecting actual conditions. Conflicting traditions, carelessness, lack of concern for
consistency, and desire for immediate poetic effect
must all be considered. The picturesque tale of
Offa and Thryth, introduced to emphasize the
amiability of Hygd, in which reminiscences of the
old Anglian king, Offa, are mingled with the folk-
tale motive of the Perilous Bride, deserves special

study as an illustration of epic processes, and as being the only piece of Anglian tradition embodied in the epic. It has, however, no real connection with the subject in hand, and may be an interpolation.[10]

At this point the second part of the tale of the Swedish wars begins, complicated by a new motive, intrigue within the Swedish royal family. King Onela had two nephews who made trouble for him, Eanmund and Eadgils, the sons of his own brother, Ohthere. Just what this trouble was, we do not know; apparently they were engaged in a conspiracy to seize his throne, and got the worst of it. At any rate, they sought refuge with young King Heardred. The vengeance of Onela reached across to the sister kingdom; he attacked the Geatas, and in the resulting conflict Eanmund was slain, and Heardred himself fell in the defence of his guests. Eadgils escaped. Onela then returned in triumph to Sweden.

There are certain interesting complications in this episode, which afforded special opportunities for poetical effect. Eanmund was slain by one Weohstan, a warrior in the service of Onela. Weohstan belonged to the Wægmundingas, apparently one of the most distinguished clans of the Geatas. Weohstan's son, Wiglaf, the young retainer who comes to the aid of Beowulf in the fight with the dragon, was a Wægmunding. Beowulf's

father, Ecgtheow, and of course Beowulf himself,
are stated by the poet to have been members of
this family, but their names do not alliterate with
"W," or with each other, and it looks as if Beowulf
had been given a prominent warrior for a father,
and as if both had been arbitrarily assigned by
story-tellers to the Wægmunding clan. But why
should the Wægmunding Weohstan be serving under the Swedish king, and so fighting against his
own countrymen and their allies?

Warriors often took service under a foreign
prince, and were obliged, by the terms of this temporary alliance, to aid him in his campaigns. It
was thus, apparently, that young warriors made
the "grand tour," completing their education.
This new duty might impose obligations as binding as allegiance to the king at home. In the shifting political relations of the times, in which friends
quickly turned to foes, a man might find himself
obliged to choose between his own people and the
people of his adoption. Here, as always in such
conflicts of duty, lay effective material for tragedy.
Obviously the connection of Weohstan with the
Swedes was unusually close; his son Wiglaf is described as prince of the Swedish dynasty of the
Scylfingas, which looks as if Weohstan had married
a lady of the Swedish royal house. So, when Onela
marched against the Geatas, Weohstan chose to
throw in his fortunes with the Swedes, and it is

highly significant that he is not reproached for so doing.

Another tragic conflict of duty faced Onela himself. As was the custom, he was offered the war-gear of his dead nephew, Eanmund, by Weohstan, who slew him. But this Onela would not accept, since tribal law forbade him to kill, or to connive at the killing of, a kinsman. Further than this, it laid upon him the duty of taking vengeance for such slaughter. Onela compromised; he could not think of taking vengeance on one of his own family, and yet he was bound to reward the slayer. So he did not receive the armor of the slain youth himself, but returned it to Weohstan (2611–2619). It passed in due time to Weohstan's son, Wiglaf. But the sword which delivered the decisive blow in the fight with the dragon was perhaps the very one that had been plunged into Eanmund's heart.

In tracing the events following the death of Heardred, we must be particularly careful to distinguish historic fact from epic elaboration. The account in the poem is clear enough: Onela, after the death of Eanmund and the flight of Eadgils, wore his crown unmolested for a time. Meanwhile, Beowulf succeeded to the throne of the Geatas, but attempted no immediate revenge for Heardred's death. But the wheel of Fortune came at length full circle for Onela. His rebellious nephew,

Eadgils, later succeeded in an attempt to seize the Swedish throne, and we are told that he was aided in this by Beowulf, who thus took a kind of belated vengeance. There was no further trouble with the Swedes during Beowulf's long reign of fifty years. But with the passing of the great hero after the dragon-fight a renewal of this old feud and war with peoples to the south is prophesied, as we have seen, by the Messenger, who brings the news of Beowulf's death, and urges that the treasures won from the dragon be burned in the funeral pyre with him, for in the future the Geatas cannot wear them in pride and security:

The flame shall devour them, the fire cover them, no chieftain shall wear a precious trophy with its memories of the past, no fair maiden shall adorn herself with a necklace, but heavy-hearted, bereft of their gold, shall they continually tread the paths of exile, now that the war-leader is done with mirth, with sport and the joys of the hall. Many a spear shall be brandished, chill in the morning, raised high in hand; no sound of harp shall rouse the warriors, but the swart raven shall croak eagerly over the bodies of the fated, telling the eagle how he fared at the banquet, when he and the wolf were rifling the bodies of the slain. (3014–3027.)

While the climax of the last adventure, the slaying of the dragon, forms a fitting close to Beowulf's career, it brings his achievements as sovereign to naught. For him to die, full of age and honors, defending his people against a supernatural adversary, is glorious, but for the Geatas to suffer extinction at the hands of their hereditary foes, with all the humiliation which this entailed, is a sorry ending to the high adventure and prosperity that had gone before. No doubt the artistic effect of this catastrophe was carefully calculated; but it was an effect imposed upon the poet by historic facts that were too well known to be tampered with.

What were the actual events following the death of Heardred? In the first place, everything that is said of Beowulf must be discounted immediately. A folk-tale hero, he never really sat on the throne of the Geatas. The epic contains little to suggest that he has replaced an authentic king. The fifty years of his reign are obviously the round numbers of story-telling. Moreover, surprisingly little is told of this long reign. We can hardly suppose that, even under an ideally beneficent monarch, there would be nothing for the poet to record. The one event that sounds at all like an echo of fact is the assistance rendered by Beowulf to the Swedish prince Eadgils, in the rebellion of the latter against Onela. The slaying of Onela by Eadgils is no doubt authentic; the account of the early Swedish kings in the *Ynglingasaga* tells of a fight on the ice of Lake Wener, in which Ali (Onela) was slain by Athils (Eadgils). One of the royal mounds in Upsala may be identified with great probability as the burial-place of Eadgils. But the Scandinavian tradition represents assistance as having come to Eadgils, not from the Geatas, but from the Danes, from King Hrothulf. The Danes may have "stepped into the place originally occupied by the Geatas," but even if this is true, it does not necessarily mean that Beowulf was leader of the Geatas in this engagement. A hero of Beowulf's prowess and spirit might be expected to take an earlier and more direct revenge for the death of Heardred, since this was one of the most binding duties that lay upon the Germanic warrior. Moreover, if Beowulf helped Eadgils to gain his throne, how does it happen that the Swedes are so unfriendly at Beowulf's death, ready to fall upon the Geatas as soon as the protecting hero has expired? It may be argued that this was caused by events which the poem does not mention; but it seems odd, in view of the details given by the Messenger, that no account whatever of such events should be included. The whole situation at the death of Beowulf is not at all what might be expected of a wise and powerful monarch. The name and the nationality of his queen are not given, and nothing at all is said of her save that she lamented at his funeral, if a somewhat damaged passage is correctly so read. He had no heir, and had apparently made no provision for the succession. One is tempted to ask how he could have allowed his people to get into these difficulties if he were as wise as he is represented. While the poet is most detailed, picturesque, and precise in describing romantic adventures, he is everywhere vague in his references to the actual political events in which Beowulf was concerned after the death of Heardred, until he comes to the final downfall of the Geat people, and then preciseness begins once more. The probability is that, after the fall of Heardred, the last of his dynasty, the Geatas were soon completely subjugated by the Swedes. Another king or chieftain may have ruled for a short time. It is possible that Wiglaf is historical. The epic represents him as a youthful warrior, the son of Beowulf's uncle, who, after assisting Beowulf in the dragon-fight, is named by him as his successor. Perhaps the royal power passed to the house of the Wægmundingas, and the final disaster to the Geatas was averted for a time by Wiglaf, just as the disaster to the Anglo-Saxons after the death of Edward the Confessor was averted by Harold, an able man of another family. This would explain the connection of Beowulf, an imaginary person, with the clan of the Wægmundingas.

It is a temptation to fill in the outlines of these political events by conjecture. But this is dangerous. Disregarding so far as possible purely hypothetical occurrences, we may cautiously summarize the historical situation as follows. Upon the death of Hygelac, the throne passed to his son Heardred, a minor, who was unable to maintain himself against the Swedes, and against his southern enemies, led by the Franks, whom his father had stirred to bitter enmity. He was caught, as it were, between the upper and the nether millstone. The Swedes gave the death-blow to his kingdom. They presently swooped down, possibly using hospitality extended to rebellious Swedish princes as a pretext, and, under the leadership of Onela, killed Heardred and inflicted a crushing defeat on the Geatas. Onela was later supplanted by Eadgils. The defeated Geatas were ultimately absorbed into the Swedish kingdom, and went out of existence altogether as a separate political unit. Just before this catastrophe, the Geatas may have turned to the powerful clan of the Wægmundingas to assist them, despite the earlier alliance of Weohstan, the Wægmunding, with the Swedish royal house, and have found in young Wiglaf a temporary leader before their final overthrow.

So much for history. But poetry will not willingly suffer a great people to perish ingloriously. Poetic imagination, when it sets to work to explain or to soften a mighty calamity, often turns to wonder-tales, disguising borrowed elements by specious realism. Men knew of the fall of the Geat kingdom; that was too well-known a fact to deny, but it was within the province of poetry to postpone the catastrophe and take away much of its bitterness by inventing new and glorious adventures for a fictitious Geat king. And so Beowulf, a hero borrowed from folk-tales, was made the nephew of King Hygelac, a member of the Wægmunding family, and the last great sovereign of the Geat people. This brought into alliance with him Wiglaf, as kinsman and helper. The folk-tale champion was metamorphosed into an illustrious ruler, distinguished not only for great deeds but for the peaceful protection of his kingdom, over which he held sway for fifty years. In a similar way, singers softened the defeat of Charlemagne at Roncesvalles by making Roland, a relatively undistinguished leader historically, a nephew of the great emperor and the doer of mighty deeds. Again, Arthur, probably one of the British chiefs who temporarily stemmed the advance of the Anglo-Saxon invaders, was exalted into a great general and king, victorious at home and abroad and a champion of marvellous adventures. In time, the original historical situation which gave birth to the Arthurian legend was completely forgotten in romantic elaborations. But in the earlier period, when the struggles of the Britons against the Anglo-Saxons held a prominent place in the story, there could be no pretence that the British were finally victorious; the supernatural legend had to be invented that Arthur should come from Avalon to deliver his people.

How the fictitious Beowulf, as protecting hero and glorious sovereign, was, by exercise of poetic imagination, fitted into the line of Geat monarchs, and how his death and the final extinction of his people were explained as due to the curse resting on the dragon's gold, will be traced in a later chapter. Historic facts, with which we are here concerned, gave him his setting, but could adorn his exploits with little of definite political importance. After the epic account is closed, he remains, despite all his royal dignities, a strayed reveller from fairyland.

IV

THE TALE OF FINNSBURG

QUITE unconnected with the main business of the epic is the tragic story of the feud between Danes and Frisians, the paraphrase of the lay sung by Hrothgar's minstrel at the ceremonial banquet after the slaying of the demon Grendel (1068–1159). It far transcends in dramatic interest the historical legends which have just been reviewed, and it is purely realistic, with no intrusion of the supernatural, and with little epic exaggeration. Actual events may well be mirrored in it, although there is unfortunately little to aid in determining this. No historical documents or poetic narratives, except the *Finnsburg Fragment*, give other versions of the story. But its general character is plain. Even if it is not a record of fact, imaginatively treated, it is a record of what might have been fact, true to the spirit and customs of the times. The chief emphasis lies upon human passions, upon the tragic crises which confronted men and women in the unsettled yet highly conventional life of the Heroic Age. Certain typical situations, frequently utilized for poetic effect elsewhere in *Beowulf* and in Germanic story-telling in general, stand forth with great vividness. The shadows are as strong as the high lights; much is left in obscurity. The minstrel's own words are not quoted, as many editions suggest, but summarized, just as in the song sung in Beowulf's honor during the return from the Haunted Mere (871–915). The way in which this paraphrase is arranged shows that the Finnsburg story as a whole was perfectly familiar, and that a knowledge of its outlines was taken for granted by the *Beowulf* poet. He was thus free to get special effects by stressing tragic and pathetic situations. This allusive method is tantalizing for us to-day; the course of events has to be reconstructed by conjecture and by study of analogous material. Patient labor has yielded a reasonably satisfying and connected narrative, but with many obscurities of detail. A completely different interpretation of the main outlines is by no means beyond the bounds of possibility.

We are singularly fortunate in being able to supplement the ninety lines of the minstrel's lay by a detailed treatment of one scene, in a little less than fifty lines, which is not elaborated in the epic. Dr. George Hickes published in his *Thesaurus*, in the year after the Battle of Blenheim, some verses copied from a leaf bound in with a manuscript of homilies in the episcopal library in Lambeth Palace. Unfortunately, this leaf has since been lost, so that we are obliged to rely upon Hickes's transcript. There is no reason, however, to doubt the genuineness of the lines. Hickes was a conscientious though not always accurate scholar, and, despite some obvious errors in the copying, the passage stands the test of our better knowledge of Anglo-Saxon well. The proper names and the localization at Finnsburg connect it beyond any doubt with the narrative in the epic. By common consent, it has long been known as the *Finnsburg Fragment*, in contradistinction to the *Finnsburg Episode* (1063-1159) in *Beowulf*. It is defective both at the beginning and at the end. How many lines have been lost, no one can tell. It seems probable, from internal stylistic evidence, that not a great deal is missing, and that, if it were preserved in its entirety, it would form a good illustration of the Anglo-Saxon short epic lay. It contrasts sharply with the *Episode* in treatment. The latter is retrospective, stressing, in the outlines of a complicated story, special scenes of pathos, tragedy, and revenge. The *Fragment* gives a vivid and detailed account of a single scene, a night attack upon a hall, and its successful defence. The reader must bear in mind that, though telling a scene in the same story, the *Fragment* is absolutely independent of the *Episode*.[1]

The circumstances under which the minstrel sang his lay in Hrothgar's hall are important for an interpretation of the story. The subject was

selected with a view to giving pleasure to the
feasting Danish warriors, celebrating the triumph
of a foreign hero, who had performed a feat that
they had themselves striven in vain to accomplish.
This might well be a little galling to them. That it
actually was so is shown by the speech of Unferth
at the banquet before the fight with Grendel. So
the court poet adroitly selected a tale of Danish
heroism and Danish vengeance, a tale of the complete and satisfying victory of the Danes over their
ancient enemies, the Frisians. And this would
have been equally pleasing for Beowulf to hear.
His own people were no friends to the Frisians;
Hygelac later selected their coast as the objective
point of the great raiding expedition in which he
lost his life, and in the later part of the epic
Frisian enmity against the Geatas is much emphasized. The whole *Episode* must be read, then,
with the grand climax at the end in mind: the absolute and complete vengeance of the Danes for the
injury inflicted upon them by the Frisians.

The foundations of the tale are laid, as so often,
in inter-tribal feud. Nothing is said of the ultimate
causes of this deep-seated hatred; it seems probable that it was an ancient grudge, temporarily
healed, but ready to break out with renewed
intensity. Historically, Danes and Frisians were
foes; raiding expeditions along the coast seem to
have been frequent. The opponents of the Danes

are sometimes called Frisians and sometimes Eotens in the *Episode* (the word occurs only in the
genitive *Eotena* and in the dative *Eotenum*). It
looks as if the Eotens were the Jutes, or *Ēotan*, and
as if the poet had confused *Ēotan* with *eotenas*,
"monsters," "giants." He seems to have fallen
into this error elsewhere. The Danish king Heremod was sent into exile *mid eotenum* (902), which
has sometimes been taken to mean "amongst
monsters," and sometimes "amongst the Jutes."
That the latter is really the meaning of the word
in this place seems clear from a passage in the
Swedish chronicle of Messenius, in which the
Danish king Lotherus, who appears to have inherited the adventures of Heremod, is stated to
have taken refuge among the Jutes, *superatusque
in Jutiam profugit*. I believe that we are to assume
that the Frisian king commanded a mixed body
of Frisians and Jutes, and that the poet used now
the one name and now the other, for the sake
of variety, and in deference to the demands of
alliteration. It has already been noted that the
larger political groups were composed of different
tribes, and that in epic narrative reference might
be made to one or another of these tribes, by a
kind of ethnographic metonymy. In the present
instance, alliteration is particularly easy for the
poet if he can refer to the opponents of the Danes
as Eotens, since this word can alliterate with any

other word beginning with a vowel or diphthong. Dr. Chambers believes that it is important for the plot to distinguish sharply between Frisians and Eotens, and that the latter are the true villains of the drama. We shall return to this point later; for the present the story may be outlined in the simpler and more usually accepted fashion.[2]

In a nutshell, the action is as follows. A band of Danes under their prince, Hnæf, are attacked at night, while quartered in a hall as guests of Finn, king of the Frisians. Many warriors on both sides are slain, among them Hnæf. Since they have fought indecisively, and to utter exhaustion on both sides, a truce is arranged, whereby the Danes are to remain for the winter under the overlordship of the Frisian king, and be treated with all honor. In the spring, Hengest, the leader of the Danes, is driven by the restlessness of his men to take vengeance on the Frisians. In the ensuing attack, Finn is killed, and his queen and treasure are taken back to Denmark in triumph. The whole tale falls naturally into two parts: the events preceding and following the long winter during which the Danes brood darkly on schemes of revenge. In the first part, the poet is most interested in the scene after the hall-fight, with the terms of the truce, which are set forth in detail, the funeral of the slain warriors, and the despair of Hildeburg, the queen of Finn, a sister of Hnæf, who has lost both a brother and a son, fighting on opposite sides. In the second part, the slow on-coming of spring is pictured, and the mental struggle of Hengest, torn between fidelity to his oath to Finn and the duty of vengeance for his dead prince.

We must now look at the *Episode* in detail. The opening lines (1063 ff.), which give the setting of the whole, and introduce the paraphrase of the minstrel's lay, are important:

> Then was there mingled song and music before the battle-chieftain of Healfdene [Hrothgar]; the harp was struck, a lay often extemporized. Then it fell to the lot of Hrothgar's minstrel, across the mead-benches, to sing of a joyful thing to hear in the hall, the swift attack falling on warriors of Finn.[3]

The poet thus alludes at the outset to the end of the tale, the moment for which the listening warriors in the hall waited, "the swift attack falling on warriors of Finn," the final vengeance of the Danes. There was no objection to anticipating the outcome, since this was already known. Interest in heroic story lay, not in suspense, but in opportunities for emotional effect afforded by tragic complications and for alluring details of narrative.

After the brief introduction, the story proper begins, with the attack on the Danes and the death of Hnæf. Since this was a temporary triumph for the Frisians, and would be no very agreeable subject for the feasting Danish warriors to linger over, it is quickly dismissed, in two lines, and the poet concentrates attention on the woes of Queen Hildeburg. The *Finnsburg Fragment*, which describes this attack fully, can do so with no loss of dramatic effect, since it is in no way connected with the setting of the lay in Hrothgar's hall. Queen Hildeburg, we are told, "could in no wise praise the good faith of the Eotens" — the typical Anglo-Saxon method of saying that she could well accuse them of treachery. Did Finn invite the Danes to his court with the design of murdering them? Or did some unlucky word or deed set the ancient quarrel new abroach, and lead to a tragic violation of hospitality? Were the Danes themselves in some degree responsible for the quarrel? We cannot tell. It is easy, however, to recognize typical situations of Germanic poetry, — the princess married as a "peace-weaver" to a foreign king, who has earlier been hostile to her people; the treacherous hospitality with murder looming up darkly in the background; the bloody hall-fight after a night-attack; and the sufferings of the unhappy lady. The details and treatment of these situations vary from tale to tale, but there are striking parallels in the story of Ingeld and Freawaru, in the scene at the court of Attila in the Nibelung legends, in the crime of King Siggeir and the dreadful revenge of Signy in the Volsung story.

It is noteworthy that the first point which the *Beowulf* poet selects for emphasis is the tragic conflict in the heart of Hildeburg. Her pathetic desolation as she stands in the gray morning, looking at the bodies of her son and her brother, loathing the treachery that has caused it all, sorrowing for the hard-pressed kinsmen from her homeland, yet bound by years of marriage to their hated foeman — all this is the very bone and sinew of Germanic lyric and epic poetry.

Not less significant is the fact that the poet devotes twenty lines to the truce concluded after the hall-fight. This, indeed, does require explanation. The strict ethics of the *comitatus* made it a disgrace to survive the death of a leader, unless he could be fully avenged; and in this instance, not only is the Frisian king not killed in reprisal, but the Danish warriors agree to accept his overlordship. For the satisfaction of the listening Danish warriors in Hrothgar's hall, the extraordinary circumstances that led to this arrangement had to be fully explained. It is clear that the Frisian party suffered great losses in the hall-fight; "battle snatched away all the thanes of Finn, save a few survivors" (1080). But, on the other hand, the Danes, a relatively small body at the start, could not conquer the Frisians, especially after the loss of their leader, Hnæf. Both sides had fought to a standstill, and to utter exhaustion. At this

point, Finn made a proposition to the Danes: they
were to have another hall, all their own, with a
high-seat for the chief; they would have equal
rights with his own men, and receive from him as
much as the Frisians in the usual distributions of
treasure, — provided they would accept him as
their lord. It was a dreadful situation for the
Danes; Finn was the *bana* of Hnæf (1102), the
man who bore the technical responsibility for his
death, even though the actual slaying had been
done by somebody else. To accept him as their
over-lord was a terrible breach of tribal custom.
But what were they to do? Winter was upon them;
they could not take ship and return home; they
had to have food and shelter, and they had fought
so long (five days, says the *Fragment*) that they
could fight no more. It was an *impasse;* an irreconcilable conflict between human endurance and
the ethics of a rigid code. So the Danes finally
accepted Finn's terms. All the emphasis, as would
be expected in a telling of the tale to Danes, is
upon the promises made by the Frisians and their
allies. Finn expressly agreed that his enemies
should have every consideration. If any Frisian
should taunt the Danes with having taken service
with the *bana* of their lord, the sword should be
the end of him. The situation was a dreadful and
impossible one, but "it was forced upon them"
(1103). They had no choice. Just here lay the

fascination of the tale for a Germanic audience. We have noted already that poets loved to draw themes for drama from conflicts between different aspects of tribal duty, or between such obligations and the facts of human life. The situation was not comfortable for the Frisians; it was big with tragic possibilities for them. They must have recognized that the truce could be only a temporary expedient for getting through the winter, until the sea should be navigable in the spring, and the Danes could leave for their own country. Later on, there would inevitably be fresh trouble; the duty of revenge would assert itself once more.

The funeral of the dead warriors of both parties is etched in a few vivid lines. A huge pyre was erected, adorned with armor and gold. Upon it were placed, among the rest, Hnæf the Dane and his nephew, the son of the Frisian king. Beside the fire stood the heartbroken Frisian queen. The flames sprang up, crackling and roaring, the bodies burst with the heat, blood poured down the pyre beneath the curling smoke. When all was over, the Frisian warriors returned to their own homes,[4] and all settled down for the winter. The Danes, with heavy hearts and grievous wounds, occupied their hall, while the winter storms raged outside.

Here the first part of the tale ends. Before tracing the tragic sequel, we must look with some care at the account of the hall-fight in which Hnæf

lost his life, as told in the *Fragment*. This is a remarkable piece of rapid and vivid narrative. The
Danes are quartered in a hall by themselves. Apparently they are the honored guests of Finn; if
there have been presentiments or foreshadowings
of trouble, we are not informed of them. The
"battle-young" Hnæf keeps watch while his followers sleep. Suddenly a gleam in the moonlight
attracts his attention. Is it a dragon flying through
the air? is it the first beams of dawn? is it a fire
in the gable of the hall? No, an attack! Their
shining armor has betrayed the stealthy traitors.
Hnæf rouses his men, they rush to arms; Sigeferth and Eaha defend one door, and Ordlaf and
Guthlaf the other. Outside the hall Garulf, son of
Guthlaf, calls out in a clear voice, asking the name
of the defender at the door within. The proud
answer comes back: "Sigeferth is my name; I am
prince of the Secgan, a wandering champion known
far and wide. Many woes and hard fights have
I survived; as for you, it remains to be seen what
fate you will suffer at my hands." Guthlaf, not
heeding the counsel of a more prudent companion,
Guthere, — the definiteness of the names gives
great realism to the scene, — rushes to the attack,
and is the first of the besiegers to fall. The fight
is on, the raven hovers above, swords gleam as if
all Finnsburg were in flames! Well do the thanes
of Hnæf repay the generosity of their leader. Five

days they fight, and no one of them falls; they defend the hall successfully. Then one of the besiegers retires, the king (Finn) asks after the wounded,—and the *Fragment* is at an end.

On the whole, all this agrees very well with the narrative in the *Episode*. We should indeed expect the divergences to be greater, in view of the characteristic shiftings of epic narrative. There are one or two minor inconsistencies. The Ordlaf of the *Fragment* is no doubt the Oslaf of the *Episode*. Garulf, the impetuous young hero who first attacks, is called "son of Guthlaf," and Guthlaf was one of the defenders of the doors. If they are father and son, why are they fighting on opposite sides? Possibly circumstances have allied the two with different parties — a common device to arouse interest in Germanic poetry; possibly the father of Garulf is another Guthlaf than the Dane inside the hall; possibly the phrase "Guthlaf's son" (*F.* 35) is a scribal error for "Guthere's son" (cf. *F.* 20). Again, the *Episode* apparently states that not only Hnæf but others (1084) fell; the *Fragment* states certainly that no one of the defenders fell. This looks like epic exaggeration, a desire to exalt the supreme valor of the Danes. The *Episode* would have no point without the death of Hnæf and the obligation of vengeance, which motivate the entire tragic situation. In the *Fragment*, a detached lay, apparently, no such event was required. However,

in discussion of the narrative as a whole, the discrepancies between the two accounts may be dismissed as of little importance.

The second part of the story has been aptly
termed "the tragedy of Hengest." [5] He was apparently not of royal blood, but the chief retainer
of the dead Hnæf, the ablest man in the party, on
whom the command of the Danes devolved. His
position was one of extreme difficulty and delicacy.
He and his men were in a foreign land, in the dead
of winter, among bitter enemies. They were bound
by oath to keep the peace, and he, as leader, was
additionally responsible. They all longed to return home, but this was impossible until spring.
Desire for revenge and a burning sense of wrong
filled their hearts. Decision as to future action
depended upon Hengest. They could, of course,
mature a plan for revenge to be executed after
they had left Finn's domains. But could they
leave without striking a blow at the *bana* of their
lord Hnæf? Nothing but the oath to Finn stood
in their way, but this oath was of the most solemn
and binding character, allegiance to an over-lord.
In this dilemma, Hengest temporized. Finally
spring came, the bosom of the earth grew fair,
the stormy sea subsided — and the restless Danes
could contain themselves no longer. One day
the son of Hunlaf came to him, bearing a sword,
the edges of which "were well known among the

Eotens," — which probably means that it had done service earlier in the hall-fight, — and formally presented it to him.[6] Hunlaf was apparently (on the evidence of the *Skjoldungasaga*) a brother of the princes Guthlaf and Oslaf (Ordlaf). Perhaps he had been killed in the hall-fight, and his son was especially desirous of vengeance for his slain father. At all events, the presentation of the sword was a call to action, and Hengest wavered no longer. He recognized the superior claim of immediate vengeance. And "horrid bale fell upon Finn in his own home." Just what happened is not told; probably the Danes surprised the Frisians in an unguarded moment, after the long months of inaction. But one thing is clear: that the final attack upon Finn and his men forms the great climax of the story, the whole point of the telling of the tale at Hrothgar's feast. Danish revenge was accomplished with dreadful thoroughness. Grim exultation and bitter reproach accompanied it; Guthlaf and Oslaf cast in Finn's teeth all the woes that had befallen them since that first fateful journey across the sea to Finnsburg. Finn was slain in his own hall, which ran red with the blood of his men. Hengest and his followers, taking with them all Finn's treasures and his unhappy queen, sailed back to their own country in triumph.

Is not this final victory clouded by dishonor? Does not the fact that Hengest proved false to his oath to Finn place him and his warriors in a bad light? No offence had been given by the Frisian party, so far as we know, since the conclusion of the truce; they had played the game fairly. Would it not have been a more satisfying tale, from the Danish point of view, if Hengest had waited until, after a stay in his own land, he could return and wipe out the old score? The submission to Finn had obviously been only an expedient for getting through the winter; it cannot have been thought of by either party as a permanent arrangement. Finn could not have expected that the Danes would remain with him after a return to their own land became possible, but he had every reason to think that they might observe the terms of the oath until after their stay in his domains was over. Does not the whole tale, then, involve the moral shame of the Danes, despite the satisfaction of the great duty of blood-revenge?

No. If this had been the case, the lay could hardly have been sung to gladden the feasting warriors in the hall of Hrothgar. In the first place, Hengest had to choose between conflicting moral obligations. He finally chose the one which seemed to him the more imperative, and which seemed so to his men. It is hard for us at the present day to realize the shame felt by a Germanic warrior if he failed in his full duty to his leader, or the disgrace of having to give allegiance to the slayer of his prince. Nothing could obliterate such humiliation, even though sealed by a forced oath, excepting thorough and bloody revenge. Moreover, early conceptions of the sanctity of an oath were different from those of to-day. Jiriczek, in commenting upon the story of the Nibelungs, points out that, while blood-vengeance was the holiest of duties and good faith the noblest of virtues,

Germanic conceptions of good faith did not exclude crime and treachery, deceit and the breaking of oaths, for this conception was, as history and poetry show, in no wise an abstract ethical law, of general application to everyone; it first gained inner sanctity and universality through the influence of Christianity. To the Germanic warrior, keeping faith was only a matter of personal relationship, grounded in morals and manners, between peoples connected by ties of blood, marriage, hereditary or voluntary service; against enemies, whether of the family or of the over-lord, or of the individual himself, bad faith, treachery, even the breaking of oaths, were regarded as permissible. And so heinous treachery may accompany the highest virtue: Hagen faithlessly murders Siegfried as the avenger of his insulted lord, to whom he is faithful unto death; Kriemhilt, who attacks her own brothers, commits the crime out of fidelity to Siegfried.[7]

So Hengest, when confronted with the supreme duty of taking vengeance for his lord, finds in oaths sworn to an enemy under compulsion no permanent and binding sanctity.

A very different view of the whole story is taken
by Professor Chambers, whose wide and accurate
knowledge of early ethnographic and social conditions makes his opinion of great importance.[8]
He thinks that the blame for the attack upon the
hall rests with the Eotens and not the Frisians,
because Hildeburg "could not praise the good
faith of the Eotens." He recognizes that different
tribal names might severally be employed for a
combined force taken as a whole, but he is not
willing to concede that the forces under Finn may
in this story be referred to, now as Frisians and
now as Eotens. His theory is that Finn's own men
"wake to find a battle in progress" and are drawn
in on the side of the Eotens, their allies. But there
is nothing to support this in the *Episode;* it is
pure hypothesis. He continues his reconstruction:
"Finn's son joins in the attack, perhaps in order
to avenge some young comrade in arms; and is
slain, possibly by Hnæf. Then Finn *has* to inter-
vene." But nothing is said in the text about
avenging a young comrade, or the slaying of Finn's
son by Hnæf. It seems to me dangerous to erect
an imaginative structure to motivate so important an event as the forced intervention of Finn,
which is also imaginary. Professor Chambers
thinks that Finn is "blameless," though he is
called the *bana* of Hnæf. But the word *bana*, to
quote a note from his own edition of the poem,

"must mean 'slayer,' not merely 'foe.'" Finn either slew Hnæf himself, or was regarded as responsible for·his death, as a chief was responsible for the acts of his retainers, according to Germanic custom. I do not see how *bana* can be "a perfectly neutral word," especially since the *Episode* tells us that the agreement was that the Danes should not be taunted because they were following the *bana* of their lord. If Finn's responsibility was a mere technicality, why should the Danes be so carefully guarded from this reproach? "Surely," says Professor Chambers, "a man may be touchy about being taunted, without being regarded as having done anything disgraceful." But it *was* disgraceful, according to the code, for warriors to give allegiance to the man responsible for the death of their lord; there is no getting around that. The point is that extraordinary circumstances, for which the code did not provide, forced the Danes into that position. How seriously the taunting was taken is shown by the lines that follow. If any Frisian did let his tongue get the better of him, the sword should be his punishment.⁹ Professor Chambers, however, will not allow that the compact was possible. "It is strange enough in any case that Hnæf's retainers should make terms with the slayer of their lord. But it is not merely strange, it is absolutely unintelligible, if we are to suppose that Finn has not merely slain Hnæf, but has lured him into his power, and then slain him while a guest." But this, to my mind, is just where the tragic tension comes in. It was against all tradition, but it *had* to be. The terrible position into which Finn forced the Danes is balanced at the end by the heavy retribution which fell upon him, — his death, the spoiling of his treasure, the abduction of his queen. Why this final emphasis upon the humiliation of the Frisians, if the Eotens are the guilty ones? If we make Finn blameless, Hengest's compact with him reasonable, and the final disasters to Finn unfortunate accidents, the whole story seems to me to burst like a pricked bubble. But if we regard it as a tale of a great wrong, of a compact unthinkable but inevitable, of a great mental struggle, and of complete and overmastering revenge, it becomes tense and tragic, a striking instance of those conflicts between the social code and circumstances which the Germanic poets loved to depict, and a theme far more suited to the occasion for which it was sung in Hrothgar's hall, a tale of complete and crushing revenge upon a treacherous enemy.

May it not be, too, that the story of Queen Hildeburg was here designedly brought into connection with the tragedy in store for Queen Wealhtheow, which must have been well known to the people for whom the poet of *Beowulf* wrote? The

downfall of the Danish royal house has been reviewed in the last chapter. The irony of it all is
heightened by the rejoicings that fill the hall of
Hrothgar, and by the happiness that is at present
the lot of Wealhtheow. Of such contrasts the
Germanic poets were exceedingly fond, as many
passages in *Beowulf* illustrate. The telling of the
story of Hildeburg in the presence of a queen who
was herself of another people than that of her husband, whose efforts to keep the peace were destined to come to naught, and whose daughter
Freawaru was to experience much the same melancholy destiny as the wife of King Finn, is surely
not without significance.

The interpretation of the story has all the fascination of a puzzle, perhaps of an insoluble one.
A completely different explanation has been proposed by Professor R. A. Williams, of the University of Belfast, who believes that the Nibelung
story, which somewhat resembles the tale of
Finnsburg, will supply the missing portions. But
great epic tales constantly shift and alter in events
and motivation, so that resemblances are no
guaranty of further identity. Different versions
of the same theme often show the widest divergences.[10]

Further detailed discussion of the Finnsburg
story obviously cannot be attempted here. Many
obscurities must remain, until new evidence turns

up. Had the poet of *Beowulf* striven to make his narrative baffling and obscure, while preserving his general artistic aim, he could not have succeeded better. He has left us unsatisfied, but he has nevertheless allowed us to catch the blurred outlines of a great and moving tragedy. Its wild passion strikes, like a vivid cross-light, athwart the placid epic atmosphere of its setting. It would lend itself readily to dramatic form, with its sharply contrasted scenes — the treacherous attack on the hall in the moonlight, the breaking of dawn on the slain warriors and the weeping queen, the blazing pyre lighting up the grim and blood-stained faces of deadly enemies, the long, gloomy winter vigil of the desperate and humiliated Danes, the secret presentation of the sword, the fierce attack on Finn's hall amid curses and reproaches, and the final voyage of the treasure-laden ship with the triumphant Danes taking a last look at the bloodstained Frisian land. It is finer matter than the tale of Œdipus, in that pursuing Fate lies in men's own passions, not in external influences determining their destinies. Somewhere in the lost poetry of the Heroic Age there lies, perhaps, an epic narrative not unworthy of the greatness of the theme.

V

SCYLD AND BRECA

IN THE preceding pages we have been dealing with historical conditions, or with imaginative but mainly realistic elaborations of those conditions. We now turn to themes in which the supernatural is the essential part of the narrative, in which the element of fantasy is not secondary but fundamental, though rendered speciously plausible by its historic setting, and by realistic detail. These themes are far more difficult of investigation. In dealing with historical or semi-historical personages, shadowy though they may be, and obscured by the mists of time, we come to grips, after all, with fact. But nothing is more elusive than the shifting processes of popular imagination. Rigorous attention to method is here especially necessary; the temptation to analyze the picturesque fantasies of the past by giving rein to our own imagination must be sternly repressed. The true guidance comes in a study of the beliefs of early peoples, and of the survivals of those beliefs in modern times. Even here the ways are often dark. An analysis of the supernatural material in *Beowulf* will depend a good deal upon the investigator's general beliefs in regard to early mythological processes and the transmission of popular material, matters which have been hotly discussed for generations, and about which final and satisfactory evidence is very hard to obtain. Scholarly fashions have changed here far more than in historical investigation. In general, the methods and results of the older students of historical conditions have stood the test of time, while their conclusions in regard to " mythology " have been substantially modified, and in some cases wholly abandoned.

In *Beowulf* — which is, as we have seen, in no sense a primitive work of art, or one reflecting purely popular conditions — the problem is especially difficult. The whole tone of the epic is far removed from the simplicity of folk-tales, from the childlike belief that the world is ruled by a multitude of invisible deities and plagued by legions of ghostly foes. The stories that it embodies were indeed born of that habit of mind, but the sophistications of courtly life, the cultivation of a reading age, and the effects of a new and essentially monotheistic religion brought great alterations. There can be little doubt, I think, that the poet of *Beowulf* believed implicitly in the existence of spooks like Grendel and of dragons like the one that dwelt near the Eagles' Ness, but he certainly conceived them in a different fashion from that of the simple credulous fellows who trembled

at the tales of their ravages, over roaring firesides at wintertime. Beowulf himself meets his
demons clear-eyed, with the heroism that springs
not only from valor but from consciousness of
virtue, and from faith in the True God. To him
they afford occasion not only for heroic achievements, and for the protection of suffering mankind, but also for the defence of the settled orderly
happiness of the civilized state. It is the duty of
a sovereign and of those who would uphold human
sovereignty to meet and destroy them.

In studying the origins and development of the
supernatural "machinery" in *Beowulf* we must
make the effort to reconstruct the more naïve conceptions on the basis of which the later and more
artistic narrative has been composed. Direct
guidance for this in early times is lamentably lacking, however. It may be understood most clearly,
perhaps, from a study of the *Poetic Edda* and the
Prose Edda. These sources are relatively late and
sophisticated, and they have not been unaffected
by foreign elements, but they are of great importance because they reflect pagan religious conceptions, and because they are highly detailed and
explicit. They have a particular significance for
the student of *Beowulf*, since it was among the
Scandinavians that the whole background of the
supernatural in the epic may be supposed to have
originated. The general outlines of the Norse

worship are believed to be valid for Danes and
Swedes and Angles and Saxons as well, though the
evidence to support this has largely disappeared.
There were of course, in any case, great variations in pagan cults in different countries and at
different times. The deities that the Icelanders
venerated were numerous — some of them highly
important, like Odin and Thor and Balder and
Frey; while others, though ranking as major gods,
were merely personifications of different kinds of
human activity, like Bragi, the god of eloquence
and poetry, or Forseti, the god of justice and legal
arrangements. The great stories that grew up
about divine beings introduced prominent figures
like Frigg, the consort of Odin, or Freya, the sister
of Frey; others, like Hermod and Skirnir, were
virtually servants, and still others, like Idunn, the
wife of Bragi, or Nanna, the wife of Balder, were
of distinctly minor importance. There were also
the powerful Norns, the fate-goddesses, and the
Valkyries, who brought slain warriors to the joys
of Valhalla. But the Northern imagination went
much further than this; it peopled the world with
beings who were the embodiments of the elementary manifestations of Nature, — the winds, the
sea, the streams, the woods, the night, the day,
and so forth. Frequently the name of the divinity
was identical with that of the element which he
was supposed to rule, as Drifa for the snowdrift,

Jokull for the ice, or Frosti for the frost. Such rude elementary beings were often conceived as giants or dwarfs, who came into conflict with the major gods, when the latter controlled or interfered with their own activities. Hence the frequent tales of strife between gods and giants or gods and elves, in which the less powerful beings are subdued by greater divinities like Odin and Thor.[1]

This general situation is familiar to students of primitive beliefs and cults and of later literature preserving relics of earlier conditions. Classical mythology offers analogies, not only in the way that the major gods were conceived, but in the multitude of lesser deities representing forces of nature or states of culture. The highly developed civilization of Egypt retained strange survivals of early and crude worship in its beast- and bird-headed gods and goddesses. Modern African and South Sea Island tribes reveal similar highly developed polytheistic systems. To the ignorant and superstitious man the world over, the universe is alive with warring forces, good and evil. As he advances in culture and enlightenment, these forces are still familiar, but they have lost something of their earlier power to terrorize and to charm. What keeps them alive most of all, perhaps, is the tales about them that have been transmitted from generation to generation, constantly changing, but growing no less absorbing through the passage of years. In the later stages of culture, represented by the Homeric epics, the Eddic poems, and the extant monuments of Egyptian civilization, artistry has modified, refined, and systematized earlier crudities of belief, but not wholly concealed them.

Mythology is not static, but constantly changing, like language, and it is therefore impossible to arrange it, for the Germanic peoples, according to any set scheme. Odin, — the West-Germanic Woden, — the chief divinity of all, is probably a relatively late figure, who has displaced Tyr, the war-god, the analogue of the Greek Zeus, who has himself sunk to a secondary place. Thor, the thunder-god, early identified with vegetation-cults, has been largely superseded in that rôle by Frey, a divinity from another race of gods, the Vanir, — perhaps another cult which was amalgamated with that of the Æsir, — and his functions specialized in other directions. Foreign influences must be reckoned with; there are obvious confusions with classical and Christian conceptions. We sometimes find Odin identified with Mercury, and Thor with Jupiter, while Balder, the god of radiant innocence and light, has been much influenced by the figure of Christ. Each deity, then, calls for a separate investigation, and his varying functions and shifting popularity are likely to make a long and intricate story.

In many cases the activities of these deities, great and small, are clear allegories of the processes of nature or the stages of human culture, just as in classical times the alternation of winter and summer was symbolized by the tale of Proserpina and Pluto, or the arts of the metal worker embodied in the activity of Vulcan. To the Egyptians the passage of the sun through the heavens appeared as the voyage of the god Ra, encountering on his way the demons of night and darkness. In other cases, however, the stories told of the gods are not to be interpreted clearly as allegories; perhaps the allegory never existed, perhaps it has become so clouded in the mists of time as to be unintelligible. This is especially the case with minor deities, and with heroes possessed of supernormal powers. The constant tendency to confuse the heroic with the divine led to endowing mortals with supernatural attributes, and to the telling of stories of mortal adventures with supernatural embellishments. Not every contest between a god and a giant necessarily meant the warring of opposed forces of nature; not every adventure involving the supernatural is to be interpreted allegorically. And it must be remembered that a story may be transferred to other figures, and the activity of the original god or hero, which first gave it significance, forgotten.

Here, then, is the crux of the whole problem of the investigation of supernatural elements in stories that have come down from primitive sources. The task of the scholar is to distinguish sharply between beings with supernatural attributes who can be definitely set down as mythological, with clearly defined functions, and those who cannot safely be so regarded, who may be merely heroes to whom the aura of the marvellous has been transferred. Furthermore, his task is to distinguish between those supernatural tales which are clearly allegories, and those which cannot definitely be so interpreted, even though the allegory may once have existed. Later conceptions must be discounted; a subtler meaning may have later been attached to an old story which had in the beginning no such significance; the "mythological" quality may be secondary and not fundamental. Conservatism is safest; there is great danger of imagining that a legend had a deeper meaning than the evidence really warrants.

Beowulf offers admirable illustrations of these general considerations. For Scyld, the son of Scef, the founder of the Scylding or Danish royal line, the ancestor of Hrothgar, builder of the mead-hall, a supernatural origin and allegorical significance may be safely claimed. But his attributes are borrowed rather than original, and he himself is a secondary and relatively late creation. The situation is complicated, but after years of patient study and discussion its main outlines have become fairly clear. Scyld is a personification, as his name "Shield" suggests, of warlike qualities, the defence of the realm. The pretty story in the opening lines of the epic confirms this. When the Danes were forlorn and apprehensive, lacking a king, — the most miserable of all conditions for a Germanic people, — there came drifting to their shores a little child alone in a boat. They accepted him as their king, and when he grew to man's estate he justified his kingship, subduing neighboring peoples and forcing them to pay tribute. After his death he was again laid upon the bosom of a vessel richly decked with weapons and precious objects, and sent forth over the waters whence he came (1-52).

Scyld is called "Scefing" or "son of Scef," a name which, meaning "sheaf," immediately suggests a vegetation-deity. Apparently Scef was regarded by the Scandinavians as a good father for Scyld, a combination that was assisted by the alliteration of the two names. In early mythology, children did not necessarily inherit the characteristics of their fathers; a vegetation-deity might easily be conceived as begetting a warlike son. The warlike Scyld was, as we shall see, given by the Anglo-Saxons a corn-deity, Beow, as a son. Scyld and Scef (or Sceaf) were probably quite independent of each other in the beginning. Both figures were used by the Anglo-Saxons in their royal genealogies, but not as father and son. Some versions of the *Anglo-Saxon Chronicle* inform us that Scef was the child of Noah, and born in the Ark! While both Anglo-Saxons and Danes used, to a considerable extent, the same figures in the genealogies of their early kings, they did not do this consistently — persons and relationships change. It seems likely that Scyld was a being born of an epithet rather than of a god, that his name and personality were derived from the term "scyldingas" ("shield-men"), applied to the Danes, and later used as a name for a dynasty. The suffix *-ing* may mean either "possessed of" or "descended from." Consequently the shift in meaning from "shield-men" to "sons of the shield," or "sons of Shield," was natural, and the creation of a mythical founder of the line, Scyld, was easy. Such a process was not uncommon. The founder of the royal line of the Volsungs, called in *Beowulf* Wæls (897), was later in Scandinavia known as Volsung, whose name was derived from that of his people.

No one, surely, will doubt the essentially "mythological" character of Scef and Scyld. But if further evidence is needed, we can study the boat-story. This is told, in significant forms, by two later writers in England, but not of Scyld. Scef or Sceaf is the hero — the variation in the vowel is not significant. The monk Ethelwerd, who composed a chronicle in the late tenth century, and William of Malmesbury, in his *Gesta Regum Anglorum*, in the first half of the twelfth century, agree in giving the adventure to the elder figure. William says that Scef arrived *in quandam insulam Germaniae Scandzam* (a territory over which Hrothgar ruled in *Beowulf*, comprising the southern tip of the Swedish peninsula, and probably Danish lands to the south, but here mentioned as if one island), a child in a boat with a sheaf of wheat beneath his head —*puerulus posito ad caput frumenti manipulo, dormiens*. In general we shall find that *Beowulf* preserves stories in their earlier form better than documents several centuries later. But in this case it appears that the tale first belonged to a harvest-deity or a vegetation-deity, and that later confusions arose from its transference to Scyld. No version except *Beowulf* tells the boat-story of Scyld. But the effect of this transference is obvious in Ethelwerd's account. He says that Scef arrived at an island of the ocean called Scani, in a boat, surrounded by weapons (*armis circumdatus*). The primitive notion of the bringing of the blessings of fertility to a people was thus blended with the bestowal of prowess in war, producing, in Ethelwerd's chronicle, a picture that is mythologically inconsistent.[2]

The mysterious fructifying powers of vegetation have of course been allegorized in the imagination of primitive peoples all over the world. Nothing is commoner; the superstitions of obscure African tribes often recall vividly the early conditions with which we are dealing here. And in a study of these conditions the personifications of the spirit of the corn or grain which may be observed in modern folk-customs in Western Europe are most illuminating. Readers of *The Golden Bough* will remember the strange connections between the ancient rites in honor of Adonis and Cybele and Attis, on the one hand, and modern peasant and savage customs on the other. When the country folk of Germany or Russia fashion the last sheaf of the harvest into the rude semblance of a woman, dress it up, sing around it, and carry it in procession, they are continuing a custom that reaches back into the pagan worship of the fertilizing power of the corn. Especially to be noted is the fact that the fetich is frequently moved about from one place to another, in a car or wagon. The spirit resident in the last sheaf is supposed to exercise a fructifying influence upon vegetation or even upon the child-bearing of women. Sometimes this is symbolized by scattering the grain of the last sheaf. The sheaf itself is identified with the divinity supposedly resident in it. So in the beliefs that we have just been examining in connection with *Beo-*

wulf, "Sheaf" is at once the name of the god and of his habitat. A survival of some of these very beliefs may explain picturesque harvest customs in England and Scotland to-day. Their significance as propitiating or invoking the powers of reproduction in nature is doubtless largely forgotten in the rustic merry-making of modern times, but for the student of folk-lore or comparative religion their most unconsidered details often recall long-forgotten pagan rites.[3]

A particularly strange bit of evidence occurs in the English *Chronicles of Abingdon*. In the reign of King Edmund, in the middle of the tenth century, the monks of Abingdon claimed certain disputed lands on the bank of the Thames. They decided to settle the matter by putting a sheaf of wheat on a round shield, with a lighted candle on the sheaf, and observing the movements of the shield as it was borne downstream by the flood. A few of the brethren followed in a small boat. The shield indicated the territory belonging to the monks very clearly by its irregular course, *quasi digito demonstrans*. This was hardly a judgment of God, but rather of the heathen sheaf-god, who might naturally be supposed to preside over the fortunes of the broad Thames meadows. The association of the shield with the sheaf is at first glance striking, but it is probably a pure accident, of no significance. What is noteworthy is the appeal to the deity of vegetation, personified by the sheaf of wheat.[4]

When we look for evidence of the worship of fructifying deities in early Germanic times we find much that is important for the Sceaf–Scyld story. Tacitus tells in the *Germania* of the singular rites of the worship of Nerthus, the "earth-mother," the goddess of fertility who dwelt on an island in the sea. In a sacred grove stood her car, which only her priest might touch. She was identical with the male god, Njord, in Scandinavian mythology; the difference in gender appears to rest upon linguistic change, the passage of certain feminine nouns into the masculine gender, rather than upon a change in personality or function. The conceptions of sex shift readily in many of the more primitive mythological figures; either a male or a female deity could represent the reproductive power of nature, the complementary sex being supplied by a priest or a priestess, as the case might be. Frey, the principal god of fertility in the Scandinavian pantheon, was the son of Njord. He rode the ship *Skidbladnir* ("the cloud"), and dwelt at Noatun ("ship-haven"). The fertilizing rains of spring were in his power. He was sometimes identified with Ing, an ancient and obscure figure venerated by the Danes, hence the epithet "Ing-wine" or "friends of Ing" (1044, 1319). His name sometimes appears amalgamated with that of Frey, as Yngvi-Frey. He is mentioned in the Anglo-Saxon *Runic Poem* — which, though late, preserves some early traditions — as having been first seen among the East-Danes, and having departed thence over the waves.[5] Just what this signifies is not plain; but it may well point to a similar story of the bringing of the blessings of agricultural fertility, as in the case of Sceaf. The connection of these vegetation-deities with the sea, with the mention of a car or boat, is striking. Clearly, they were thought of as habitually dwelling elsewhere than in the lands over which their beneficent influence extended, and their journey to those lands was most often made in a boat, since that was the commonest means of travelling any distance in early Germanic times. The car of the goddess Nerthus, in her island home, was in all probability a sea-going vehicle.

New and striking parallels have been brought forward in recent years from Finnish and Lappish sources. These peoples, though not of Germanic stock, appear to have borrowed from the mythology of the Scandinavians, in particular from the cults of Frey and Thor. One of the most arresting instances of this is the activity of a Finnish vegetation-deity, Sämpsä Pellervoinen, who is summoned by the sea-god Ahti in the spring, when the ice breaks up, to bring fertility to the fields, — and also, it would appear, to women. Sämpsä makes his fructifying journey in a boat, his mother (or sister, or step-mother), who is also his spouse, accompanying him. Finnish legends are chiefly familiar to us through the *Kalevala*, a manufactured epic, put together in the nineteenth century on the basis of old Finnish songs by the poet Lönnrot. In this epic Sämpsä Pellervoinen sows the barren earth after the Creation.

> Pellervoinen, earth-begotten,
> Sämpsä, youth of smallest stature,
> Came to sow the barren country,
> Thickly scattering seeds about him.
> *(Runo II*, 13–16.)

Verses still current among the Finns, not utilized in the *Kalevala*, present important resemblances to the Sceaf myth. In some of these Sämpsä appears as a boy, sleeping in a boat, upon a heap of corn, with a female relative, and taking "six grains of corn," with which, presumably, the fertilization mysteries were to be accomplished. Whether or not this was borrowed from Germanic sources, it remains important testimony for the assignment to a vegetation-deity of the legend of a boy coming across the waters in a boat, lying asleep on a sheaf of wheat.[6]

In what sense we may safely speak of mythological elements in *Beowulf* will now, perhaps, be clear. Such elements may still be discerned, in faint and rationalized forms, attached to minor figures antedating the action of the poem. But there is nothing to show that Beowulf, or the other characters contemporaneous with him, are deities masking in the guise of human beings; nor can the adventures in which they engage be interpreted as allegories.

The scholars of earlier generations thought otherwise, however. That a nature-allegory underlies the main plot of *Beowulf* was long held to be too obvious to need proof. The precise details of this allegory were indeed much disputed, but as to the soundness of the general principles involved there was hardly any question until the latter part of the nineteenth century. The theory of the great German scholar Karl Müllenhoff (1818–1884) may be taken as typical. This is of importance not only on account of Müllenhoff's great and deserved reputation, but because it was the earliest systematic and authoritative explanation, the general method of which was long regarded as canonical. It is also beautifully simple and neat, and its main outlines may be described in comparatively few words.[7]

Müllenhoff distinguished three great "adventures" in the poem — the swimming-feat with Breca, the fight with the Grendel kin, and the contest with the dragon — which he regarded as originally activities of a deity, whose adversaries represented the various phases of the destructive power of the North Sea. In the spring the god overcomes this power, personified by Breca of the Brondingas. He later beats back the raging floods that inundate the Low Countries, represented by Grendel and by his dam (the latter being the depths of the sea). In the autumn he is overcome by the dragon, the victorious stormy winter ocean. It is, then, a "seasons-myth." Each spring the god comes to life, to do battle against the destructive powers of nature; and each autumn he is himself conquered by them. The attachment of the myth to the historical background of Danish and Geatic sovereigns Müllenhoff regarded as late and secondary. He believed that the adventures were earlier told of an Anglo-Saxon deity, called Beow or Beaw (the variation in the diphthong is of little moment), who in early Anglo-Saxon genealogies occupies the place of Beowulf the Dane in the epic as son of Scyld; and that later they were attached, with Beowulf the Dane as intermediary, to Beowulf prince of the Geatas. This general theory had earlier been proposed by the English scholar, Kemble. Further evidence for making Beow the antagonist of Grendel was adduced from a Wiltshire charter of the year 931, in which, in the description of a piece of land, "the enclosure of Beowa" (*beowan hamm*) and "the pool of Grendel" (*grendles mere*) are mentioned.

All this, it will be observed, is a series of unproved hypotheses. There is no evidence that such narratives were told of Beow or Beaw or Beowa; there is no evidence that they were told of Beowulf the Dane; there is no evidence that the adventures of Beowulf the Dane were transferred to Beowulf the Geat. The occurrence of place-names recalling the deity and the demon in the same locality proves nothing, unless there is some strong antecedent reason for connecting the two. The whole theory hangs in the air, a creation of the imagination. But so great was Müllenhoff's prestige that there were few to dispute him. Eduard Sievers, perhaps the greatest Germanic scholar of his generation, writing in 1895, said:

I may, I suppose, regard it as admitted that Beowulf the Geat was not originally the hero of the dragon-saga, but Beowulf the Scylding, the father of Healfdene, or rather the Scylding Beow or Beowa of the genealogies and place-names, whose name was secondarily supplanted in our epic by the name Beowulf.[8]

Other investigators, while not questioning the general processes used by Müllenhoff, produced new interpretations of the supposed myth. Laistner identified Grendel — the monster stalking through miasmatic mists at evening, and crunching the bones of his victims with his teeth — as the pestilence, which racks men's bones with fever. His adversary would then be a wind-god, blowing away such poisonous vapors. Boer believed Grendel to be "the terror of the long winter nights," and his divine opponent a light-god. E. H. Meyer spoke for storms and a lightning-god. Brandl stressed the agricultural attributes of Grendel, and suggested that he may perhaps signify "corn-grinding, the work of slaves, the sign of the conquered foe." Still other scholars perceived in Grendel a whale, or a werewolf, or even our old friend, the Lernæan hydra.[9]

Perhaps these ingenious guesses — more than one of them — have some measure of truth in them. The original conception of Grendel may have been connected with some of the darker manifestations of nature, or these may have been attached to him as the tale of his depredations was repeated by generation after generation. But it all lies too far in the mists of the past for analysis. And even if such an allegorical quality did attach itself to Grendel, that does not mean that his victorious opponent must be a deity. Supernatural demons of darkness or mist or pestilence may be slain by a mortal hero. The reason why mythological hypotheses were so readily received is really that this method of interpreting popular literature, and artistic literature based on traditional sources, was a widely accepted fashion among scholars. Müllenhoff's methods were not original with him; he applied what he had learned from others, which also happened to be regarded as sound doctrine throughout his lifetime, and applied it in an alluring and authoritative manner. The work of later "comparative mythologists" who never set themselves to analyzing *Beowulf* will be found of much assistance in comprehending the criticism of the Anglo-Saxon epic. They examined the names of the personages in a given story, and then, taking into account the evidence of related Indo-European languages, interpreted the whole allegorically, aided by study of similar myths among other peoples. So Max Müller, the celebrated German professor resident at Oxford, explained classic myths. The insubstantiality of the results of these operations became gradually visible to clearer-eyed scholars, however. It is especially disquieting that the mythologists themselves so often disagree as to the meaning of a myth. They cannot all be right. Which man shall be believed? We may apply to *Beowulf* Andrew Lang's sharp criticism of interpretations of the classical myth of Cronos.

He may be Time, or perhaps he is the Summer Heat, and a horned god, or he is the harvest god, or the god of storm and darkness, or the midnight sky, — the choice is wide; or he is the lord of dark and light, and his children are the stars, the clouds, the summer-months, the light-powers, or what you will. The mythologist has only to make his selection.[10]

Very disquieting for the supporters of mythological interpretations of the adventures of Beowulf is the fact that these do not really fit the descriptions in the poem. If Grendel personifies the wintry sea, and his dam the depths of the sea, how does it happen that they dwell in a quiet inland pool, which is described in considerable detail in one of the finest passages in the poem (1345–1376), and is confirmed as the original and not the secondary location by Scandinavian parallels? This whole matter will be discussed in the following chapter. Again, a dragon flying about in the air, and spewing fire over the countryside, does not suggest to the skeptical mind the destructive power of inundating water. The parallel to Thor's fight with the World-Serpent, which lies at the bottom of the sea, with his tail in his mouth, suggested by Müllenhoff, simply does not exist; there is no resemblance between the two stories. Still more fatal to the notion that Beowulf's exploits are a seasons-myth is the death of the dragon. When the winter-demon kills the summer-god he ought not to die too; he ought to live triumphant over his adversary, wielding uncontrolled power over the wintry sea.[11]

How, then, if Müllenhoff's elaborate theory be rejected, are we to account for a Beowulf as son of Scyld in the epic, where Beow or Beaw appears in the English genealogies? Neither Beow nor Beowulf occurs as son of Scyld in lists of early Scandinavian kings.

It seems probable that Beow or Beaw was a vegetation-hero or deity (Anglo-Saxon, *bēow*, "corn," "grain"), who had attained some popularity among the West-Germanic tribes. We know nothing of his exploits; his name may be identical with that of the Finnish Pekko ("barley"). Little is known of Pekko, either, but he seems a good deal like Sämpsä Pellervoinen; he comes from the corn-heap in the spring as a little child. Now, since the Anglo-Saxons made Beow the son of Scyld (Sceldwa) in enumerating the ancestors of their own kings, it is natural to suppose that they might also do this in setting forth the early sovereigns of the Danish house in *Beowulf*. That the name Beowulf occupies the position that Beowa should have in the epic, as son of Scyld, is probably due to the carelessness of a scribe, writing by mistake the similar-sounding and familiar name of the hero of the poem. It is possible, of course, that such a confusion might have arisen earlier, in oral transmission of the material. That the poet of *Beowulf*, expert as he was in the ramifications of story-telling, should be guilty of it, seems less likely.

Thus far we have not considered the episode in which Beowulf swims the icy sea of winter with Breca, prince of the Brondingas (499–606). This was regarded by the mythologists as of high significance. Müllenhoff put his view plainly: the hero "swam against the polar current, and may therefore be regarded as a mythical person, a divine being friendly to mankind, who in his youth, that is, the spring, subdues the violence and wildness of the wintry sea, overcoming its stormy character. This is represented by his rival or fellow-swimmer Breca." Other scholars cherished different views. To Sarrazin, Beowulf was a sun-god who "swims faster than all other beings; the dashing sea-wave (*breki*) cannot contend with him; he overtakes it very quickly." Brandl calls the episode "the depiction of a natural phenomenon in human terms; the South-Scandinavian sea is broken up and kept open in winter by the wind; in Western Norway the Gulf Stream gives clear water for sailing." Whether Breca is an opponent or companion of Beowulf, then, the incident has been held to represent the victory over the ocean of a divine power or of a personified force of nature.

A review of the story is important for its own sake, entirely apart from its supposed mythological significance.[12] Oddly enough, it has been pretty generally misunderstood. It is one of the finest pieces of narrative in the epic,— rapid, vigorous, and dramatic, and without the misuse of rhetorical devices so common in Anglo-Saxon poetry. There is no mystery about it; the meaning is plain enough on a careful examination. Perhaps it formed the subject of a separate epic lay, before it was utilized by the *Beowulf* poet. Objection has been made by Klaeber that the "disrespectful treatment of Beowulf contrasts strangely with the dignified courtesy reigning at Hrothgar's court." But the dramatic effectiveness of the contrast is evident, and a good opportunity is thus afforded for the poet to introduce into his tale an account of one of his hero's earlier exploits. If Unferth's manners seem to indicate a lapse from the high standard prevailing at the court of Hrothgar, they must be looked upon as an inheritance from the older legends which had come down from a ruder age. But the very nature of the episode justifies them; they could not be made wholly elegant without spoiling the tale, and the poet has carefully motivated Unferth's resentment.

Unferth, the son of Ecglaf, and the chief counsellor of the king, is, as we have seen already, a trouble-maker. In the midst of the feasting at Hrothgar's court on the evening of Beowulf's arrival, he drinks too much, and his ill-temper increases. It irritates him that a distinguished foreigner has come to slay the demon which no Dane has been able to dispose of: "he could not bear that any man should perform more deeds of glory than he had himself accomplished." So he attacks Beowulf bitterly, accusing him of having engaged in a contest in swimming with Breca of the

Brondingas, and of having been worsted by him. "He overcame you in swimming; he had greater strength." And furthermore: "All his boast against you did the son of Beanstan"—that is, Breca—"in very truth accomplish." Finally, Unferth prophesies Beowulf's defeat in the coming contest with Grendel.

Beowulf, retorting calmly, but with superb effect, gives Breca the lie direct, accuses him of having drunk immoderately, recalls a disgraceful episode in his past life, when he murdered his kin, or failed in his duty to his clan, and remarks that, if he were as brave as he thinks, there would be no need to fear the onslaughts of Grendel. Moreover, Beowulf relates — and this is the most interesting part of his speech — the swimming adventure as it actually happened, vindicating his own prowess. All this disposes effectively of Unferth; the incident is closed. The next morning, when Beowulf enters the hall in triumph, bearing the arm and claw of the monster as trophies, the poet remarks grimly that "the son of Ecglaf was pretty silent."

The first point that Beowulf makes in his speech is that he had "greater strength on the water, greater power to endure hardships on the waves, than any other man." Secondly, it was not a race at all; Breca could not swim faster than he, and he had no wish to be separated from Breca. The whole was the mutual performance of a difficult feat, a boyish and foolhardy business, to be sure, but not like Unferth's account of it. "We two boys — for we were still in the time of our youth — vowed and made a brag that we would risk our lives on the sea, and we did it, too." The danger was in the wintry sea, swept with storms, and concealing hideous monsters in its depths. The whole affair was primarily a trial of endurance, then, like the exploit of Grettir the Strong and his friend Bjorn, who swam at a single time the whole course of the Hitara River from the lake where it rose to the sea. According to Shakespeare, the same kind of adventure was undertaken by Cæsar and Cassius.

> For once, upon a raw and gusty day,
> The troubled Tiber chafing with her shores,
> Cæsar said to me: "Dar'st thou, Cassius, now
> Leap in with me into this angry flood,
> And swim to yonder point?" Upon the word,
> Accoutred as I was, I plunged in
> And bade him follow; so, indeed, he did.
> The torrent roar'd, and we did buffet it
> With lusty sinews, throwing it aside
> And stemming it with hearts of controversy.

We are not told what the goal of Beowulf and Breca was, if indeed there was any goal at all. Their plans were upset by rough weather, which drove them apart. Beowulf came to shore in the land of the Finns, and Breca (so Unferth says) among the Heatho-Ræmas, a name surviving in the modern district of Romerike in Norway, near

Oslo. Nor do we know the point at which they started. Beowulf never claims that he outstripped or out-distanced Breca, but that he endured the greater hardships; he was forced to encounter sea-monsters. One of them he slew at the bottom of the sea, and nine others lay dead in the light of the morning on the surface. Never has he heard of a tougher fight than that, he says, or of a man in harder straits. Neither Breca nor Unferth ever accomplished anything like that in battle-play.

It should be noted that the exploit was preceded by a formal boast, made by both Beowulf and Breca. This custom of vowing, in good set terms, to do a deed that could not in honor be abandoned, is too familiar to need comment; note Beowulf's speeches before his contests with Grendel and Grendel's dam, and the dragon. These "brags" sometimes involved emulation with another hero, which was just the reason why Unferth's slander, that Breca tried to surpass Beowulf and accomplished his boast, was dangerous and plausible. Observe how differently Beowulf himself puts the matter. It was a mutual feat of strength. "*We* asserted that we would risk our lives on the ocean, and *we* did it." Two or more men might brag that they would engage in a hazardous exploit, and succeed or fail as comrades. In the *Saga of the Jomsvikings*, Sigwald promises a dangerous deed:

As a great drinking-horn was brought to him, he stood up, took the horn, and said: "I vow to sail to Norway and attack Jarl Hakon before the third winter from this, and not to return until I have killed the Jarl or driven him out of the country, and if I have not it will be because I have lost my life." . . . Then the king called out: "Now it is your turn, O Thorkell Hafi, to speak! What will you vow to undertake? You must be bold and courageous!" "I vow," answered Thorkell, "to follow my brother Sigwald, and not to flee sooner than he, as long as I see the prow of his ship and the oars ready for action, in case he fights on the water with Jarl Hakon; but if he engages with him on shore, I will not retreat until I can see Sigwald no more in the thick of the fight, and his banner is behind me." "That was well spoken," said the king, "and you will no doubt accomplish it, for you are a doughty hero! Now it is your turn to speak, Bui Digri! We know that you will have something worthy of a man to promise, for you are rightly called the mightiest of heroes." Bui said: "This vow do I make, that I will fare northwards with Jarl Sigwald and follow him in this expedition as long as my endurance permits, and not flee from Jarl Hakon until fewer of our men remain than have fallen, and I will hold out as long as Sigwald will have me."

As to the origin of the Breca episode, nothing is known. It seems likely that it was a purely imaginary incident, invented to exalt Beowulf as a swimmer and a fighter of monsters, rather than an actual occurrence. Breca is probably as fictitious as Beowulf. He is mentioned in *Widsith* (25) as Breoca, ruling over the Brondingas, but this does not necessarily mean that he or his people ever existed, any more than King "Thyle" of the "Rondingas"—almost certainly epic personifications of "the orator" and "the warriors." Breca and the Brondingas were perhaps named after the "breaking" of the waves (Old Norse, *breki*) and the dashing of the sea (cf. modern German *Brandung*), but they are not on that account to be set down as personifications of the power of the ocean, to be viewed through the perspective of a nature-allegory. Nothing is said of them in the poem or elsewhere that would lead to such a conclusion.

In what sense mythology may be traced in *Beowulf* will now be plain. Relics of the veneration of vegetation-deities appear to have affected the figures of the early Danish kings, looming up vaguely through the mists of antiquity. Their divine attributes have, however, been almost wholly obscured by the passage of years, the inclination to rationalize, and the exaltation of other qualities, like success in war. On the other hand, no such attributes can be discerned in the main personages of the poem, Beowulf and those represented as contemporaneous with him, nor can their exploits be interpreted as allegories of the phenomena of nature or of states of culture. The chief reason for this conclusion is the total absence of convincing evidence, internal or external, and the unsatisfactory way in which allegorical hypotheses thus far proposed fit the events of the action. It may well be, however, that the allegory, if it had ever been present, would have become so altered in the course of time as to be distorted and unrecognizable. If the investigator, from his study of the general processes of early poetry, believes that a mythological foundation *must* underlie the action, there is no way of proving that he is wrong. But unless new evidence appears, there is no way for him to prove that he is right, or to explain the faded allegory convincingly. Something more than a purely imaginative reconstruction is necessary.

It is surprisingly easy to fit a nature-allegory into any simple story. One may say, for example, that he believes the nursery rhyme about Jack and Jill to be really of high antiquity, based upon an ancient day-and-night myth. Jack is the sun-god (cf. Latin *jaculum*, "javelin," "spear" — the spear-like rays of the sun); he climbs the hill of the heavens, but falls down and breaks his crown (the setting of the sun and the spreading of its rays in all directions at sunset). Jill is a feminine divinity, the moon-goddess, who also climbs the heavens, and "comes tumbling after" the sun, as the moon sets after sunset is long past. The "pail of water" is the dew, which falls upon the earth at evening, although it might also be interpreted as evening or morning showers.

This is no more absurd than much serious mythologizing has been. But the foundations of such processes no longer stand unchallenged and secure. Müllenhoff prefaced his work with the dogma that "every epic narrative [*Sage*] and the contents of every popular epic, consists of two elements, myth and history." This dogma is canonical no longer in the sense in which he meant it. Guidance in regard to the supernatural elements in *Beowulf* must be sought in definite external evidence of a very different sort, which is set forth in the two chapters that follow.

VI

GRENDEL AND HIS DAM

"HEATHENISM," says Santayana, "is a good word. It conveys, as no other word can, the sense of vast multitudes tossing in darkness, harassed by demons of their own choice." [1] Of such origin, no matter what we conceive their significance to have been, were the monsters in *Beowulf*, pagan incarnations of joyless evil. Their attributes embody what men most feared in the world about, — the strength of the bear, the poison of the serpent, the swooping attack of the eagle, the hideous destruction of fire, the mysteries of lonely waters, the nameless terror that walketh in darkness. The imagination of countless generations has moulded them; they are not merely personifications of some one aspect of nature or of physical life, but composites, revealing, even in the artistic and formal treatment of epic, something of their complicated ancestry.

The Grendel brood are in some respects more interesting than the dragon, because rarer in European story-telling. They are pagan in origin, beyond a doubt, but Christian and Hebrew tradition have lent them new terrors, in connecting

them with Cain and the devils spawned as his
descendants. It seems doubtful, however, if they
owe to those traditions their half-human shape.
In their latest guise, they are almost to be reckoned as bear-demons, so much have they taken
on the aspect of that dreaded animal. And the
bear is a beast that walks like a man. Brute and
hero share common characteristics in early times;
the ambition of the slayer was to possess qualities
as terrible as those of the beasts that he overcame.
In days when mere physical strength served men
best it was natural to believe that drinking the
blood or eating the heart of a wild animal would
give its strength and courage. So Beowulf, whose
very name appears to mean "bear," has the super-
human strength, the prowess in wrestling, which
match him evenly with a demon like Grendel.[2]
When the antecedents of Grendel and his dam are
examined, however, it becomes clear that they
are only secondarily bear-monsters. Earlier, they
were water-demons. So much of this, indeed,
still remains in the epic that Müllenhoff and others,
as will be remembered, made it the point of departure for mythological hypotheses. But Müllenhoff was quite mistaken in the nature of the
demons. They are not spirits of the vasty deep,
but of inland waters. A study of Scandinavian
analogues shows that they were earlier conceived
to be waterfall-trolls, and this is still observable

in the Anglo-Saxon. Etymology further bears it out: Grendel used to be connected with *grindan*, "grind," and the monster explained as "the grinder," who crushes his enemy, bear-fashion, in his powerful teeth. More convincing, however, is the connection of the word *grendel* with *grund*, the depths or bottom of a body of water. It is there that Grendel and his dam may be found (cf. *grund-hyrde*, 2136; *grund-wong*, 1496, etc.; *mere-grund*, 2100, etc.). The name Grendel appears to survive in English place-names, which can be traced in Anglo-Saxon documents, and it is noticeable that these localities are not near the sea, but inland regions — *grindeles pytt* (a "pit" filled with water?); *grendles mere* ("pool"); *gryndeles sylle* ("swamp"); *grindles bec* ("brook"). Examination of these places as they exist to-day confirms this. In a marsh or lake, then, in the mysterious depths below, it would appear that a water-monster, a *grendel*, was supposed to dwell. We shall see later how this English conception has supplanted that of the waterfall-troll, producing in *Beowulf* a curiously mixed and inconsistent idea of the demon dwellings. Perhaps the word *grendel* was a generic term for a water-monster; perhaps the localities just mentioned were named with the Grendel of the Beowulf tale in mind; who can tell? In Shakespeare's day, hobgoblins were called "pucks" ("as I am *an* honest Puck," "else *the*

Puck a liar call"); but we, and very likely those who saw *A Midsummer Night's Dream* on Shakespeare's stage, have felt that "Puck" is almost as distinctive a personal appellation as Robin Goodfellow.[3]

The Grendel of the epic, at any rate, is very much of an individual; in no other tale does a devastating monster of his name appear. And his "mother" is of equal importance. The story told of them contains very marked and individual features which set it apart and relate it to similar stories in various parts of the world. These narratives, for the most part popular tales, preserve a recognizable framework of incident which recurs again and again, no matter how widely separated the tellings may be in time and place. Very strange, too, are the correspondences in details, which link a version in Japan with one in Germany, perhaps, or one in Iceland with another in India. While Grendel is not a type, then, like the dragon, he and his dam are central figures in a type-story, which is not confined to European territory. It is clear from these tales that the adventure with the mother of Grendel is not a later elaboration of the Grendel-contest, as scholars used to think; it is an integral part of the type-story.

The killing of Grendel and his dam is the kernel of the epic, the central theme of all the earlier action. It has been much altered by its connection with the Scandinavian royal houses, and by courtly and religious influences, but its essential simplicity and its naïve and "popular" character are evident. If we would pluck out the heart of its mystery, we must disregard non-essentials, and listen to it as a tale told among simple people with childlike imaginations. The more aristocratic circles which have felt its spell also have their testimony to give. For it has pushed its way (not, of course, in just the form in which it appears in *Beowulf*) into historical and legendary narratives, attaching itself both to real and to imaginary heroes. In such folk-tales and narratives we have something tangible upon which to base conclusions as to the history of the materials in *Beowulf*, not, like the web of the nature-mythologists, a fabric spun out of the gossamer of imagination.

It is important to emphasize at this point that the dragon-story was originally entirely separate from the adventure with the two demons in the haunted hall and beneath the water. Never, except in *Beowulf*, has it been found connected with those adventures. In a few of the variants of the type-story to which the Grendel-fight belongs, the terrors of the subterranean adventure are increased by introducing a dragon or dragons, but these do not suggest the closing episode of *Beowulf*, while the folk-tales and other narratives which do show vague resemblances to the dragon-fight in the epic present no incidents analogous to the Grendel-contests. This is very significant. The mythologists assumed that the Grendel and dragon episodes were parts of one and the same early myth. This assumption, which, as we have seen, is improbable for other reasons, is again contradicted by the evidence of popular story. If these two themes had originally been united, we should expect traces of this connection to survive in later times.

The importance of systematic study of *märchen*, both for their own sake and for the light that they throw upon sophisticated literature, has long been recognized. Only in comparatively recent times, however, has such study fully come into its own. Scholars busy with the reconstructions of comparative mythology were sometimes inclined to look with disdain upon those who collected nursery tales and professed to draw serious conclusions from studying them. Yet the beginnings of the long trails which lead through the forest of folk-tales were blazed long since, under the stimulus of the awakened interest in early literature in the late eighteenth and early nineteenth centuries. The *Household Tales* of the brothers Grimm, published in 1812–1815, cleared out an immense amount of timber, and opened up vistas to other workers. The learned and suggestive comments of the

Grimms revealed plainly the great significance of such tales for literary origins, and inspired others to make collections in other fields. As the century advanced, a similar service was done for Danish ballads by Grundtvig, whose edition (published 1851–1890) was the model used by Professor Child in his great collection of English and Scottish ballads (1882–1898). Anthropology and folk-lore lent their aid; it was perceived that knowledge of the early beliefs and imaginative processes of mankind are best understood by studying the survivals that have come down to modern times, and observing the habits of peoples in a similar grade of culture to-day. It is hard to classify scholars satisfactorily according to their theories. Mannhardt (1831–1880), for example, who began as a meteorological mythologist, broke sharply away and became a pioneer in investigating popular customs and superstitions, and explaining their true significance. He was not without distinguished followers in Germany, while England also produced an extremely able group of scholars — Tylor, Frazer, Andrew Lang, E. S. Hartland, Alfred Nutt, and others. The classical example of the folk-loristic method, Frazer's *Golden Bough*, probing in minute fashion the worship of the Arician Diana, points a suggestive way to the elucidation of primitive custom in *Beowulf*. But our concern must rather be with the assis-

tance given by folk-tales in explaining the supernatural episodes in the epic.

The nursery tales with which we are all most
familiar do not represent popular material in its
purity; they have been considerably modernized
and altered. Those that we remember best —
*Cinderella, Hop o' my Thumb, The Sleeping Beauty
in the Wood, Little Red Riding Hood,* and the like
— have been much influenced by the fancy of
Charles Perrault, who gave to them the airs and
graces of the court of Louis XIV, which loved to
take even its shepherds and milkmaids as creations
of art rather than of nature. In the *Household
Tales* of the Grimms the truer estate of these old
stories may be seen — the simple and sometimes
even crude and vulgar forms which they assumed
when they were the possession and delight of the
people, a part of the stock of traditional narrative
handed down orally from generation to generation.
The first thing necessary in studying folk-tales is
to eliminate "literary" accretions. We are then
in a position to estimate properly the influence
that they have exercised in earlier days upon more
sophisticated narratives.[4]

Consider *Cinderella,* one of the most widespread
and beloved of all tales, which may be examined
in its popular forms, as varied and shifting as the
combinations in a kaleidoscope, in the great collection issued by the British Folk-Lore Society. Its

incidents were readily attached to heroines, real
or imaginary, who had a more dignified place in
story-telling. When we read, in the Old Norse
saga which bears his name, of the marriage of the
Viking chief, Ragnar Lothbrok, to a beautiful girl,
brought up in squalor and poverty, who satisfied
his bridal tests, we recognize the central incident
of the Cinderella *märchen*. The episode of the
slipper is told of King Rother, an historical Lombard king of the seventh century, whose fortunes
were retold centuries later, with imaginative elaborations. Historic tradition, passing into legend,
borrows, of course, only such elements from popular tales as it chooses, omitting and adapting with
the utmost freedom. The story of the Sleeping
Beauty in the Wood, foreshadowed in an Egyptian
papyrus of the Twentieth Dynasty, attached itself
to Sigurd and Brynhild, and became one of the
central features of their legend. Sigurd rides
through the fire to rescue Brynhild, just as the
prince penetrates the encircling hedge of the magic
castle, and wakes the warrior-maiden plunged into
slumber by the sleep-thorn of Odin, which we
recognize as the spindle of the old crone in the
tower in the nursery version. Sigurd and Brynhild
were themselves imaginary characters, but they
were given reality and dignity, and their supernatural adventures plausibility, by their connection with historical Burgundian kings of the fifth

century. Again, admirable illustrations of the significance of folk-tales as revealing the meaning of episodes in romantic literature are afforded by Arthurian romance. Thus Nutt has shown the bearing of Celtic folk-tales upon the Grail legends; Kittredge, upon *Gawain and the Green Knight* and the werewolf story of *Arthur and Gorlagon;* Brown, upon the *Yvain* of Chrétien de Troyes; Maynadier, upon Chaucer's *Wife of Bath's Tale.* Familiar as this method of investigation is at the present time, it is a distinctly modern development; the significance of such collection and analysis of folk-tales for the content of more "artistic" literature was not generally appreciated fifty years ago. Nor need we stop with the Middle Ages. Every student of *Hamlet* knows how the old folk-tale attached to the Amlethus of Saxo Grammaticus affected, despite all subsequent alterations, the supreme achievement of Shakespeare. I have elsewhere attempted to show how detailed study of popular tales and customs, and their modifications in more sophisticated literature, often throw the strongest light upon perplexing problems in Shakespeare's plays — the degradation of Cressida, the strange wager in *Cymbeline*, the unsavory plots and puzzling characterization in *All's Well that Ends Well* and *Measure for Measure.* By careful study of the way in which men of earlier days understood situations that seem strange to us, we can see how those situations presented themselves to Shakespeare's audiences, and influenced the creations of the great dramatist himself.[5]

Resemblances between the supernatural plot-material in *Beowulf* and popular tales had been observed by various scholars, but detailed investigation really began with the work of Friedrich Panzer, who, in 1910, published carefully tabulated plots of a large number of *märchen* illustrating the Grendel adventures, and similar material illustrating the dragon adventure. The former are far the more important and convincing. Despite all differences, the *märchen* resembling the story of Grendel and his dam preserve a common framework, which is of the utmost importance as showing what the earlier form of that story must have been. Panzer's work, while exhibiting errors of judgment and critical shortcomings, must be regarded as a landmark in the investigation of *Beowulf*. It struck boldly out into an almost unexplored field, and demonstrated the significance of the results thus gained. Over two hundred variants of the *märchen* that underlies the Grendel episodes were listed, and others have since been noted. Of course no enumeration can ever be complete. New analogues will turn up from time to time. But Panzer presented material enough to show beyond question that the tale is of wide geographical distribution and of great antiquity.

His variants cover the Scandinavian countries, including Iceland, also Germany, the Low Countries, Celtic territory, the Faroe Islands, — just the regions where one might expect historical traditions of Scandinavian kings to have been affected by folk-tales, — and Romanic, Slavic, and Baltic territory, Finland, and India. Although most of the tales have been recovered in very recent times, it is evident that they cannot have sprung from *Beowulf* itself, or from any of its analogues in the sagas.[6]

Classification of folk-tales and construction of a type-tale is hazardous business. No two stories are alike. Each consists of a series of episodes, but these episodes are often differently motivated and worked out, and complicated by the introduction of other elements. Every new story-teller arranges the material according to his own individual fancy, sometimes so freely that the underlying pattern is hardly recognizable. Sometimes, indeed, the differences are so striking that it is wisest to exclude a tale from the "type" altogether. No two collectors, then, would arrive at the same classification. Nor can they hope to gather all extant versions into their nets. But this is of little consequence. What is of importance is to show that, in spite of all divergences, a common pattern is really visible. Panzer's method is to construct this common pattern, and to illustrate it, incident by incident, from his collections. This is obviously somewhat dangerous, and may lead to false conclusions. By taking many different colors and lines from many different pictures one can put together almost any kind of picture that one pleases. That this would be an unjust criticism of Panzer's book is evident when the tales themselves are read. For the only really satisfactory way to judge a type-story is to examine a very considerable number of the individual stories, regarded as wholes, with particular attention to framework and incident. Unfortunately such a proceeding is not possible in a brief analysis and review; it demands a disproportionate amount of space. We may therefore look at the main structural outlines which Panzer discerns beneath the earlier versions of the story.

The type-tale has been named "The Bear's Son," because, in so many variants, the hero is brought up by bears, or is of bear-parentage or with distinct physical characteristics which suggest the bear. The main part of the tale is twofold: the double contest of a young hero with supernatural beings, first in a house or hall above ground, and then in the underworld. Or, to give the outline a little more fully, a youth, untried in valor and little esteemed, overcomes a demon in a lonely house, after his companions or elder brothers have failed. The demon escapes, and his bloody footprints lead to a subterranean lair, into which the hero descends, generally being lowered by a rope. Here he kills one or more supernatural beings (sometimes making use of a magic sword), and frees imprisoned princesses. His treacherous companions, who were to have drawn him up to the surface again, leave him in the demon realm, but he finds means at last to return, and under cover of disguise takes vengeance upon them and finally marries the fairest of the princesses. Many of the tales lay special emphasis upon the hero's birth, bear-parentage, or youthful deeds. Others begin with the princesses, the daughters of a king whose domains are plagued by the demons, and who offers the rescuer, in good fairy-tale fashion, the opportunity of becoming his son-in-law. The Defence of the Hall, then, is really only the prologue to a more difficult subterranean adventure. The end of the story shows, on the whole, less variation than the beginning.

It is evident that when the folk-tale of "The Bear's Son" was attached to a prince of the royal house of the Geatas, just as the imaginary Nibelung adventures were brought into connection with historical Burgundian kings, only such portions could be used as were suited to the historical setting. Much had to be omitted, and the gap filled by other incidents extraneous to the folk-tale. The princesses were necessarily left out altogether. The epic shows no interest whatever in romantic love, nor does Beowulf ever exhibit any sign of attachment to the gentler sex. It would appear that his wife lamented him at his funeral, but beyond this we learn nothing. The folk-tale themes of the faithlessness of the hero's companions, and his revenge upon them, were not well suited to an heroic epic, composed in a time when the greatest stress was laid upon the duty of the warrior to support his chief, even unto death. What was obviously of chief interest in the folk-tale were the two great combats with the demons, so these were kept, with many details: the champion's slothful youth, the loss of the demon's arm, the bloodstained footprints leading to the underground lair, the fire in the hall below, the use of a magic sword, which in the folk-tales often hangs on the wall. Much descriptive and incidental matter was introduced, entirely foreign to the style of the *märchen*, — the sea-voyage, the parley with the coast guard, the reception at Hrothgar's court, the banquets and present-giving, the long summary of the Finnsburg lay sung by Hrothgar's poet, the quarrel with Unferth, and the account of the swimming-exploit with Breca.

The adaptation of folk-tale to epic sometimes left inconsistencies, which are explained in a striking way when the variants of the Bear's Son *märchen* are studied. When Beowulf first keeps watch at night in the haunted hall, he does not attack Grendel immediately, but waits until the monster has killed and eaten one of his companions, the luckless Hondscio (739–745; 2076). Why does not Beowulf go to the aid of his friend? Germanic custom, it will be remembered, insisted particularly on such assistance. But Beowulf calmly allows him to suffer a horrible death, and this is never made a subject of reproach. Moreover, the other thanes sleep quietly through it all, though they have come to Denmark with the express purpose of purifying the hall from the nightly visitations of the cannibal monster. The epic poet lamely motivated Beowulf's inaction: "The mighty one, the kinsman of Hygelac, watched to see how the evil scather would act as he attacked." Turn to the folk-tales, and the situation is clear: the younger hero had to wait until his older or more renowned companions had fought and failed. Reminiscences of the cowardice and treachery of the young hero's companions in the subterranean adventure appear in the epic — in the emphasis upon Unferth's cowardice (1468–1472), and in the curious departure of the Danes, who see blood in the water and immediately decide it must be that of the hero, and go home. The folk-tale provides the explanation, — the desertion of the faithless comrades. This could of course have no place in a Germanic epic, unless an issue were made of it, and a special effect gained, as in the dragon episode. Again, Beowulf finds the dead body of Grendel lying in the hall beneath the water, and strikes off the head. The *märchen* show why: the demon, who had been wounded in the earlier fight, had fled thither, and there received his death-blow. Some details in this part of the story which recall the folk-tales will be noted: the fire burning in the hall under the waves, the day's journey [7] through the water to reach the bottom, the fruitless attack with the hero's own weapon, the removal of the demon's head as a trophy, and so forth.

These considerations make it obvious that the popular tales cannot be a degraded form of the epic material. They give the substance; the epic, the shadow. Where the epic motivation is hazy, unconvincing, or contradictory, that in the *märchen* is crystal-clear. Where the one is cast wholly in the mould of courtly life and heroic custom, the other shows no trace of such matters. The more one studies *Beowulf*, the more plainly one sees behind it vague shapes, not only of different stories, but of different forms of such stories.

It is of the highest importance to remember that the *märchen*, both in its independent form and as attached to Beowulf, continued to circulate in Scandinavian territory, long after the material had been brought to England and worked up in epic form. So good a tale was not to be forgotten; it formed a favorite adornment of the adventures of the heroes of the prose sagas. These later narratives deserve careful study. Conclusions of the greatest significance for *Beowulf* may be drawn from the tale of Grettir the Strong, while what is told of Bothvar Bjarki, in the *Saga of Hrolf Kraki* and related material, and incidents in the stories of Orm Storolfsson and of Samson the Fair, serve to indicate still further the popularity of the theme. The exact literary relationships of these analogues are hard to determine, but their general character, and the light that they throw upon *Beowulf*, must be briefly examined.

The most noteworthy of all is the *Saga of Grettir the Strong*, which affords an interesting picture of life in Iceland in the days when Canute was ruling England. Grettir is as much an historical character as Canute himself. His adventures, which were written down at the end of the thirteenth or the beginning of the fourteenth century, are much embellished with supernatural features and bits of floating story, among which stand out prominently the two fights of the Bear's Son type, in a hall and under water. Grettir is a rawboned outlaw, but with underlying honor and kindliness. His exploits have been rationalized, but the demon-fights have not suffered as many changes as they did in England in being forced into the mould of a courtly epic among a foreign people. Comparison of the saga with *Beowulf* shows clearly what kind of monsters the Scandinavians conceived the Grendel kin to be, and defines the geographical location in which the underlying *märchen* took shape. A summary of the most important part of the saga will help to make this clear.

In Barthadal, at a place called Sandheaps (Sandhaugar), a man named Thorstein had mysteriously vanished at Christmas-time, while his wife was away at service at the church. The following year, when the wife was absent for the same reason, the man-servant whom she had left at home likewise vanished, and there were again signs of a struggle, so that men said that evil spirits were at work. When Grettir heard of this, he determined to pass Christmas-tide there. During his stay at the farm, he took the name of Guest. When the good-wife went off to church, as usual, Grettir remained alone behind. Towards midnight in came a huge she-troll, with a chopping-tray in one hand and a great knife in the other. Grettir leaped at her, and they wrestled up and down the room. She tried to escape, but Grettir held her fast, so that she could get out only after they had carried away all the woodwork around the door on their shoulders. She dragged Grettir down to a steep rocky cliff above the river. Long they wrestled there, but finally Grettir drew his knife, and cut off her arm. She then plunged down into the waterfall. Grettir lay long on the cliff, but finally got back to the farm, and went to bed.

When the good-wife returned home, she found her house turned upside down, and heard the story of the fight from Grettir. He told her his real name also. The priest, whose name was Stein, was brought to hear the tale, and said that he could not believe it. After a little time had passed, Grettir chanced to meet the priest, and asked him to come with him to the river, and see for himself what the case really was. The priest consented. "And when they came to the waterfall, they saw a cave beneath the overhanging rock; the sheer precipice was so high that no one could climb up, and it was nearly ten fathoms from above to the water." Grettir fastened a rope with a stone in one end of it to the cliff, and threw it down into the water. Leaving the priest to watch the rope, he then dived under the waterfall, "and that was difficult, because the force of the water was great, and he had to dive to the very bottom before he could get up under the fall. There was a little projection, and he climbed up on that. There was a great cave under the waterfall, and the water poured down in front of it from the top of the cliff." A great fire was burning in the cave. Grettir was immediately attacked by a giant, who thrust at him with his *hepti-sax*, — a kind of pike with a wooden handle, — but Grettir hewed the shaft in two. The giant tried to reach a sword hanging behind him, but Grettir clove the giant's chest and belly, so that his entrails fell into the water. The priest above, seeing the blood, concluded that Grettir had been killed, stopped watching the rope, and went back home.

Grettir gave the giant one blow after another, until he lay dead. Then Grettir explored the cave, and found gold, and the bones of two men, which he put into a bag. He then went out of the cave, and shook the rope, but since the priest was not there to pull him up, he had to pull himself up alone, hand over hand. Later

on Grettir told the priest the tale and remarked that he
had not watched the rope faithfully, which the priest
admitted. Thereafter there was no more trouble from
trolls in Barthadal.[8]

The entire passage as it stands in the original
should of course be read. But even in a brief summary the outlines of the folk-tale are clearly recognizable, with some details far better preserved
than in *Beowulf*, such as the rope by which Grettir
ascends from the cavern, and Stein, the name of
the watcher above, found in various forms in the
folk-tales as belonging to one of the hero's faithless comrades. The princesses and all that goes
with them are lacking, of course; princesses were
scarce in eleventh-century Iceland. Comparison
of *Beowulf* with the saga shows special similarities: the blood in the water convinces the priest
that the hero is dead, just as it convinced the
Danes in their watch at the Haunted Mere; a
similar, though not identical, phrase is used of the
weapon with which Beowulf fights in the cave,
— *hæft-mēce* in Anglo-Saxon, *hepti-sax* in Icelandic.
The divergences are obvious: the hero fights a
female demon in the hall, and does not hew off
her arm until he is close to her lair; in the underground realm he fights a male demon. The sex
of supernatural monsters is not constant in early
story; it shifts in the Bear's Son tales, and the poet
feels so little that Grendel's dam is a woman that

he sometimes uses the masculine pronoun in referring to her. The whole adventure in the cave
is clumsily motivated as an attempt on Grettir's
part to convince the skeptical priest of the existence of the demons. In spite of all differences,
however, it has always been recognized that there
must be an unusually close relationship between
the account in the Anglo-Saxon epic and that in
the saga. Either the latter was influenced directly
or indirectly by the Beowulf tale, or both sprang
from the same early source. Certainty is difficult
to attain, but a guess may be hazarded.

It appears most probable that both *Beowulf* and
the account in the *Grettissaga* were derived from
the same form, or very similar forms, of the Bear's
Son *märchen*, which may possibly have been taken
over into the saga as one of the lays narrated of
Beowulf, or, to speak more accurately, his Scandinavian counterpart, who was perhaps named
Bjólfr. Some five centuries elapsed between the
composition of the epic and that of the saga, and
considerable discrepancies are therefore to be expected. The exploits of Grettir are much rationalized, of course, as those of a well-known historical
personage were bound to be. One thing is obvious:
that the straightforward account in the saga cannot have been derived, even indirectly, from the
epic. The saga is clear where the epic is confused;
it preserves the original form of the story so much

better that it may even be used to explain obscure incidents and description in the Anglo-Saxon.

As an illustration, let us see how the tale of Grettir serves to show the original conception of the demon lair, and the nature of Grendel and his dam — matters which have been much blurred in *Beowulf*.⁹ The most definite description of the dwelling of the Grendel brood comes from the lips of Hrothgar (1357–1376), just before the expedition to the Haunted Mere. An understanding of this passage is all the more important, since it is one of the finest pieces of description in all Anglo-Saxon poetry, and a familiar "purple patch" in *Beowulf*. Hrothgar, in the heaviness of his heart, after the bloody work of the preceding night, tells once more of the two night-haunting monsters, and especially of the one who has repeatedly attacked his mead-hall.

> To him have dwellers upon earth in days of yore
> 1355 Given the name Grendel; his father know they not,
> If a dark spirit did indeed in times gone by
> Live as his sire. In a darksome land they dwell,
> Dales where wolves couch, windy crags,
> Fearsome fen-trails, where the mountain-stream
> 1360 In the mists of the heights descendeth,
> A flood beneath the rocks. Not far is it
> In reckoning of miles that the mere standeth;
> Hoar-frosted trees hang round about it,
> A fast-rooted thicket overspreadeth the water.
> 1365 There night after night a marvel is manifest,
> Fire on the flood. So wise is no one
> Of the race of men as to know what lurketh below.

Though the heath-goer, harried by hounds,
The stag with sturdy antlers, seek the forest,
1370 Pursued from afar, he will yield his life,
He will die on the bank, sooner than there
To hide his head. Uncanny is the spot;
Up the watery spray ascendeth,
Dark to the welkin, when the wind wakens
1375 Dismal weather, till the air darkles,
The heavens weep.

This is a vivid picture of what may be seen in Norway at the present day — a waterfall breaking over beetling cliffs, which seem to overhang it, into a pool below. The spray rises to the sky in a fine mist; gray trees grow round about. This we may believe to have been the conception of the demon-dwelling in the Scandinavian folk-tale underlying both *Beowulf* and the saga. I might translate the Anglo-Saxon word *fyrgen-strēam* in line 1359 (literally "mountain-stream") as "waterfall," because I believe that is clearly indicated by *niþer gewīteð* ("descendeth") in the following line. Apparently the Anglo-Saxons had no special word for "waterfall," since it was not to them a familiar natural phenomenon.

Now when we turn to the *Grettissaga*, we find that the setting of Grettir's adventure under the water corresponds in quite an extraordinary way to the passage just quoted from *Beowulf*, and that the details of that adventure often make the situation in the Anglo-Saxon more comprehensible.

Beowulf dived into the water, and, after a struggle with the she-demon at the bottom of the pool, reached a cave where a fire was burning, a place in which the water did not touch him, "nor could the sudden grip of the flood strike him on account of the roof of the hall" (1515-1516). Take this "hall" as a cave under a waterfall, and the whole scene clears up. The poet of *Beowulf* did not visualize things as clearly as the saga writer. Moreover, confusions set in as soon as the tale of waterfall-trolls was taken out of waterfall country, and transported to the Continental homes of the Anglo-Saxons and to Britain, in neither of which are waterfalls common. The epic poet's description is blurred in just the way a man would blur the description of a scene that he did not clearly understand. Perhaps he had never seen a waterfall; and if he had, it was probably different from the lofty Scandinavian forces. Still other confusing elements entered the tale; the Haunted Mere was made more terrible by adding sea-beasts (1425-1441), which has naturally seemed to connect the demons with the sea. Beowulf was a great slayer of nickers (422, 574), and it looks as if the poet or one of his predecessors had awkwardly introduced deep-sea beasts into an inland pool. Again, the relationship of Grendel and his kin to Cain led to locating their dwelling in some passages (103, 162, 710, 764, 820, 851) in the moors

and fens, the "desert and waste places" where
the demons descended from Cain were supposed
to dwell. How important the waterfall was felt
to be in the Scandinavian story is shown by the
fact that Sandhaugar in the Barthadal, where
Grettir met his trolls, according to the Icelandic
saga, quite lacks waterfall scenery. The river is
"an unimportant stream which runs in rather a
shallow sandy bed." But the saga writer had to
put a waterfall in if his hero were to fight water-
fall-demons, and fortunately he knew how one
looked better than his English brother who wrote
Beowulf. Mythologists have spent much time in
discussing whether the demons in the epic are to
be connected primarily with the sea, or with darkness, or with pestilence, or something else. It is
plain that they were waterfall-trolls, whose original
nature and characteristics have been somewhat
obscured. The belief that such beings haunt the
falls is still common in Norway. Visitors to Ber-
gen will recall the monument to Ole Bull, in which
the master stands on the rocks above, playing his
violin, while the *nøkken* in the cave beneath the
waterfall listens to the music, pausing as he strikes
his harp. The water-sprite is held to be well
versed in music; sometimes he teaches mortals to
play, and some folk-melodies are said to have been
derived in this way.[10] In many other versions of
the Bear's Son material, of course, the demons are

differently conceived; in Anglo-Saxon, other traits have been added to those proper to waterfall trolls.

There are curious echoes of these incidents elsewhere in the *Grettissaga*. A fight with a brown bear recalls a bit the contests with Grendel.[11] The bear left its den at night, destroying men and cattle; the den was in a cliff by the water, in a cave made by overhanging rocks, to which a narrow path led along a sheer precipice. A hero named Bjorn ("the bear") tried to kill the beast, lying down and covering himself with his shield; but the bear was too much for him. Grettir then tried his hand, wrestled with the bear, and cut off its paw; finally he plunged his sword into its heart. He then returned to his companions, carrying the paw as a trophy. Again, Grettir's fight with the ghost of a shepherd named Glam, who had killed beasts and men, and terrorized the whole neighborhood, is worth noting. Grettir awaited the spook alone at night, lying down in the hall, and when Glam entered, they wrestled up and down, breaking the woodwork to pieces. Glam strove to get out, and Grettir to hold him. Too much weight must not be attached to these obvious reminiscences of the Bear's Son tale; they merely serve to suggest that the writer of the saga was so fond of it that he could not keep it out of his head.

How the visualization of the monsters of the *märchen* as waterfall-trolls persisted in later Scandinavian literature may be seen in the thirteenth- or fourteenth-century *Saga of Samson the Fair*.[12] This, like many of the later sagas, is a curious combination of heroic and romantic elements, but it is a good story; as the writer says at the end, "it will not seem a long evening when this saga is read." Here a tale of a female troll dwelling in a cave under a waterfall is combined with that of a supernatural seducer, her son, who is skilled in harping, familiar in the ballads of *Lady Isabel and the Elf-Knight* and its many analogues in different countries. We have just seen that the waterfall-troll was believed to be especially versed in music. Apart from one episode, the tale bears no resemblance to *Beowulf*. Since the saga is very little known, a brief analysis of the situation which leads up to the incident that recalls *Beowulf* may be desirable.

Arthur, king of England, had a son named Samson the Fair. Samson was given to a foster-father, Salmon, who had a wife, Olempya. After Samson had been with them for eleven years, Salmon died, and Olempya went to live in Scotland.

Samson fell in love with Valentina, the daughter of King Garland of Ireland, who came to stay at Arthur's court as a hostage. When she went back to her father's country, Samson set out to win his spurs as a knight.

King Garland had possessions in Scotland, and went thither, taking Valentina with him. There she fell under the spell of Kvintalin, son of a miller named Gallyn, who was thought to have begotten him on a she-troll who lived under the mill-force. Kvintalin, who was skilled in all kinds of craft, could play the harp so beautifully that he could entice girls out into the forest. He lured Valentina into the woods, and took her mantle and jewels, but she was saved by Olempya, who took her into her own castle, and played tricks to deceive Kvintalin. Valentina's father sailed home without his daughter.

Samson, on arriving in Ireland, asked news of Valentina. Her father said that he did not know what had become of her, so Samson went out in search of her, and journeyed to Scotland. He stayed awhile with Jarl Finnlaug, who told him of Gallyn the miller. Samson found Gallyn at his mill, "and beneath them was a deep ravine with swiftly rushing water." Samson promised Gallyn money if he would assist him in finding Valentina.

"While they were talking, Samson was standing at the edge of the fall, and the first thing he knew he was seized by both feet and pushed over into the stream. He had to match his strength against a huge she-troll. They were dashed about hard and long, and drawn downwards to the bottom. It was a matter of life and death to Samson to get the upper hand of her when they reached the bottom, and just about then he reached for the knife which he carried in his belt and which Valentina had given to him. He plunged the knife into the belly of the she-troll, so that all the entrails fell out. After he was freed from her clutches, he dived under the force, and immediately perceived the mouth of a cave, but he was so weakened that he had to lie a considerable time. When he came to himself after this labor, he girded up his clothes, and went into the cave, and he thought he might never come out. He went a long distance through the cave, wondering at the size and structure of it very much, and presently he came to a side-cave, where he found woman's gear, precious objects, gold, and silver. There was a couch with remarkably beautiful hangings, and the bed-clothes were of the same sort. In the cave he found the kirtle and mantle of the Princess Valentina, with her diadem and girdle. He took from these what he de-sired, and went to the end of the cave, where he found a big door at last, let down in a cleft, but not locked, and after he had got it open with much difficulty, for it was heavy, he saw before him a large and beautiful forest." After staying awhile with Jarl Finnlaug, Sam-son returned home.

The resemblances between this and the *Beowulf* material must not be unduly emphasized. But they do exist. A she-troll dwelling under a water-fall has begotten a son, a supernatural being who haunts the forests. She is killed, like Grendel's dam, in a struggle under the waters. Afterwards the hero dives under the fall, and comes to a cave in which he finds precious objects. Gallyn the miller, seeing blood in the stream, immediately concludes, like the watchers in the tales of Beowulf and Grettir, that the hero has been killed. The whole episode is, of course, a mere insertion in a narrative of quite different character, and it has been still further altered by combination with the legend of a demon who lures a lady to his home beneath the waves, or of a supernatural harper who attempts to entice the king's daughter away, and gets thrown in himself, as into "Wearie's Well" in one version of *Lady Isabel and the Elf-Knight*. This new theme might attach itself easily to the story of a waterfall-troll; we have already noted that the *nøkken* is noted for his musical accomplishments. But it destroys all resemblance between Kvintalin and the male demon of the Bear's Son tale. Professor Child, who called attention to this saga in discussing the ramifications of the ballad of *Lady Isabel*, thought that "Quintalin's mother, who is a complete counterpart to Grendel's, was probably borrowed from *Beówulf*." [13] But I think that it would be more correct to say that she was borrowed from the folk-tales still current in Scandinavian territory, which had earlier given birth to the English lays that formed the basis of the epic. The specific resemblances are not so close as to make it probable that there is influence from the Anglo-Saxon poem, even at second or third hand, and the probabilities are all against it. Once more we have to reckon with the perpetuation and popularity of this old theme in variant forms on Scandinavian soil.

Reminiscences of the double fight against a she-demon and a giant appear in the tale of Orm Storolfsson in the *Flateyjarbók*. These are slight and secondary, but unmistakable. Orm was an historical character, but marvellous deeds were attached to him, just as to Grettir. The story of one exploit tells how a female demon in the shape of a terrible black cat (*ketta*) attacked the companions of a warrior named Asbjorn, devouring some and tearing others to pieces. Asbjorn did not take vengeance on her, but sought out a giant named Brusi in a cave. In the resulting fight Asbjorn was killed. When news of this came to Orm in Iceland, he sailed with about twenty companions to Sandeyjar (Sand-Isles), sought out the cave, and killed the giantess in cat-form by wrestling with her and breaking her back. He then tackled Brusi, and wrestled with him a long time, finally breaking his back, too. Brusi asked him, before he died, to hew off his head. Orm "cut the blood-eagle" on Brusi's back, burned him and the giantess in a fire, and left the cave, taking gold and silver with him.

All this looks very much like a faded and altered version of the two fights of the Bear's Son type. The *Ormssaga* is late, — later than the *Grettissaga*, — and, like many narratives of this period based on old traditional material, occasionally inconsequent. For example, it is not clear why Asbjorn went off to fight the giant Brusi instead of taking revenge on the she-monster for the death of his fellows. Other accounts are preserved in Swedish and Faroe ballads, probably based on

Icelandic ballads derived from the story above. There is no possible doubt that the compiler of the adventures of Orm and Asbjorn borrowed not only incidents but words and phrases from the *Grettis-saga*. He may also have known other versions of the Bear's Son tale. Certain details are interesting: the location at Sand-Isles; the wrestling powers of Orm; the gold and silver in the cave; and the giant's request that Orm cut off his head.[14]

We may now turn to another analogue, the *Saga of Hrolf Kraki*, which serves to show the continued existence of the Beowulf material in Scandinavian territory, not in the simpler form of the Bear's Son *märchen*, but attached to historical personages of Denmark and the northern Scandinavian peninsula. Perhaps the troll-fights of Grettir and of Samson and of Orm may have been influenced by versions that had been given such an historical setting; but there is nothing to show it, and much to make it more reasonable to trace them to folk-tales, or to literary material based on folk-tales. In the *Hrólfssaga*, however, the situation is entirely different: the setting is the most striking part of the resemblance to *Beowulf*; indeed, if it were not for this we should not recognize the incidents of the folk-tale at all. But when both historical tradition and popular tale are taken into account, the parallel to *Beowulf* becomes too close to be accidental. Scholars are not agreed as to the relation between *Beowulf* on the one hand and the *Hrólfssaga* and related Scandinavian sources on the other, but the whole problem is illuminating for epic processes, and a tentative solution may at least be suggested.[15]

It has been pointed out in an earlier chapter that Hrothulf, the nephew of Hrothgar, who became king after the death of Hrothgar's son Hrethric, achieved a remarkable celebrity in the north, where he was commonly known as Hrolf Kraki. His court was imagined as a centre of chivalry, to which the most renowned champions resorted. Saint Olaf is reported to have said that, if he were to be likened to any of the old pagan kings, it would be to Hrolf Kraki. Chief among Hrolf's warriors, as the stories ran, was one Bjarki, the "little bear," who was also called "Bjarki the Warlike" ("Bothvar Bjarki"). In the saga, the epithet Bothvar has supplanted the original name in most passages. Now, as the fame of Hrothgar was transferred to Hrothulf, some features of Beowulf's troll-slayings at Hrothgar's court were apparently transferred likewise to Hrothulf's champion, Bjarki. It will be remembered that in *Beowulf* Hrothulf is represented as sharing the place of honor in the hall with Hrothgar, and as almost enjoying equality in the government of the realm. We are dealing, in considering the *Hrólfssaga*, not with Anglo-Saxon traditions, however, but with the Scandinavian form of those traditions; it would be more correct, then, to speak of Hrothgar as Hroar, and of Hrothulf as Hrolf. In the shifting of a tale from one hero to another, some alterations are to be expected. The earlier Scandinavian form of the story has not been preserved, of course, but in any case it must have been very different from the Anglo-Saxon epic, which was an independent development on foreign soil. So we cannot really compare the version in the *Hrólfs-saga* with its earlier prototype in the Scandinavian Beowulf legends, but only with the English off-shoot of those legends. Moreover, about six centuries elapsed between the composition of the epic in England and the Old Norse saga. In so long a period of time, great changes must of necessity take place in any story.

The *Saga of Hrolf Kraki* shows its late date in many ways. It is a queer jumble of old and new, of romantic and heroic elements, of nobility and childishness, of realism and the supernatural, set down in an age when the old tales had lost much of their earlier authority and validity. Like Sir Thomas Malory, whose activity falls less than a century later, the compiler worked from earlier written sources, but unlike Sir Thomas, he quite failed to subdue the various legends before him to a consistent artistic purpose, and often degraded them by trivialities and burlesque. The greater part of the saga is taken up with the adventures of other warriors than Hrolf; as in the *Morte Darthur*, the titular hero gains chief interest through his tragic death. Despite all this, the saga preserves much valuable early tradition. To the same period belong Icelandic ballads, or *rímur*, which narrate episodes in the career of Bjarki. A third form of the material appears in the Latin of Saxo Grammaticus, some two centuries earlier. These will be considered presently; the account in the *Hrólfs-saga* may first be reviewed.

Bothvar Bjarki, the son of Bjorn ("the bear"), a man who through magic could assume bear-shape, and the grandson of King Hring of Uppdalir, came to the court of King Hrolf Kraki at Hleidargard (Lethra) after a stay with his brother Thorir, ruler of the Gautar (Geatas). On his way he took refuge for the night at the house of a peasant. The good-wife told him of the ill-treatment of her son Hott by the warriors at court, and begged that Bothvar would protect him. Bothvar did so; on arriving at the royal hall he found that Hott, in the extreme of cowardice, had taken refuge under a pile of bones, and he made Hott come out and sit beside him. At dinner the king's warriors amused themselves by throwing bones at the two men. Suddenly Bothvar seized a bone, hurled it back, and killed the thrower. This made him respected; the affair was settled, and Bothvar became one of the retainers of the king.

"And as the Yule-feast approached, the men grew depressed. Bothvar asked Hott the reason; he told him that a beast had already come two successive winters, a great and terrible one — 'and it has wings on its back and flies about continually; two autumns it has already sought us here, and it does great damage; no weapon wounds it, but the king's champions, the best warriors of all, don't come home at this time.' Bothvar said, 'The hall isn't as well defended as I thought, if a beast can destroy the domain and property of the king.' Hott answered, 'That is no beast, it is rather the greatest of monsters [*hit mesta trǫll*].' Now came the Yule-even; and the king said, 'Now I desire that the men be still and quiet in the night, and I forbid them all to run any risk on account of the beast; let the cattle fare as fate wills; my men I do not care to lose.' All promised to act as the king commanded. But Bothvar crept secretly out in the night; he made Hott go with him, but Hott went only because he was forced to, crying that it would surely be the death of him. Bothvar told him it would turn out better. They went out of the hall, and Bothvar had to carry him, so full of fear was he. Now they saw the beast, and Hott shrieked as loud as he could, and cried that the beast was going to swallow him. Bothvar commanded the dog [Hott] to keep still, and threw him down in the moss, and there he lay in unspeakable terror, and didn't even dare to run home. Then Bothvar attacked the beast, but it chanced that the sword stuck in the sheath when he wanted to draw it; then he pulled so hard at the sword that it flew out of the sheath, and he plunged it immediately with such force under the shoulder of the beast that it penetrated the heart, and hard and heavily fell the beast down on the ground dead. Then Bothvar went over to where Hott was lying. He took him up and carried him over to the place where the beast lay dead. Hott trembled frightfully. Bothvar said, 'Now you must drink the blood of the beast.' For a long time he was loth to do this, but he finally did n't dare to do otherwise. Bothvar made him drink two big gulps, and eat some of the beast's heart; then Bothvar grappled with him, and they struggled long with each other. Bothvar said, 'Now you have become very strong, and I don't believe that you will be afraid of the troop of King Hrolf any longer.' Hott answered, 'I shall not fear them any more, nor shall I be afraid of you henceforth.' 'That is well, comrade Hott' [said Bothvar], 'and now we will set up the beast, and arrange it so that the others will think it alive.' They did so. Then they went in and were quiet; no one knew what they had done.

"The king asked in the morning whether they knew anything of the beast; whether it had showed itself anywhere in the night; they told him that the cattle were all safe and sound in the folds. The king bade his men see if they could not find some indication that it had come thither. The warders obeyed, came quickly back again and told the king that the beast was advancing rapidly to attack the town. The king bade his men be courageous, [and said] each one should help, according as he had courage for it, and proceed against this monster. It was done as the king commanded; they made themselves ready for it. The king looked at the beast and said, 'I don't see that the beast moves, but who will undertake the task and attack it?' Bothvar answered, 'A brave man might be able to satisfy his curiosity about this! Comrade Hott, destroy this evil talk about you; men say that there is neither strength nor courage in you; go up and kill the beast, you see nobody else wants to.' 'Yes,' said Hott, 'I will undertake it.' The king said, 'I don't know whence this courage has come to you, Hott; you have changed marvellously in a short time.' Hott said, 'Give me your sword Gullinhjalti, which you are bearing, and I will kill the beast or die in the attempt.' King Hrolf said, 'This sword can only be borne by a man who is both brave and daring.' Hott answered, 'You shall be convinced that I am such a man.' The king said, 'Who knows whether your character has n't changed more than appearances show? Take the sword and may you have good fortune!' Then Hott attacked the beast and struck at it as soon as he was near enough so that he could hit it, and the beast fell down dead. Bothvar said, 'Look, lord, what he has done!' The king replied, 'Truly he has changed much, but Hott alone did n't kill the beast; you were the man who did it.' Bothvar said, 'It may be so.' The king said, 'I knew as soon as you came here that only few men could compare with you, but this seems to me your most illustrious deed, that you have made a warrior out of Hott, who appeared little born to great good fortune. And now I wish him called Hott no longer; he shall from this day be named Hjalti — thou shalt be called after the sword Gullinhjalti.'"

The resemblances to *Beowulf* are obvious. Bothvar Bjarki, a prince of a royal house in the north, comes, like Beowulf, from the land of the Gautar (Geatas), where a relative is king, to Hleidargard in Denmark (Lethra, the probable site of Hrothgar's hall), to the court of Hrolf, king of the Danes, the Hrothulf of *Beowulf*. Here a monster, invulnerable to swords, has made attacks which the Danes have not been able to repulse. When

Bothvar arrives at the court, he becomes involved in a quarrel with one of the king's men, and discomfits him, in a ruder way, but as effectively, as Beowulf silenced Unferth. Bothvar then slays the monster at night, becoming son-in-law to the king, as Beowulf was made the adopted son of Hrothgar. The name "Bjarki" curiously parallels "Beowulf" in meaning. Bothvar Bjarki's bear characteristics are borne out by his parentage, and by the fact that he later fights in defence of the king in bear shape. There is a curious correspondence, too, between the sword Gullinhjalti, with which the dead troll is struck by Hott, and the sword with a golden hilt, the old demonic weapon which Beowulf found in the cave, and with which he struck off the head of the dead Grendel. This has been much discussed; some scholars have denied that there is any connection between the epithets, but it would hardly seem that their likeness is the result of chance.

There are great discrepancies between the account in the Anglo-Saxon epic and that in the saga. Nothing remains of the double fight, with the male and the female demons. The monster killed by Bjarki does not suggest Grendel; he is much more like a dragon. The winged troll has supplanted the waterfall-troll. Possibly, if the dragon episode had already been attached to Beowulf in Scandinavia, and was still told of him, this might have affected the earlier Bear's Son adventure. But dragons were so common that a writer with his head full of the débris of story-telling might have got his dragon from a variety of sources. There is nothing in *Beowulf* to correspond to the strange trick played on the king by the smiting of the dead troll by Hott-Hjalti; indeed, the figure of Bjarki's friend and companion is clearly a late intrusion into the story, and very ill-managed. The whole tone of the narrative in the saga is far removed from the grave earnestness of the epic. Nevertheless, the Icelandic appears to preserve recollections of the tale of Beowulf's adventures, battered, time-worn, trivialized, overgrown with other material, but still recognizable.

In the Icelandic *rímur*, or ballads, and in Saxo Grammaticus, more of the heroic temper of the tale is preserved, and the events are more rationalized. In the ballads, Bjarki kills a she-wolf and makes Hjalti drink its blood; Hjalti gives evidence of his prowess by slaying a gray bear. It would appear that Hjalti was the original name of Bjarki's companion, not Hott, as in the saga, which is rich in inept elaborations. The ballads add one important point, first emphasized by Professor Chambers, which shows, like a flash of light, the dependence of all this on the figure of Beowulf or Bjólfr: they state that Bjarki aided Athils in his struggle against Ali, which is obviously a recol-

lection of the assistance rendered by Beowulf to
Eadgils in his hostilities with Onela.

Saxo's account lacks much that is told in the
saga. Bjarki and Hjalti are first introduced at the
bridal banquet of Agnar, who is marrying Rolf's
sister. Nothing is said of Hjalti's cowardice;
Bjarki throws a bone at a feaster who had struck
Hjalti in a similar fashion, and fights a duel with
Agnar and kills him. He later marries Agnar's
bride himself, after overcoming those who en-
deavored to avenge the dead man. "When he was
triumphing in these deeds of prowess, a beast of
the forest furnished him fresh laurels. For he met
a huge bear in a thicket, and slew it with a javelin;
and then bade his companion Hjalte put his lips
to the beast and drink the blood that came out,
that he might be the stronger afterwards. For it
was believed that a draught of this sort caused
an increase of bodily strength." Saxo describes at
length the great contest between Rolf and Hiartuar
(Hrothulf and Heoroweard), devoting much space
to a paraphrase of the famous "Lay of Bjarki,"
in which Hjalti spurs on Bjarki to the final combat. The substance of this song, says Saxo, is
found in an ancient Danish lay, "which is repeated by heart by many conversant with antiquity." [16] And so we may believe that Saxo
learned of other lays of Bjarki from oral tradition,
though his whole account gives the impression of

a tale imperfectly understood, save for the Bjarki lay and the circumstances that explain it. He has preserved nothing recognizable of the Grendel-fight, unless it be paralleled in the brief and tame account of the contest with the gray bear.

The relationships of these different accounts of the Bjarki story have been long discussed by scholars. No certainty has ever been reached, nor, in my judgment, is it possible, unless new evidence comes to light. All that caution will permit us to say is that reminiscences of the Beowulf tale, not in its Anglo-Saxon form, but as it lived on in Scandinavian territory, were attached to Bjarki, and may still be seen, gleaming faintly through the complexities of later story-telling. The exact ways in which such borrowings took place are, indeed, not of great consequence for our survey of epic tradition. The main point to observe is how, despite all changes in the passing of years, the old tale preserved something of its original setting and incident, through a study of which we may better understand its earlier history.

VII

THE DRAGON

"AMONG all the kindes of Serpents, there is none comparable to the Dragon, or that affordeth and yeeldeth so much plentiful matter in History for the ample discovery of the nature thereof." These words of the pious Edward Topsell, naturalist and contemporary of Shakespeare, in his *Historie of Serpents*,[1] may well be pondered by those who follow the trail of dragons through the story-telling of Western Europe. There is indeed so much "plentiful matter" that classification and genealogizing can accomplish but little. Topsell, following Conrad Gesner, arranged his dragons in scientific groups: Class I, with wings but no feet; Class II, with both wings and feet; Class III, with neither wings nor feet. Modern scholars have tried a different method, based on dragon heroes rather than on the beasts themselves, — the victorious youth who wins treasure (Sigurd type); the hero who frees a maiden (St. George type); the hero who slays a dragon to protect mankind (Thor type). Such a classification, however, gives a false confidence. The incidents are not constant; the "types" borrow from each other, — in short, the dragon (noted, as St. Augustine put it, *propter insidias*) wriggles slyly out of categories, and no scholar has been able to bind him fast.

The dragon was so well known on Germanic soil that the poet of *Beowulf* did not even give him a name. His kind was so common, and the adventures in which heroes met them so numerous, that no type-story can satisfactorily. be constructed into which the narrative of *Beowulf* will fit. Most of the incidents of the fight itself may be paralleled in folk-tales, and in literature based on popular sources, but there is no analogue, or group of analogues, which really shows close resemblances to the narrative in *Beowulf*. Resemblances to scattered elements from different sources are a very different matter from the constantly recurring narrative framework of the Bear's Son tale.[2] The dragon episode has no analogues of any consequence, because there is so little about it which is distinctive. The dragon fits Beowulf as any dragon fits any hero. The really individual parts of the adventure, the accounts of the deposition of the hoard in the earth, and the circumstances leading up to its plundering, have little to do with the dragon himself.

Our method of investigation, then, must be quite different from that of the narratives of Grendel and his dam. There we have highly individual monsters fitting into a type-story found in various localities all over the world. In the dragon we have a monster which is not individualized, but a type, occurring in stories so varied that they show little recognizable and recurring framework.

No one can tell just how the dragon came to be added to the tale. It seems probable, however, that after the Bear's Son — slayer of two demonic beings, one in a hall and the other underground — had been made into a great Scandinavian warrior and prince, and his adventures placed in an historic setting, a suitable and glorious death had to be provided for him. So the dragon episode was added. When a hero once becomes popular, the story of his whole career is likely to be demanded. A great slayer of trolls and a mighty king ought not to die in his bed, tamely, but in glorious combat with a worthy foe, and the dragon was ready to hand, in the treasure-house of story — a familiar and a fearful adversary. Beowulf could not survive, for, after all, he was mortal; in an earlier form of the tale he seems to have perished through the curse resting on the dragon's gold. But his glory was nevertheless increased in that he defended his people from a fearful scourge, and won for them renown and treasure.[3]

The poet is rather shy of definite description of the dragon, as is his habit when dealing with the supernatural. A monster is more fearful if pictured in the imagination. This is sound art, but the dragon was too familiar to need much comment. He was apparently regarded much as we look upon the hippopotamus or the rhinoceros — a strange animal, not met with every day, to be sure, but not outside the pale of ordinary human experience. Less than a hundred years after *Beowulf* was composed, the people of Northumbria beheld dragons in the air, and dire misfortunes followed. In the time of Chaucer, so Thomas of Walsingham informs us, a dragon near Ludlow was subdued by the incantations of a Saracen physician, and much treasure extracted from his lair. The grave descriptions of the dragon in mediæval bestiaries are familiar; there too he appears as a curious but not unauthenticated feature of natural history. As for *Beowulf*, a fairly vivid picture may be reconstructed by putting together details from various passages. The monster was in serpent form, with a long coiling body, about fifty feet long (an indefinite largish number, like the fifty years of Beowulf's reign). He was provided with wings, and had the usual red-hot insides. His breath was poisonous, his bite mortal, he exhaled steam, he spewed out fire as he flew through the air. He was not proof against his own fires, however; he was singed by his own coals in death, as the dragon slain by Sigemund (897) was consumed by his own heat. Like the Grendel-brood, he made his raids at night, and he had to get back before daybreak. Like them, he was invulnerable to ordinary swords; for even Beowulf's famous Nægling broke, and it required the supernatural weapon possessed by Wiglaf (2616) to pierce the scaly hide. Like them, he took pleasure in his feud with mankind, but we have been told that "no single phrase or descriptive epithet applied to the firedrake can be tortured into any connection with devils, or creatures of evil in the Christian sense." [4] The dragon was quiescent until disturbed; his raids were not made, like Grendel's, out of devilish malice, but in defence of his treasure. Altogether, he was a somewhat more genial adversary.

The dragon's lair deserves especial notice. It was in a burial mound, on a rocky height near the sea. There the monster had brooded over his treasure for three hundred years. A hot stream, effluvia from his burning insides, no doubt, issued from the mound. That such was the common haunt of the dragon, we have plenty of testimony, as in the Anglo-Saxon *Gnomic Verses*, curious commonplaces which may be described as inverted riddles. The riddle gives facts in regard to an object, and asks its name; the gnome names the object, and describes it in formal fashion.

The spear, the missile adorned with gold, is held in the hand . . . the mast standeth on the ship, the supporter of the sail. The sword, the noble weapon, hangs on the thigh. The dragon lieth on the grave-mound, old, exultant in treasure.[5]

In similar fashion the epic mentions the dragon as a commonplace of natural history.

The flaming dragon seeketh mounds, naked and hateful reptile; he flieth by night, encompassed by fire; him dwellers on earth fear exceedingly. It is his nature to seek out treasure in the earth, where, old in winters, he guardeth heathen gold; he profiteth naught thereby. (2272–2277.)

This was just what the dragon of *Beowulf* had done.

The old night-scather found the joyous hoard of treasure lying open. . . . So the foe of the people guarded well an enormous treasure three hundred winters in the earth, until a mortal awakened wrath in his heart. (2270 ff.)

There are still to be observed, not only in England, but in the Scandinavian kingdoms, Germany, France, and other countries of Western Europe, the remains of ancient burial mounds, some of them dating as far back as the Stone Age. At the time when *Beowulf* was written, then, they were already of high antiquity, and regarded with superstition as strange relics of the misty past. Precious objects, often made of gold, which were interred with the dead, led to frequent violations, against which heavy legal penalties were devised. It is easy to understand the effect that these tombs, constructed in strange fashion of massive stones, containing secret chambers and passages filled with dead men's bones and curiously wrought weapons and ornaments, must have exercised upon the popular imagination. Well might they be supposed to be the work of giants (2717), protected by magic spells (3052), and inhabited by dragons. They were usually built upon dominating heights; in *Beowulf* the dragon's barrow is on or very near a hill called the Eagles' Ness, in a desolate place by the shore, with the waves breaking beneath. The description of this cliff in relation to the action of the story is hazy, as is usual in the epic. But the mound itself is very clearly visualized. This particular tomb was, of course, imaginary, but when the archæological evidence in regard to burial mounds in general is carefully studied, and compared with the description in the poem, it is easy to see that actual observation has been at work. This description in *Beowulf* fits perfectly a well-recognized type of mound, dating at the earliest from the Stone Age, which is held to have ended in Europe about 2000 B.C. — a type that is still observable in England and the Scandinavian countries.[6]

It belongs to the variety termed by archæologists "megalithic passage-graves." A flat spot was chosen, generally upon a height, and one or more chambers were then constructed of large flat stones set on end, roofed with thinner slabs placed horizontally on top. The whole was then covered with earth, in rounded mound-shape, and a passage left from the exterior to the chambers within.

This passage was also built of flat stones, and roofed over, with a covering of earth, forming a part of the same mound as the main structure. The entrance was closed with one or more blocks, and others might also be placed across parts of the passage. In Sweden "the chamber in a passage-grave is not infrequently as much as twenty-four feet long, or more, nine feet broad, and nearly six feet high. ·The passage is narrower and lower, but sometimes as long as the chamber." [7] In the British Isles there seems to have been a tendency to cut up the central chamber into smaller connecting rooms. There are some differences, also, in the method of covering the chambers, but the indications in the epic are not precise enough to show whether the description is based upon specifically English conditions. It is interesting to note that the Anglo-Saxon phrase *enta geweorc*, "the work of giants," is paralleled in the Danish *jætte-stue*, "giant-chamber," a term that has passed into archæological usage.

The dragon's barrow in *Beowulf* was built upon a height (2212, etc.); it was covered by a mound of earth, and hence is called an "earth-hall" (2410, 2515, 2719, etc.) or "earth-house" (2232). It had an overhead covering of arches of stone, resting on pillars or supporting stones (2718). A passage led into the interior (2213), — though it is conceivable that this may refer to the path leading up to the barrow, — a passage so long that when the Geat warriors entered to get the treasure, one had to carry a light. The dragon found the mound "open" (2271), that is, the stone or stones closing the entrance had fallen down. So he entered, and lay coiled about the treasure in glittering rings. But after the passage of three centuries, the hoard was rifled at last; a precious cup was stolen, which later came into the possession of Beowulf (2404, 2405). When the dragon awoke, and perceived the theft, "sniffing along the stone wall" of the interior (2288), and circling around about the mound on the outside, the intruder had made good his escape. Waiting "with difficulty" until evening, the time for creatures of evil to fare abroad, the dragon took his revenge by "burning the bright courts," spewing hot coals upon the countryside, and striking terror to the hearts of the people. Beowulf, aged but valiant, resolved to deliver his people, and went, with eleven companions and armed with a shield of iron, to the barrow, the thief himself guiding them to the spot. After resting awhile on the headland, Beowulf advanced to the mound, shouting in beneath the hoary stone, and rousing the monster. The earth resounded, poisonous breath issued like steam from the entrance, the huge serpent crawled writhing from his lair, and the fight was on.

A study of this episode as a whole is important for an understanding of the methods of the epic poet. Different and contradictory accounts of the early history of the treasure exist side by side, as it were, but it seems possible to make a fairly safe guess as to how these contradictions arose, and which form of the narrative is earlier. The original motivation, which has been obscured by elaborations of secondary importance, and often overlooked by readers and even by scholars, is of great importance for the episode as a whole, and for the epic design. Furthermore, the events which led to the plundering of the hoard by the thief have, I think, been generally misunderstood. In this connection our brief examination of Germanic social and legal customs earlier in this study will be of assistance. This question must be postponed, however, while we first look at the history of the treasure before the dragon found it.

The epic presents two separate and distinct conceptions of the way in which the gold came to be deposited in the earth. The older and more important passage (3047–3075) states that the treasure was buried by illustrious chieftains, who laid a curse upon it. The poet has just described the dragon as lying stark in death, singed by his own internal fires. He now continues:

3047   Beside [the dragon] were heaped chalices and flagons,
       flat vessels lay there, and a precious sword
       eaten through by rust, which for a thousand winters

3050   had lain there in the bosom of the earth.
         For that heritage was huge in sum,
         the gold of men of yore, protected by a spell,
         that the hall of rings might be disturbed
         by none of the race of men, unless God himself,
3055   the true King of Glories, should grant to whom he
            would
            — he is the protector of mankind — to ope the hoard,
         even to whatever man it should seem to him meet.

After a few lines, the poet repeats the curse-motive.

3062   Uncertain it is
         where a brave man will reach the end
         of his destined days, when longer he may not,
3065   a man among his kin, dwell in the mead-hall.
         So was it with Beowulf when he sought the warder of
            the mount,
         deadly enmities; he himself knew not
         in what wise his parting from the world should be.
         For till the day of doom had they laid a mighty curse
            upon it,
3070   the far-famed chiefs, who there had placed the gold,
         that the man should pay the penalty of his sins,
         be confined in idol-fanes, bound in the bonds of hell,
         tormented with tortures, if he plundered that place,
         unless he, eager for gold, had very zealously
3075   given heed in the past to the grace of the Lord.

Unfortunately, the close of this latter passage is most obscure in the Anglo-Saxon; I have given the rendering that seems to me most convincing, and best in accord with the context.[8]

It is not hard to conjecture the changes which have taken place in this part of the story, in pass-

ing from pagan into Christian hands. Originally
the tale ran somewhat as follows. A thousand
years ago, illustrious chieftains buried the gold,
with spells to protect it, pronouncing a curse upon
those who should disturb it. When the hoard was
plundered, the curse operated immediately; the
dragon began his fearful ravages. Moreover, Beowulf himself fell a victim to the ancient spell, since
a cup stolen from the treasure had come into his
possession (2404, 2405); it was his fate to fall in
combat with the dragon. In similar fashion the
Nibelungen Hoard brought evil and death upon
its possessors, and finally upon Sigurd himself.

More than all this, the curse lay heavy upon the
Geatas after Beowulf's own death. He rejoiced
that he had won the gold for his people in slaying
the dragon (2794), and asked that he might look
upon it in his dying hour (2747 ff.). This is tragic
irony; he did not know the reason of his death
(3067), he did not know that in securing the gold
for his people he was bringing upon them misfortunes that would pursue them fatefully for
years. For after his death the treasure passed into
their possession; the warriors removed it from the
dragon's lair. The Messenger says it shall be
burned on the funeral pyre (3014), but when this
pyre is prepared, there is no mention of the treasure. Helmets, shields, and bright coats of mail
serve as adornment (3139), and it is expressly

stated that the treasure was placed in the barrow erected about the pyre after it was burned out (3163). Had the gold been consumed, it might have lifted the curse. Fire is a great purifier. But it still remained in the possession of the Geatas. We have seen earlier that the historic downfall of this people, and their absorption by their hereditary enemies, the Swedes, was probably, in popular story, softened by the introduction of the great protecting warrior Beowulf. The curse-motive provided at once the explanation of the final death of the peerless hero Beowulf and of the extinction of his people as a great political power, so graphically foreshadowed in the epic (3015 ff.).

Such we may believe to have been the earlier form of the tale. But this, in the epic as we have it, is confused with later conceptions. In the first place, the power of a pagan curse was inconsistent with the power of the Christian God, constantly emphasized by the poet. So in the two passages just quoted, in which the curse is mentioned, the poet hastens to say that God could nullify the power of the spells and the curse if he chose. No one could disturb the treasure in the mound unless God should permit it (3052-3057); the man who disturbed the gold should suffer for it, through the operation of the curse, unless [though] eager for gold,[9] he had zealously served the Lord (3071-3075) [who would protect him]. Furthermore, the

connection of the curse with the death of Beowulf
is subordinated as far as possible in the epic. But
the poet was powerless to alter the fact that Beowulf was killed by the dragon, and that his people
came to grief when he no longer ruled over them.
The story was too well known to make radical
alterations of the leading themes possible. Logi-
cally, Beowulf ought to have been saved by the
Christian God, who is superior to the incantations
of dead heathen, and who careth for his own, but
Beowulf was not saved in the traditional story, so
there was nothing for it but to allow the curse and
the spells to work, after all, and the dragon to kill
him off. But it was possible to keep the curse-
motive in the background, and disguise it by further elaborations of the tale.

Great prominence is, therefore, given in the
epic to another and totally different account of the
way in which the gold was buried in the ground in
the beginning. Here there is no mention of any
curse upon it, and the whole scene is changed: instead of the "illustrious chiefs" (3070), a solitary
man, the last survivor of his race, concealed the
treasure in the earth.

2231   Many such things there were
    in the earth-house, treasures of old,
    the mighty heritage of a noble race,
    which, in years gone by, a man — I know not who —
2235 in this spot prudently concealed,
    precious possessions. Death had claimed his kin

in days of yore, and this one surviving
of the warriors of the folk, the last of all,
a treasure-keeper mourning friends departed, awaited
    a like fate, —
2240   that he but for a little might enjoy
the treasures of old time. A barrow all prepared
stood on the flat ground near the waves,
new beside the ness, secure in its structure;
and therein did the shepherd of the rings
2245   bear a deal of the treasures of noble men,
decorated gold, and a few words spake:
"Hold now, O Earth, since heroes cannot,
what warriors have owned. Lo, from thy bosom once
good men obtained it; war-death claimed them,
2250   horrid life-bale, all the men
belonging to my people; they have given up life,
they have looked their last on the joys of the hall.
    I have no sword-attendant,
no one to polish the cup with its golden patines,
the precious vessel; the warriors have departed.
2255   The doughty helmet, adorned with gold,
must lose its plates; the attendants sleep in death,
whose office was to brighten the battle-mask;
the coat of mail, which in battle survived
the biting of swords when shields were crashing,
2260   crumbles now that its wearer is gone; the ring-locked
byrny cannot, since the war-lord is dead, fare afar
on the hero's shoulders. Now there is no joy of the
    harp,
no cheer of the glee-wood, no good hawk
swoopeth through the hall, nor doth the courser swift
2265   strike with his hoofs the courts. Death hath indeed
claimed many of the race of men."
Thus, sad at heart, gave utterance to sorrow
the survivor of his race, sadly wandered
day and night, till the surging of death
struck at his soul.

Stylistically this is in striking contrast to the other account of the deposition of the gold. It is lyrical and elegiac, full of the pathos that lies in the decay of glory. It suggests vividly the tone of the so-called "Northumbrian lyrics" in Anglo-Saxon. *The Wanderer*, perhaps the finest of these, recalls, in theme and treatment, the above passage. The feelings of an exile who once enjoyed association with kin and lord are portrayed (7 ff.); death has claimed them (23, 61); he or another stands among the ruins of once brilliant halls, and laments the passing of the glorious dead.

92 Where is now the steed? Where the rider? Where is
      the giver of rings?
   Where are the seats of the feasters, where the joys of
      the hall?
   Alas for the bright cup! Alas for the byrnied chief!
95 Alas for the power of the prince! How hath time flown
      by,
   vanished beneath the helm of night, as if it ne'er had
      been!
   Where once beloved warriors gathered, standeth now
   a wall of wondrous height, adorned with dragons.
   The warriors fell before the might of the spears,
100 weapons greedy of slaughter, inexorable fate!

The "solitary survivor" passage just quoted from *Beowulf* gives every indication of being a late elaboration made in England by an Anglo-Saxon poet. It is thoroughly in the spirit of Northumbrian lyric verse of the eighth century, and, as Axel Olrik has noted, not Scandinavian in tone.

"The old hero, nameless and not much individual-ized, with his complaint for vanished glories, is typical for English poetry, and does not remind one of the characters in Scandinavian poetry." [10] In introducing this new account of the burial of the gold, then, the poet of *Beowulf* was able still further to subordinate the curse-motive of the original story, and at the same time to add a deco-rative elegiac interlude in the taste of his time in northern England. But he left enough of the older form of the tale to produce a disturbing inconsis-tency, — disturbing, if one reads the poem with sufficient care to notice it.

The point is of some importance for another reason. Critics [11] have conjectured that in the earlier form of the story the solitary hero burying the gold was himself metamorphosed into the dragon, as Fafnir, the son of Hreithmar, was changed into the dragon of the Rhine-Gold. But if this solitary hero is really a late and secondary addition to the tale, such a theory cannot stand. Moreover, the surviving scion of the noble race is not impelled by greed; he feels his own death near, and despairs of further joy in this life. And it is expressly stated in the poem that the dragon found the hoard standing open, and that, since it is the nature of dragons to seek out treasure over which to brood, although it profits them nothing, he settled down to guard it (2270 ff.). All this is quite at variance with the idea that the man who buried the gold turned into the dragon. It may be that the poet borrowed his "solitary survivor" from an episode of the Beowulf story already in existence, but produced in Northumbria, and not representing an earlier form of the tale. He seems elsewhere to have utilized variant conceptions, regardless of consistency. On the other hand, this new motivation of the burying of the treasure, with its opportunities for conventional lyrical pathos, may have been original with him. There seems to be no way to decide.

We now come to another part of the tale, which I believe to have been generally misunderstood. How the hoard was actually plundered by a thief is set forth in two passages (2214–2231; 2278–2293). These do not embody dissimilar conceptions, but different aspects of the same series of events. Unfortunately, the manuscript is so much damaged in the earlier passage that only about six lines can be satisfactorily read. And the whole story is obscured by the allusive, hind-foremost, disconnected fashion of much Anglo-Saxon narrative verse. Reduced to its lowest terms, and set in chronological sequence, the train of events is about as follows. The dragon guarded the treasure unmolested for three hundred years, until a man penetrated into his mound, and stole a cup, and possibly other treasures, while the monster slept.

This man did not commit the theft "of his own accord" — he acted from "dire necessity" (2221–2223). Moreover, he was "an outcast from the hall," and "fled the blows of hatred." Why he had been forced to leave, we are not informed, but his stealing of the cup was in any case clearly a desperate expedient to get something of value with which to buy peace and restoration to his place in the community (2282). The ruler who arranged the settlement was, no doubt, Beowulf himself. We are told that he came into possession of the precious cup, which was used, in one version of the tale, to motivate his death, on account of the curse attached to the dragon gold. The offence committed may have been one for which Beowulf himself could call the culprit to account, which would explain his retaining possession of the cup. Or he may have acted as mediator for another chieftain of the tribes which made up his kingdom. The details of the story, which were probably familiar to the poet and his hearers, are not given. But in any case the immediate purpose of the theft was fulfilled; the boon of the wretched man, the fugitive from court, was granted (2284). A far greater trouble resulted: the dragon, in revenge for the loss of his treasure, fared forth at night, scorching the countryside with his fiery breath, and striking terror far and wide. Then the aged Beowulf resolved to slay the monster, and with a band of followers made his way to the dragon's lair. The wretched man who had earlier penetrated into this desolate spot and plundered the hoard acted as guide. "He went against his will," says the poet, grimly, and indeed anyone who had once ventured near the dragon had no taste for more of him.

It was suggested many years ago that the man who stole the cup was a slave, and this theory has gained much currency. The authority of Grundtvig, who first proposed it, lent it weight, but its sole and only support is the conjectural emendation of a word in a damaged line (2223), for which various readings are possible. If a conjecture is often enough repeated, it gets in time to be accepted as canonical. There is nothing else in the poem to support the idea that the thief was a slave, and recent discussion of the matter serves, to my mind, to make it less plausible than ever.[12] The situation is amply explained by a well-known procedure in early Germanic justice: the payment by a freeman of a sum of money, or its equivalent in value, for the settlement of an offence. We have already in an earlier chapter had occasion to notice this, and to observe how Beowulf's own father, Ecgtheow, was forced to flee from the court of the Geatas because he had killed a man, whereupon he took refuge with the Danes, and Hrothgar compounded the feud by sending gold to the kinsmen of the slain men, and apparently binding Ecgtheow by oath to keep the peace. Possibly the offence for which the fugitive in the dragon-tale was seeking immunity was, like Ecgtheow's, a murder. In any case, it is well to remember that a man did not have to be a slave to be a wretched outcast from tribal society, and that the chances are distinctly against this particular culprit's being a slave. The poet is not interested in slaves; they are not mentioned in the epic.

In sharp contrast to the reminiscences of the past, told in part by the poet, and in part by Beowulf himself, before he encounters the dragon, is the description of the fight itself. This is vivid, but unhurried. The aged hero advances alone to the dragon's barrow, and shouts his defiance in through the stone arch of the entrance. Hot steam pours forth; the earth quakes — "there was no great occasion for seeking friendship." Curled and writhing, the monster advances; the hero stands his ground and strikes, but his sword will not pierce the scaly hide, and his shield affords less protection than he had hoped. The rage of the dragon waxes; flame and smoke pour forth, and both contestants prepare for another onslaught. At this point Wiglaf, Beowulf's young cousin, the prince of the Wægmundingas, comes to his kinsman's assistance, carrying a marvellous sword forged by etins. A description of this sword and a longish speech delay the narrative. Presently the youth rushes into the fiery reek, his shield is consumed, he takes refuge beneath the shield of Beowulf, who thereupon strikes with his sword Nægling once more, but so great is the force of the blow that the weapon is broken. A third time the dragon advances, and this time fastens his deadly fangs in Beowulf's neck, inflicting a mortal wound. But Wiglaf, though his hand is scorched with flame, strikes the monster "a little lower down," in the soft parts of the body, presumably, whereupon the fire begins to slacken, and Beowulf, drawing his short sword, cuts the dragon in two. But the venom in the wound does its work quickly; the last hour of the hero has come. Wiglaf unlaces his helmet, brings him water, and receives his dying instructions. His eyes are gladdened by the sight of the treasures which have been won. With his last breath, Beowulf designates Wiglaf, the last survivor of their clan, as his successor, since he himself dies childless.

All this needs little elucidation. The same is true of the scenes that follow — the announcement of Beowulf's death by the eloquent Messenger, the plundering of the hoard by the Geat warriors, the building of the bale-fire upon the Whale's Ness, the funeral laments and ceremonies, the erection of a beacon on the headland around the smoking brands, while the twelve chosen warriors encircle it on horseback, uttering solemn praises of the dead hero as they ride. Many picturesque details, many interesting glimpses of primitive funeral customs are revealed, which must presently be briefly discussed. What is not so clearly obvious, even on a careful reading, is that the whole climax of the poem is designed to celebrate the two great ideals of Germanic warrior-life: the conduct of the perfect retainer and the conduct of the perfect king. As we have seen, the poet is never happier than when he is illustrating, by concrete action, the great fundamental principles upon which the society of his time was founded.

It is a matter of pride with Beowulf that he encounters the dragon single-handed. "It is no undertaking for you" he tells his thanes (2532). He even apologizes for meeting the monster with shield and coat of mail; he would fain match him, strength for strength, as he did Grendel, but the poison and fire of his adversary make it sportsmanlike to have some advantage on his own side (2518 ff.). The craven thanes need no urging to stay away; they flee into the wood, leaving their lord to his fate, an unspeakably shameful and disgraceful proceeding. At this point Wiglaf, the ideal retainer, addresses them with bitter words: they, the chosen ones, the recipients of favor and treasure, are recreant to their duty now that their lord is in mortal danger. So he, though a young and untried warrior, refuses to join them, but rushes to assist his lord. It was his baptism of fire; never before had he stood in the press of battle (2625). And again, when all is over, Wiglaf reproaches the recreant thanes yet more bitterly.

How little shall ye and your kin have joy in the taking of treasure, the bestowal of swords, the happiness of home! Every man of your kindred shall be deprived of his land-rights, when athelings far away shall learn of your flight, of your inglorious deed. Death is better for any warrior than dishonor! (2884–2891.)

This attribution of abject cowardice and faithlessness to the *comitatus* of the hero, in an age which emphasized courage and fidelity above all things, is most striking. Apart from this particular episode, there is no intimation in the poem that the Geatas were in any way lacking in the attributes of a noble people, worthy to surround their chieftain. Their later defeat at the hands of the Swedes is suggested as a misfortune, not a disgrace. Did the poet of *Beowulf* introduce the cowardice of the thanes into the tale, or get it from older tradition? We have no means of deciding, but the latter would be more in accord with his usual practice. In that case, what explains its place in the story? Was it designed to emphasize the paralyzing terror inspired by the dragon, a terror so great that warriors would forget their most sacred duties? Was the curse of the gold already attacking, not only Beowulf, but his people?

The constantly shifting motivation of epic tradition is hard to follow. There can, however, be no doubt as to the artistic effect of the theme in the completed epic; it throws the strongest light upon the heroism of the single faithful retainer.

It may be that this heroism had a foundation in fact, in no way connected with a dragon. In examining the historical basis of the poem in an earlier chapter, we have seen that Wiglaf, of the powerful house of the Wægmundingas, may actually have become leader or king of the Geatas on the death of Heardred, and that his defence of his people may have staved off their downfall for a while, although, in later song and story, he was crowded into a secondary place when the folk-tale champion, Beowulf, was introduced into the royal line. Reminiscences of the achievements of Wiglaf appear, however, in his association with the greater hero, who is made his kinsman, and particularly in his assumption of the royal power at Beowulf's death. As the aged hero feels his end approaching, he says that he would fain leave his war-gear to his son, had he been granted one (2729). But, like Arthur, he dies childless. So he gives his own golden necklace, his helmet, and his coat of mail to the valiant young thane, telling him to care for the needs of the people (2800). This is not merely a token of appreciation for the help which has been rendered him; Wiglaf is the natural successor to the throne, as Beowulf's only surviving kinsman (2813). The later speech of Wiglaf to the retainers, in which he tells them that they shall be deprived of their land-rights, is comprehensible from the lips of so young a warrior only if he is already assuming an authority superior to theirs. Both fact and fancy may well have combined, then, in furnishing the poet materials for the idealization of the perfect retainer, a theme only lightly suggested elsewhere in the epic. There are hints of it in Beowulf's devotion to his sovereign, Hygelac, whose death he avenged, and in his disinterested service to the son of Hygelac. But nowhere is the supreme duty of fidelity to over-lord set forth in so dramatic and telling a fashion as in the devotion of Wiglaf, which knows no compromise with fear or self-interest.

Wiglaf fades quickly into the background, however, and the epic closes, as it should, with the apotheosis of Beowulf. The controlling theme of the whole poem, which gives it unity, bridging the long gap of fifty years in Beowulf's life, and placing the originally separate Grendel and dragon adventures in logical relation to each other, is the glorification of the ideal hero and king. The epic is not a biography, but a *Heldenleben;* it opens with a great exploit, the purifying of Hrothgar's hall, narrating other feats in passing, such as the swim with Breca, the revenge for Hygelac and the escape from the Franks, and it closes in a blaze of glory, in the hero's magnificent death in the contest with the dragon. There is little in the poem to disturb this conception. In the oral traditions which had clustered about the figure of Beowulf there may perhaps have been scenes of humor or love, as in the *Poetic Edda*. If these existed, they were rejected by the epic poet as inconsistent with his theme. His work is held in restraint by that didactic seriousness so characteristic of Germanic heroic narrative. Only rarely does an echo of the folk-tale Beowulf meet our ears, and then so subordinated as to seem of little consequence. Such is the hint of the hero's boyhood, when he was neglected, despised as slothful, and not honored at the mead-bench (2183 ff.). The Male Cinderella is the right sort of fellow for fireside yarns; he does not belong in courtly society. To begin an epic celebrating an ideal prince and king by introducing this folk-tale theme would be to court disaster. The poet makes no such mistake. He first introduces Beowulf as "good among the Geatas . . . noble and mighty" (195-198), and only when his poem is two thirds done does he drop the casual remark about the despised boyhood, — a remark best viewed as an inadvertence, in view of the sustained artistic purpose which dominates the whole.

How far the characteristics of the ideal monarch, as set forth in the epic, are due to the final poet, and how far to earlier tradition, is an unanswerable question. There can be no doubt, however, that later and more sophisticated conceptions have been superimposed upon earlier and ruder notions. The cultivated society of a northern court in the days of the Venerable Bede would surely have admired a somewhat different sort of sovereign from the early Anglian colonists. There exists, unfortunately, no earlier form of the Beowulf legends from which to draw conclusions. We are more fortunate with King Arthur. Two very different conceptions of Arthur and his court are preserved in the Welsh *Mabinogion*, a collection dating in its present form from the end of the eleventh to the end of the thirteenth century, and containing both early and late material.[13] The tale of *Kilhwch and Olwen*, in which Arthur is depicted as a primitive king surrounded by the half-supernatural warriors of folk-tales, forms a striking contrast to the polished and courtly sovereign of *The Lady of the Fountain*. *Beowulf* is, in a sense, in this later stage of literary and social development, because it presents a highly civilized and sophisticated time, conscious of etiquette, and with well-formulated and gentle ideals, although of course a chivalry very different from that of the twelfth century. No stage of the Beowulf story has been preserved which may stand as parallel to *Kilhwch and Olwen*. The Bear's Son

folk-tales and the dragon-stories of popular tradition [14] do not represent the hero as a Germanic
prince or king; he is the typical champion of folk-
tales.

The spiritual deepening of the story, in setting
forth Beowulf's relations to his clan, to his king, —
in the days before he became king himself, — and
to his people is doubtless due in part to the pagan
traditions which had come down to the Anglo-
Saxons from Continental days. In England these
conceptions of the best qualities of kingship as a
Germanic institution, and of fidelity to over-lord
and kindred, were further refined by education
and by Latin culture, and by the softening influences of Christianity. All this is revealed most
clearly in the closing scenes, as the shadows close
in about the aged hero. His illustrious qualities as
a monarch are set forth in the closing adventure in
the poet's own comments, in the speeches of Wiglaf and of the Messenger, in the whole course of the
action, and finally, in Beowulf's own summary of
his reign.

I ruled this people for fifty winters; there was no king
of all my neighbors who dared attack or intimidate me.
I awaited what time might bring forth, held well mine
own, sought no enmities, swore no false oaths.[15] In all
this, though sick unto death with my wounds, may
I have joy. And the Lord cannot hold against me the
violent death of kinsmen, in my hour of passing. (2732–
2743.)

It is highly significant that, in days of constant warfare and violence and self-seeking in the northern kingdoms of England, these wise and temperate words could have been written. Armed strength is, indeed, necessary for national safety; but next to this, the happiness of a people is best secured by a stable and quiet domestic policy, by scrupulous adherence to agreements, by forbearance under provocation, by avoidance of bloodshed, and by taking no part in foreign quarrels. It is a lesson which the twentieth century might well take to heart.

The closing scene of the poem, Beowulf's funeral, is a formal "set-piece" of epic narrative. It should be compared with the briefer but not less vivid account of the burning of the dead warriors of both parties at the close of the *Finnsburg Episode* (1107–1124). The lair of the dragon was at a headland called the Eagles' Ness (3031); the barrow of Beowulf was, according to the dying instructions of the hero, erected on another promontory jutting out into the sea, called the Whale's Ness (2805, 3136), a barrow built around the brands of the funeral pyre. The mound was to stand as a memorial of the dead warrior, that his people might not forget him, and that seafarers might recognize it and call it "the barrow of Beowulf." It was strongly built, and decorated with helmets, shields, and coats of mail (3137 ff.). Within the mound the dragon's treasure was, according to one passage (3163–3168), deposited. The solemn rite of burning was accompanied by the lamentations of the warriors (3149), among whom appears, in all probability, the widow of Beowulf, like Andromache bewailing the dead Hector. Unfortunately, the passage is much damaged, but it may be read, with some emendations, in a way which is probably not far from the original wording.

Likewise the wife, with tresses bound up, sang, sad at heart, a lay of lamentation for Beowulf, repeated again and again that she feared for herself days of sorrow, a deal of bloody contests, the dread of an enemy, humiliation and the distress of captivity.

The later Swedish victory already casts its shadows upon her. Nothing is said elsewhere of Beowulf's wife. If we wish to rationalize the situation, we may picture the lady as Hygd, the former consort of Hygelac, who was apparently younger than her first husband (1926), and who may well have offered herself to Beowulf, with the crown and royal power, at Hygelac's death. Although he chose rather to support Heardred, Hygelac's son, he might well, according to early custom, have married Hygd when he himself became king. But this is conjecture. The mourning widow is a part of the poetical machinery; as Professor Gummere says, "a *praefica* . . . belonged to the Germanic funeral." In like manner, Hildeburg sang of her sorrow at the pyre which consumed her son and her brother (1117, 1118).

Not less interesting are the picturesque rites after the body has been consumed, and the beacon built. The riding in a circle about the remains of the dead is paralleled, as has often been noted, in the account of the funeral of Attila in the *De Origine Actibusque Getarum*, commonly called the *Getica*, of Jordanes, an account written in the middle of the sixth century, at the same time, roughly speaking, as the main historical events related in the Anglo-Saxon epic. This passage is often cited, but not in full, and it may be worth while to examine it a little in detail.[16] Jordanes was not himself a Goth, but of Germanic stock friendly to the Goths. He was not a warrior, but a small cleric. While he based his narrative mainly on a lost work of Cassiodorus, he was himself neither a clear nor an elegant writer. The passage in which he sets forth the funeral of Attila is of priceless value, however, as giving us a glimpse of primitive funeral customs, even though the accuracy of his account has been questioned.

Jordanes tells how Attila, on the night of his marriage to a beautiful girl named Ildico, died, overcome by sleep and drink, of a hemorrhage in the throat, and how he was found in the morning, unwounded, but covered with blood, while the maiden wept beneath her veil.

Then, as the custom of that people is, they cut off a part of their hair, and disfigured their countenances with gaping wounds, that a distinguished warrior might be mourned not with female cries and tears, but with the blood of men.

A marvel which happened at the time of his death is then related, and a description of the funeral follows.

I cannot omit telling a few of the many ways in which his remains were honored by his own people. In the midst of the plains, in silken tents, the corpse was placed, a solemn spectacle for the wondering view of men. And the most excellent knights [*equites*] of all the Hunnish people, moving in circus fashion [*in modum circensium cursibus;* that is, in a circle] about the spot where he had been placed, made mention of his achievements in a lay of lamentation in such wise as follows: "Attila, illustrious king of the Huns, son of Mundzuc, master of most mighty peoples, who with a power unknown before alone held the Scythian and Germanic realms, and struck terror into both parts of the Roman world by capturing states, and, that what remained might not be subjected to pillage, received, appeased by prayers, a yearly tribute, fell in death after he had accomplished all these things through the coming of good fortune, — not through the wounds of his enemies, nor by the treason of his own folk, but among a well-protected people, rejoicing as he did in pleasure, and untroubled by sorrow. Who would expect this end, which no one thinks may be avenged?" After he had been mourned in such lamentations, they celebrated a *strava*, as they call it, over his tomb, with great revelry, and, combining two things contrary to each other, manifested grief proper to a funeral with intermingled revelry, burying the body secretly at night in the earth. His barrow they provided first with gold, then with silver, then with solid iron, thus conveying the idea that all things are suited to a very mighty king: iron, because he conquered men; gold and silver, because he won the adornment of both states; they added the arms of enemies gained in slaughter, horse-trappings rich with the splendor of varied gems, and insignia of diverse sorts, by which courtly splendor is maintained. And, that human curiosity might be removed from such treasures, they killed those assigned to the work, — a horrid recompense, — and instant death fell upon the buriers along with the buried.

The point of view here is clearly that of one observing the customs of an alien people (*ut gentis illius mos est*), and we are expressly told that the funeral of Attila was conducted *a sua gente*. It has been maintained that Hunnish conditions are here set forth, but probably the whole affair was affected by Germanic, especially Gothic, customs, since Attila had among his followers subordinate Germanic chiefs. It is noticeable that the corpse of Attila was buried rather than burned, but this is, I think, more likely to be a survival of an old and very widespread custom, antedating that of cremation, than a concession to Christian prohibitions against burning the body, which might have been obeyed by Gothic warriors in Attila's retinue who were Arian Christians. It is difficult to say how far the burial of treasure in the barrow, and the riding about the corpse, as described by Jordanes, are evidences of purely Germanic conditions. Nevertheless, the resemblances which these present to the account in the Anglo-Saxon epic merit very careful consideration.[17]

It seems most probable that the account of Beowulf's funeral was written by a Christian poet who was archaizing, on the basis of tradition, and not always consistently or accurately. The church indeed frowned sternly upon cremation, but in describing Continental conditions two centuries or so earlier the poet could well be pardoned for retaining a ceremonial as picturesque as the lighting of a bale-fire for the dead. It is highly probable that, in the traditions he was following, such scenes were made the occasion for considerable poetic elaboration. Observe the effectiveness of the burning pyre in the *Finnsburg Episode*. To sacrifice a scene like this, or the detailed account of the burning of Beowulf, would have been to miss opportunities for picturesque effect, and perhaps to disappoint auditors who were expectant of such descriptions. The representation of the personages of the story as pious Christians is not uniformly sustained throughout the poem; consider, in addition to the pagan bale-fires, the passage in which it is expressly stated that the Danes knew not God, and prayed to the Devil in their distress (175-

183), or that in which the Geatas consult omens in
the heathen fashion (204), as reported by Tacitus.
The older view, which is still held by some scholars, that the descriptions of heathen conditions in
the poem have been superficially Christianized by
other hands, does not appear convincing. The
burning of the dead was still practised in some districts where Christianity had been established, and
a vivid recollection of it must have lingered long
after the custom had ceased. There is a chance
that the poet of *Beowulf*, though a Christian, may
have witnessed a cremation; among the Christian
Saxons on the Continent the rite survived until the
severity of the edicts of Charlemagne put a stop
to it. The description in *Beowulf*, however, is sufficiently explained as a literary performance based
upon existing traditions.[18]

How little this description represents purely
Germanic conditions, how much it is a part of the
poetical "machinery" of that stage of social development sometimes called the Heroic Age, is
shown by the burials in the Homeric poems. The
Iliad affords striking pictures of the burning of the
corpses of Patroclus and of Hector (xxiii, 135 ff.;
xxiv, 785 ff.; compare also the account of the burning of the dead, vii, 421 ff.), while the resemblances
to *Beowulf* of similar passages in the *Odyssey* are
especially striking.

So soon as early Dawn shone forth, the rosy-fingered, I sent forth my fellows to the house of Circe to fetch the body of the dead Elpenor. And speedily we cut billets of wood and sadly we buried him, where the furthest headland runs out into the sea, shedding big tears. But when the dead man was burned and the arms of the dead, we piled a barrow and dragged up thereon a pillar, and on the topmost mound we set the shapen oar. (*Odyssey*, XII, 8 ff.)

Thus for seventeen days and nights continually did we all bewail thee, immortal gods and mortal men. On the eighteenth day we gave thy body to the flames, and many well-fatted sheep we slew around thee, and kine of shambling gait. So thou wert burned in the garments of the gods, and in much unguents and in sweet honey, and many heroes of the Achaeans moved mail-clad around the pyre when thou wast burning, both footmen and horse, and great was the noise that arose. But when the flame of Hephaestus had utterly abolished thee, lo, in the morning we gathered together thy white bones, Achilles, and bestowed them in unmixed wine and in unguents. Thy mother gave a twy-handled golden urn, and said that it was the gift of Dionysus, and the workmanship of renowned Hephaestus. Therein lie thy white bones, great Achilles, and mingled with them the bones of Patroclus son of Menoetias, that is dead, but apart is the dust of Antilochus, whom thou didst honour above all thy other companions, after Patroclus that was dead. Then over them did we pile a great and goodly tomb, we the holy host of Argive warriors, high on a jutting headland over wide Hellespont, that it might be far seen from off the sea by men that now are, and by those that shall be hereafter. (*Odyssey*, XXIV, 63 ff.) [19]

The closing lines of the Anglo-Saxon epic deserve special attention. They give the substance of the elegiac lay sung by the warriors riding solemnly about the barrow of Beowulf, after the body has been totally consumed, and a wall built about it with a beacon above. At the funeral of Attila, according to Jordanes, the warriors sung their dirge *in modum circensium cursibus ambientes*, while the body was still lying in state, but before burial. In both cases, the elegy itself is of great interest. It looks as if Jordanes had preserved, in his crabbed Latin, the substance of a genuine old lay in the vernacular, perhaps the very lay actually sung at the obsequies of the Hunnish chieftain. The lyrical coloring, especially of the opening, is noteworthy: "*Praecipuus Hunorum rex Attila, patre genitus Mundzucco, fortissimarum gentium dominus.*" It has even been thought possible to distinguish in it traces of Gothic alliterative verse.[20] Saxo Grammaticus, it will be remembered, rendered vernacular lays into Latin prose so closely that one of them has been conjecturally restored to its original form. The poet of *Beowulf* does not give the actual wording of the lay sung by the warriors, or of that uttered by the woman, perhaps the wife of Beowulf, during the actual consumption of the hero's body. We are fortunate, however, in having an elegiac lament in the exact words of the vernacular, in Hrothgar's outburst over the dead

Æschere. Here the strong lyrical coloring of the Anglo-Saxon is noteworthy, especially if it be read aloud.

> Ne frīn þū æfter sǣlum; sorh is genīwod
> Denigea lēodum. Dēad is Æschere,
> Yrmenlāfes yldra brōþor,
> min rūn-wita ond mīn rǣd-bora,
> eaxl-gestealla, ðonne wē on orlege
> hafelan weredon, þonne hniton fēþan,
> eoferas cnysedan. Swylc scolde eorl wesan,
> æþeling ǣr-gōd, swylc Æschere wæs.[21]

The classification of these early elegiac passages and their relation to the development of the lyric are puzzling and difficult problems. Perhaps "the earliest form of elegiac poetry is the funeral song of remote antiquity." [22] It should be observed, however, that the lay sung by Beowulf's warriors appears to have been considerably colored by Christian conceptions. We can speak, of course, only of the paraphrase given by the poet. It has been noted that the lines "sound like an echo of divine service." [23] They are, in any case, singularly elevated in tone, forming a fitting epitaph for a hero whose virtues, as set forth in the long narrative preceding, are a mingling of heathen valor and desire for glory, on the one hand, and Christian gentleness and kindness on the other. They close, in superb fashion, an epic in the grand style:

Then about the mound rode the battle-brave heroes, sons of æthelings, twelve in all; they were minded to utter their sorrow, to lament their king, to weave a lay, to commemorate the hero. They praised his glorious achievements and fittingly celebrated his mighty deeds. For it is meet that a man exalt his lord in speech, make manifest his affection for him, when he must be separated from this mortal body. So the people of the Geatas, his hearth-companions, mourned the passing of their lord; they said that he had been, mighty king, the mildest and gentlest of men, the kindest unto his people, and the most desirous of praise.

VIII

DEVELOPMENT AND COMPOSITION
OF THE EPIC

WE HAVE now reached the final stage of our discussion. In the preceding chapters the principal historical and imaginative traditions in *Beowulf* have been analyzed, and their origins and literary relationships reviewed. It now remains to attempt a far more difficult task, to trace the combination of the several component parts and the evolution of the whole narrative from its beginnings to the completed epic. This naturally means repetition, in briefer form, of much that has been said already. But such repetition is valuable by way of summary, and of presentation in vivid and connected fashion. In addition, a careful survey of the conditions in England under which the epic took final shape is necessary, since those conditions go far to explain peculiarities in its spirit and literary method.

Analysis of preceding stages of development is particularly hazardous, since we have, to guide us, absolutely no extant version of any part of the tale, or indeed any Germanic literature at all, of earlier date than the completed poem. I am not including charters, laws, inscriptions, and the like, under "literature." All the Scandinavian analogues are much later; indeed, the earliest extant Scandinavian verse falls more than a century after the composition of the Anglo-Saxon epic. It is very difficult to date the oldest Anglo-Saxon verse with accuracy; possibly some few portions may ante-date *Beowulf*, but it is wisest to consider these as contemporary. We are, then, obliged to rely almost wholly upon analysis of the poem as it now stands, upon what is known of early poetic processes in general, upon testimony from Latin sources, and upon the evidence of later documents and later popular tradition. Reconstructions of the genesis of *Beowulf*, moreover, like that of the Arthurian legends, depend very largely, as we have seen, upon the solution of difficult problems of folk-lore, ethnography, "mythology," metrics, language, and the ways of story-telling in general. Complete agreement among scholars in such matters is in the nature of things impossible.

An outline of development must, then, be largely a matter of guesswork — a series of hypotheses that cannot be proved, although they rest upon definite and tangible evidence. If we take such a reconstruction for what it is worth, however, not regarding it as in any way final, we can at all events get some idea of the complexity of the growth of the epic, and of the advance in artistry of its completed form as compared with what had

gone before. The trouble will be, not that our outline will be too elaborate, but that it will not be
elaborate enough. The endless shiftings of story-
telling cannot be perceived with any clearness.
Early traditions must have been largely oral; both
historical and supernatural themes were transmitted from generation to generation by word of
mouth. It seems unlikely that they got into written form before they reached England, and even
then they must long have been perpetuated in the
memories of those who loved them, that is to say,
long after the present poem was composed. If
there are gleams of light here and there to guide us
on our way, they will shine upon only a very few
of the multitude of singers and story-tellers who
made the achievement of the final poet possible.

We begin with the folk-tale of "The Bear's
Son," the adventures of the young hero who fights
victoriously in hard encounters two supernatural
beings, one in a dwelling, and the other beneath the surface of the earth. This tale, which
is widely distributed not only in Europe but in
other parts of the globe as well, preserves a very
distinct and clearly recognizable pattern, though
the setting and the details of the narrative vary
widely. In investigating its appearance in *Beowulf*, we must start with the hypothetical Norwegian versions, since later analogues — like the
Grettissaga and the *Saga of Samson the Fair*, which

show close resemblances to the Anglo-Saxon poem, but could not have been based upon it, even indirectly — lay the scene of the adventure with the underground demon in rocky country, at a waterfall, with a cave beneath; and since the descriptions of the lair of the monsters in *Beowulf* show waterfall scenery to have been the original underlying conception, though blurred and half forgotten. In Norway such scenery would have been familiar, and would have moulded the characteristic folk-tale, in the days preceding the shaping of the epic legends. Iceland was not colonized until long after, and Denmark does not afford this peculiar variety of landscape. Some idea of the nature of this folk-tale may be gained from modern survivals, which, in spite of the greatest diversity of incident, nevertheless show extraordinary resemblances to *Beowulf* and to its Scandinavian analogues of a literary character, and even make clear episodes which are obscure in them. The whole character of the folk-tale was, however, radically altered by being put into an historical setting of the sixth century. The hero was made nephew to King Hygelac of the Geatas, an indisputably historical character, and the troll adventures were laid at the court of an equally famous contemporary, Hrothgar of the Danes. This combination gave immediately to the exploits of fairyland the dignity and plausibility of heroic story.

Incidents of the folk-tale which were felt to be unsuitable to the new setting, like the rescue of princesses in the underground realm, were discarded, and the hero himself was made a great Scandinavian prince and king. His name "Beowulf" (we do not know the earlier Scandinavian form) probably means "bear," and it seems likely that this was taken over from the folk-tales. So were his prowess in wrestling, like the bear's "hug," the supernatural strength of his grasp (that of thirty men), his ability to exist under water, the legend of his slothful youth, and the like.

Whether he was confused or identified with some figure in the Geat royal house, whose position he occupied, and whose name was supplanted by his own, we do not know. It appears unlikely, however, that this was the case. If it did actually happen, most of the attributes of the figure in question were lost in the process of amalgamation. Beowulf was, to be sure, given a father named Ecgtheow (to use the Anglo-Saxon equivalent of the name), who may have been historical, and he was further identified with the Geatic clan of the Wægmundingas, which was probably historical. Young Wiglaf, whom, according to the epic, he designated as his successor to the crown, looks like a genuine member of the Wægmunding clan. But Ecgtheow is not convincing as a Wægmunding; we should expect a name alliterating on

"W." Other details that would be expected if Beowulf had stepped into the place of a royal prince are lacking, — his mother's name and the name of his consort, for example. The poem is extremely rich in historical reminiscences, but in these Beowulf, great sovereign as he is stated to be, has little part. His participation in the Geat–Swedish feuds, which are described in such minute detail, is singularly colorless and unconvincing, and his connection with the historical raid of Hygelac into the Low Countries is that of a champion of fairyland, — swimming away to his northern home, carrying thirty suits of armor. His troll and dragon slayings have naturally no integral connection with the historic background, and are rather lamely motivated as friendly acts in aid of a neighboring king, and in defence of his own people. The story in its late Anglo-Saxon form, then, while avowedly presenting Beowulf as an ideal Germanic prince, really gives precise information only in regard to his supernatural adventures.

The characteristic waterfall scenery of the subterranean adventure, clear in some of the Scandinavian analogues, and recognizable although blurred in *Beowulf*, makes it probable, as we have just seen, that the underlying folk-tale material took shape in what is to-day Norwegian territory, or at all events in the mountainous districts of the northern Scandinavian peninsula. But this does not mean, of course, that the combination of folk-tale and history was effected on Norwegian soil. The landscape setting had extraordinary persistency when the tale was told in other countries, even when it was localized in a region of quite different character, where no waterfall existed, as in the *Grettissaga*. Peoples in the flat, lake-dotted territory of southern Sweden, where the Geatas appear to have been settled, or the equally flat landscape of Denmark, might well have told it, and have effected at the same time the combination with the historical elements. Where is it most likely that this took place?

We may hazard the guess that the insertion of Beowulf into the royal line of the Geatas was made by the singers of that people. The poem tells of their constant and bitter hostilities with their powerful neighbors, the Swedes, and their friendly relations with the Danes. This may well reflect actual conditions. It is certain that the Geatas were defeated by the Swedes and absorbed by them, an event that may conjecturally be set about the middle of the sixth century. It is very clearly foreshadowed at the end of the poem. The circumstances of the final struggle are not clear, but it appears likely that, after the disastrous expedition of Hygelac against the Franks, advantage was taken by the Swedes of the weakened condition of their opponents, and a final and decisive victory gained. Perhaps the leadership was assumed by the Wægmunding house. To this house Beowulf assigns the defence of his kingdom at his death. Perhaps Wiglaf was the successor of Hygelac's son, Heardred, and the last king of the Geatas. Certainly the long and glorious fifty-year reign of Beowulf is pure fiction. But it is easy to see how this might have been invented by singers anxious to soften the final defeat, to add another brilliant chapter to the annals of their countrymen before the final catastrophe.

On the other hand, it is perfectly conceivable that the introduction of Beowulf and his exploits into the circle of Geat sovereigns may have been made by Danish minstrels, through sympathy with their neighbors to the north, with whom they were on terms of friendship, and that the praises of the Danish dynasty, with which the Anglo-Saxon poem opens, are a relic of this, and not merely the minstrel's conventional assurance that the listeners are to be regaled with a tale of a people worthy of remembrance. But this is not a necessary assumption, and there does seem to be a special reason for thinking that the desperate fortunes of the Geatas, who were engaged in a life-and-death struggle with their hereditary foes, may have given to that aggregation of tribes a solidarity and a patriotism like that which united the scattered and quarrelsome English after the days of King Alfred, and that this may have resulted in the exaggeration of native heroic traditions.

By whatever people we conceive such a union of folk-tale and history to have been made, the addition to it of the dragon motive is readily comprehensible. The folk-tale ends with the triumph of the hero after his double adventure with the trolls, in the haunted house and underground, and, if we may judge further by its modern analogues and by the habits of folk-tales generally, with the rosy prospect of his living a long and blissful life, the details of which are left to the imagination. But historical legend is quite a different business; it calls for an explanation not only of the hero's life and chief exploits, but also of his glorious death. So a new element was added to round out Beowulf's career, a desperate struggle with a fire-drake, in which he perished, — not defeated, since the monster was slain, but himself a victim of fate or of overwhelming odds. This new episode was quite unconnected with the tale of "The Bear's Son." Dragons were so common in popular story that a poet could scarcely have found a more convenient and plausible way of disposing of his hero. We are fortunately able, through careful analysis of the narrative in *Beowulf*, to see with some clearness what the outlines of the older dragon-story were. They have been overlaid by later conceptions, characteristic of Anglo-Saxon poetry, which have blurred, but not wholly concealed, the outlines of the earlier narrative.

These earlier outlines appear to have been as follows: a dragon had long guarded a treasure in Beowulf's domains, which was rifled by a man desirous of getting an object of value with which to compose a feud. In revenge the dragon attacked the Geatas with fire and flame. A curse had been laid upon the hoard in days of old by those who had put it in the earth, and Beowulf himself, in receiving a portion of the treasure, and acting as mediator in compounding the feud, unconsciously brought this doom upon his own head. When he met the dragon in single combat, he was fated to fall in the encounter. This left his people undefended. His warriors ruthlessly plundered the lair, after the death of the dragon, and so upon them too the curse descended; they were doomed to defeat at the hands of their hereditary foes, the Swedes. Thus the death of Beowulf and the overthrow of his people were at once explained in a way detracting no whit from their valor, but carrying with it the inevitability of Fate. In the Anglo-Saxon epic this simple older conception has been overlaid by a new account, in the style of the Northumbrian lyrics, of the way in which the gold was deposited in the earth. The solitary survivor of a noble race put it there. This new motivation emphasized the transitoriness of earthly glories, the lost joys of the wine-hall, with complete forgetfulness of the curse that had at once explained the calamities at the end of the poem and given tragic emphasis to the whole. But the older theme was, curiously enough, not wholly suppressed, reappearing in a brief later passage, in such fashion that its significance has been very generally missed.

We must be wary of assuming too orderly and logical a development of narrative traditions. Folk-tales circulate orally, but when they reach the dignity of heroic story, by combination with historical elements, and at the same time assume more sophisticated form, the possibility of written transmission has to be reckoned with. The heroic lay in verse (*Heldenlied*) appears to have been cultivated by the Germanic peoples of the northern and western groups at least as early as the fifth century,[1] and it is to this type that we have to look for the stages of development immediately preceding the epic form of *Beowulf*. The chances seem to be that it persisted orally and not in written form down to the time when the *Beowulf* poet worked, but on this point there is no certainty. Short lays may have been committed to writing in the seventh century. Then, too, there must have been traditions handed down from one generation to another without the adornment of poetry; men cannot always have recounted the deeds of heroes as if they were minstrels singing in a hall. The main thing to keep in mind is the endless complexity of story-telling in days when all free men took a keen interest in perpetuating tradition. Furthermore, it is impossible to be sure how the various combinations of material were actually effected. Was the dragon-adventure attached to Beowulf before the stories reached England? Was this done by the poet himself, in order to round out his material in epic form, as many scholars have assumed, or had it already been done by others, telling in shorter form the end of the hero's life? One guess is as good as another; the truth lies buried in the mists of time.

According to our best knowledge, these traditions had reached England, at least by the first quarter of the eighth century, and had been put into elaborate form by a Northumbrian or Mercian poet. How and where did the English get them? One thing is clear, — they must have been in their possession for a considerable time: "the proper names . . . are in all cases so correctly transliterated as to necessitate the assumption that they were brought across early, at the time of the settlement of Britain or very shortly after, and underwent phonetic development side by side with the other words in the English language. Had they been brought across from Scandinavia at a later date, much confusion must have ensued in the forms." [2] The English can hardly have got them before the middle of the sixth century, at the earliest; the best evidence places the death of Hygelac at about A.D. 516, and even if the overthrow of his successor or successors and the fall of his kingdom followed shortly thereafter, a quarter of a century should surely be allowed for the development of the legends and their transmission to England. It seems altogether likely that in England they first developed among peoples of Anglian stock; the Anglians had settled that part of the island where they were put into epic form; there is Anglian but no southern tradition in the poem; and the subject-matter would have made a particular appeal to people of Anglian lineage if, as we have conjectured, it first assumed its historical setting among Geatas or Danes. The Angles were closely allied to the Scandinavians in origin, and even in their new homes in northern England were not, at this early period, unlike the Scandinavians in their manners and customs. [3] They had occupied, while in their Continental seats, lands that were later settled by Danes. "The territory of the numerous race who settled all the north-eastern coast of Britain . . . undoubtedly extended over all Schleswig, some of the Danish isles, and possibly over part of Jutland in the fifth and sixth centuries." [4] Information in regard to the time of their settlement in Britain is unfortunately scanty. The most probable hypothesis seems to me that the *Beowulf* legends were brought across to Britain by late colonists or singers from the motherland in the second half of the sixth century. It does not appear probable that there was much communication between England and this territory or the north generally in the seventh and eighth centuries. All the allusions in the poem to Continental affairs belong in the early sixth century or earlier; there are none of later date, which might have been expected had the material been brought to England in the seventh century. Moreover, the early possession of the tale in Britain is shown by the modifications and misunderstandings in the legends that have been examined here — in the changed versions of the waterfall scenery of the second adventure and in the variants of the dragon-story. These have so far entered into the fibre of the completed epic as to make it clear that the story had for many years been transferred from its original Scandinavian homeland, and had developed independently in a new country.

The foregoing conclusions contradict the hypothesis that the poem is translated from the Scandinavian, which is, indeed, little accepted at the present day. It is improbable enough for other reasons: *Beowulf* is quite unlike Scandinavian poetry in form; the attempt made by Hermann

Möller [5] to show that it was originally stanzaic, like Scandinavian poetry, results in proving how much violence must be done to it to force it into that mould. Furthermore, its pathetic, elegiac, leisurely manner contrasts vividly with the dramatic quality and passionate emotion of the Scandinavian lays, which are, in the Homeric sense, not "epic" at all. The fundamental metrical principles of West Germanic and North Germanic verse appear to be identical, but the two groups were already sharply differentiated in the earliest extant poetry. A Scandinavian poem of the seventh or eighth century, from a land still pagan and lacking in the gentler culture of Northumbria, would have presented a strange contrast to the courtly, refined, and Christian spirit of *Beowulf*. Careful research has shown that the Christian elements are in all probability not interpolated, but an integral part of the epic.[6]

The Scandinavian analogues are of the highest importance, however. While the story was developing on English soil, it continued to circulate independently in Scandinavian territory, both as folk-tale and as semi-historical legend. Later analogues, attached not to Beowulf but to other personages, historical or quasi-historical, may be borrowed from either of these forms; it is often hard to tell which. It appears likely, however, that the tales of Grettir, of Orm (based in part on

Grettir), and of Samson the Fair are derived from folk-tale tradition; those dealing with Bothvar Bjarki rather from the historic traditions. There is least ambiguity about the modern Danish and Swedish and Norwegian *märchen*. Most of these are clearly the descendants of folk-tales centuries back. All this later Scandinavian material, particularly that in the *Grettissaga*, gives the most valuable evidence in regard to the development of the Anglo-Saxon epic, but it must be used with great care. The relations between *Beowulf* and the legends relating to Bjarki and Hrolf Kraki are peculiarly difficult to trace with accuracy.

I am obliged to take issue with Professor Klaeber when he says:

> There is no evidence to show that "a Bēowulf legend" had gradually grown up out of popular stories that had been brought over to England by the migrating Angles. If such were the case, it would be inexplicable why the exclusive interest in Scandinavian legends remained virtually unimpaired, and why in particular such a minute attention to the fortunes of Northern dynasties continued to be manifested in the epic.[7]

The answer seems clear. Interest in Scandinavian legend remained unimpaired, just as it did in Germanic legend generally. How keen this interest was, all the remains of pagan verse in Anglo-Saxon illustrate — *Widsith*, *Deor*, *Waldhere*, the Northumbrian lyrics. In these, genuine native traditions play a very small part. The Angles were interested in the fortunes of northern dynasties, just as the Northerners themselves were in the foreign dynasties in the southern legends that went to make up the great Volsung–Niblung story — Frankish, Burgundian, and Hunnish. The historical elements were better preserved in Anglo-Saxon, since neither the lapse of time nor the geographical remoteness was so great as in the case of the Eddic lays. The early contiguity of Angles and Scandinavians is also to be considered. It has often been emphasized in these pages and by other writers that legend thrives best away from its own home. There seems to me no reason, then, for turning to the hypothesis of "close relations, perhaps through marriage" [8] between an Anglian court and the kingdom of Denmark, or a common meeting-ground of Danes and English in Friesland. These hypotheses are pure conjecture, rendered unlikely by the improbability of close intercourse between England and the northern part of the Continent in the seventh and eighth centuries, to which reference has already been made. It is not necessary to find any special reason for the selection of a Scandinavian subject for an English poem. The point of view of the story-teller is impartial, that of a man versed in the legends of many peoples. We must think of the traditions about Beowulf and the historical characters surrounding him not only as in oral circulation, but as the peculiar possession of professional poets, the descendants of the court minstrels of whom we read in the epic. The altered conditions under which they worked in the seventh century brought certain changes, but much in their art remained as it had been in older pagan days. The "plots" were common property, which each individual poet could develop as he liked, particularly stressing pathetic or dramatic moments, and adapting, with the adroitness of the improvisator, bygone legends to the demands of special occasions, just as the court-poet in Hrothgar's hall tells of an old feud between Danes and Frisians in such a way as to compliment his own kinsmen and their guests.

Heroic traditions were apparently current in varying forms, as would be entirely natural in poetry perpetuated orally and subject to constant improvisation and elaboration. And the epic poet, curiously enough, was not averse to combining in his narrative different and even contradictory accounts of the same episode, which brought inconsistencies in motivation and plot. It would appear that this had become to a certain extent traditional; it bears a strong analogy to the passion for variation in Anglo-Saxon verse. Ten Brink, who believed that the epic was made by dovetailing and combining epic lays, laid great stress upon variant versions.[9] Modern criticism has rejected his mechanical view of epic-making, while recognizing that in free and original composition the poet of *Beowulf* was dependent upon variant lays. In some cases passages of contemporary verse may have been introduced bodily, but it is impossible to be certain where this occurs. An enormous amount of material lay ready to the poet's hand; he fused it into a more elaborate synthesis of his own, and his originality consisted in the selection and combination of incident, the constant by-play of allusion, the deft alternation of fiction and fact, the contrast between the joyous exultation of youthful heroism and the tragic mystery of life, all leading to the final struggle between the greatest human power and an inscrutable and inexorable Fate.

That *Beowulf* was originally composed in the Anglian territory of England is hardly open to question. Practically all extant Anglo-Saxon verse, although preserved in West-Saxon transcriptions, was originally written in the north. As between Northumbria and Mercia, there is no trustworthy linguistic evidence; the varied dialectical forms probably arose in the processes of copying and recopying in the two centuries and a half intervening between the original version and the present form. The evidence afforded by the episode introducing the Anglian king, Offa, and his shrewish bride, Thryth, is discussed below. Nor is greater certainty to be attained in regard to the date of composition. The widest limits may be said to be the century from 650 to 750; conservative narrower limits, between 675 and 725. Most scholars, I think, incline to the first quarter of the eighth century.[10] The commonly accepted dating in the age of Bede remains unshaken, despite efforts to place it some two hundred years later, or to regard the poem as having, in some portions at least, existed in epic form before the change of faith, and to conclude that the appearance of the Christian element is due to revision. Both of these arguments have been reviewed in detail, and with destructive effect, by Chambers.[11] The traditional dating was arrived at in part by tests of language and syntax. In recent years there has been increasing skepticism in regard to the validity of such tests. They cannot, indeed, be applied in the somewhat mechanical fashion adopted by earlier scholars, but they do supply valuable confirmatory evidence. So with metre; there has been too much of a tendency to establish a rigid metrical system for Anglo-Saxon and to regard variations from this system as errors. Yet the testimony of metre cannot be neglected. The situation is much like the dating of Shakespeare's plays from versification. No one would presume to establish an exact chronology of the plays on such a basis. "Nevertheless, when all allowances

have been made and all due caution exercised, it
will be found that the indications of the versification corroborate and supplement the external evidences in a valuable way." [12]   We may also make
a comparison of the style, subject-matter, and vo-
cabulary of *Beowulf* with those of the Cædmonian
and Cynewulfian poems. The difficulty is that the
dating of those poems themselves is not certain.
The probabilities point to the late seventh and
early eighth centuries for *Genesis A*, *Exodus*, and
Daniel, and the late eighth or very early ninth
century for the poems of Cynewulf and his contemporaries, whose manner is often indistinguish-
able from his own. *Beowulf* appears to occupy
an intermediary place between these, showing the
influence of the traditions that produced the
Cædmonian poems on the one hand, and being
imitated in *Andreas* on the other. The whole matter is delicate and complicated; it has been held
that Cynewulf himself inserted passages in the
manner of his *Christ* into *Beowulf*.[13]   It is clear,
however, that the affiliations of the specifically
Christian passages in *Beowulf* are generally with
the more simple treatments of Old Testament
themes by the earlier school, rather than with the
New Testament subjects and lives of saints in
which Cynewulf and his group were chiefly interested. Taking everything into consideration,
we may, I think, date the poem with approximate

accuracy between 675 and 725, using round dates purely as a convenience.

Many new influences had affected the development of Anglo-Saxon literature in Britain. The Celtic peoples had opened new vistas of poetry, and taught the Anglo-Saxons much of books and letters; the scenery of northern Britain had given them fresh imaginative stimulus; they had experienced the novelty and interest of settling in a new land; the effects of the Roman occupation were not wholly extinct; Christianity had tempered the fierceness of pagan warlike spirit; the new classical culture of Northumbria, brought in by the missionaries, was far more vigorous than that which had come to the Old Saxons on the Continent. In the opening chapter the general nature of these influences has been briefly indicated, but they must now be examined in a little more detail in order to provide a proper background for the composition of the epic, and explain its characteristics.

At the opening of the seventh century, about one hundred and fifty years had elapsed since the first settlements of the Germanic tribes in Britain. Our information about the Saxon Conquest is much less definite than was formerly supposed, and even for the sixth century trustworthy records are scanty. The Anglo-Saxons came, of course, not in one great migration, but in a series of colonizations extending over many years. By about A.D. 600, however, the period of settlement and of contests with the British, the Picts, and the Scots for the right of remaining in the country was over, though hostilities with the earlier inhabitants continued well down to the Norman Conquest. A large number of small tribal settlements, each under its own chieftain, or "king," occupied roughly the eastern half of the island, from the Forth to the Channel. In these the Continental organization and traditions appear to have continued, in the beginning, with little change. As time went on, the scattered tribes gradually amalgamated into larger groups, with one powerful leader as the nominal head of each group, a process that we have already observed taking place in earlier days on the Continent. The advantages of such coöperation, particularly in fighting common enemies, were too manifest to be neglected. In days of constant struggle a small and obscure group has most to gain by affiliating itself with its stronger neighbors.

During the seventh century, the fortunes of the larger kingdoms can be followed with some exactness. In the Saxon territory in the south lay Essex, Sussex, and Wessex, with settlements of the Jutes in the Isle of Wight and the adjoining mainland. In the midlands were East and Middle Anglia, and the very important kingdom of Mercia to the west. Still farther north, stretching along the east coast to the borders of Scotland, lay Northumbria, comprising the great Anglian states of Bernicia and Deira, which were in the seventh century sometimes independent and sometimes united under a single monarch. On the east coast of modern Scotland lay the Picts, to the west of them the Scots, while the western portions of the island were in the hands of the dispossessed Celts.

Some caution must be exercised in assuming a sharp separation of these different political and linguistic divisions. It has been argued that the Angles and the Saxons had already been fused into one people while still on the Continent, so that the Conquest was the work of two nationalities, Anglo-Saxons and Jutes, instead of three.[14] This hypothesis has not commanded general acceptance, but it is clear that the different groups of invaders were much alike in race, language, and culture, that they early felt the necessity of unity in defence against common enemies, and that the gradual civilizing of the island tended to draw them closer together, despite sharp political animosities. The name "Anglo-Saxon" appears to have originated on the Continent, the earliest recorded occurrence of it being "Angli Saxones" in the *Historia Langobardorum* of Paul the Deacon in the late eighth century. Though used by writers in England in the ninth and tenth centuries, the phrase was forgotten until it was revived by Camden in his *Britannia* in the sixteenth century. The terms commonly used in Britain down to the Norman Conquest were, for the country as a whole, "Angelcynn," or "Angel-þēod"; for the language, "englisc." [15] When the Saxons were referred to, "Seaxan" was generally used in the narrower sense. Perhaps this is not without significance for the continued importance of the Anglian elements, even after the Scandinavian incursions. The name "Anglo-Saxon," however, represents fairly the chief peoples in England before the Norman Conquest, and its retention to-day in speaking of them and of their language is far less ambiguous than the frequently used "Old English."

Having fought the natives with some success, the Anglo-Saxons had leisure, in the seventh century, to fight each other. History concerns itself mainly in this period with the north, in particular with wars between the Northumbrians and Mercians, and the continued defence of both peoples against the Britons. The seventh century marks the height of Northumbrian power; the eighth, the supremacy of Mercia. Of greater importance than any inter-tribal victories or defeats, however, was the introduction and spread of Christianity. The first three quarters of the seventh century were occupied with fighting and with religious conversions, with truces and relapses into heathendom. A quieter period followed; from

679 to 714, — to give exact dates, — the northern part of the island enjoyed extraordinary prosperity, tranquillity, and culture.

The early establishment of Christianity in Britain, from the third and fourth centuries, had had little effect upon the Anglo-Saxons. We do not know much about the earlier church, but it was sufficiently organized to send representatives to a council at Arles, and sufficiently vigorous to produce the heretic Pelagius. The Celtic Christians felt no enthusiasm about converting the Anglo-Saxons; this had to wait for the well-known mission of Augustine in 597. Augustine found his task far easier than he had anticipated; he was not destined, as he feared, to wear the martyr's crown The conversion of Kent was quickly followed by missionary activity in the north, and by a general readiness on the part of the pagan tribes to give the new religion a fair trial. Augustine tried to get the Celtic bishops to help him in organizing the country into bishoprics, but with no success. Missionaries sent along the coast were partially successful in East Anglia, and completely so in Northumbria, where, at the court of King Eadwine, the apostle Paulinus achieved the results so strikingly set forth by Bede. The era of peace and prosperity under Eadwine was, however, short; he was slain by the heathen Penda of Mercia in 633, and Paulinus and the queen of Eadwine had to flee to the south. There was some feeling among the Northumbrians that Christianity had brought ill fortune, that perhaps the old gods were best. Bernicia and Deira were both ruled for a short time by kings who had returned to the faith of their fathers.

Meanwhile, however, northern Britain was being converted by the Irish. Saint Patrick had established Christianity in Ireland at about the time of the first Anglo-Saxon settlements in Britain. His pious work was continued in the next century by missionaries to the Continent, and especially by Saint Columba on the holy island of Iona, one of the inner Hebrides, south of Mull. Thence apostles were sent to the Angles, the Picts, and the Scots. The Irish church differed in organization and in details of observance from the Roman. It encouraged monasteries, its bishops being really less powerful than its abbots; it favored asceticism, and it clung passionately to its own reckoning of the date of Easter and its own fashion of priestly tonsure. After the death of Eadwine, it made its influence felt in Northumbria through the favor of the powerful King Oswald (634–642), whose chief spiritual guide was Aidan, an Irish monk from Iona. Oswald met the same fate as Eadwine: he was slain by the stout old heathen, Penda. But Aidan and his priests did not flee, as Paulinus had done. They remained, and

the Irish influence remained as well. The powerful Bernician king, Oswy (642–671), who finally
defeated and slew Penda, had been baptized at
Iona, and was a devout and practical Christian.
One cannot, however, forbear admiring Penda,
fighting bravely to the end of a green old age,
sticking unwaveringly to his own gods, but tolerant
of disciples of the new faith provided they were
constant to it, and even allowing his own son to
embrace it.

It is extremely important to observe the dual
influence of the Irish and Roman churches, and
the occasional persistence of heathen worship, in
order to understand the genesis of *Beowulf*. The
facts are well known, but they must be briefly
summarized. The Irish ecclesiastics at Oswy's
court found in the Roman organization, with its
mother church at Canterbury, a powerful opponent. Oswy's rule ultimately extended over all
Northumbria, and over northern Mercia, with
the homage of Essex, Wessex, and East Anglia.
He had to take a broad view, therefore, and
when the two churches came to an open trial of
strength at the famous Synod of Whitby (664),
he had to consider carefully which was likely to
provide the best spiritual government for England.
There is no doubt that he chose wisely in favoring
the Romans, though he concealed his real motives.
The Romans were far superior in organization and

administration; they were firmly entrenched in the south, and their close relations with the Continental churches and with the central government at Rome promised far greater permanence than the loosely organized Irish system. Oswy's judgment was decisive; after the Synod of Whitby the Irish were never again a power in the English church. But this must not blind us to their influence upon letters.

Many Englishmen went at this time to Ireland for study; King Aldfrith of Northumbria, as Bede informs us, endured voluntary exile on account of his love of wisdom. The Irish schools were fully abreast of the best knowledge of their day. The Seven Liberal Arts were cultivated, on the basis of the celebrated treatise of Martianus Capella, as handmaids to the study of theology. The Church Fathers and such of the Latin classics as were then accessible were eagerly studied, and Greek and Hebrew were not unknown.[16] Book-making received particular attention. The distinctive Irish writing, introduced into England at the time of the missionary enterprises sent out from Iona, became the foundation of English script. The different style practised by the Roman priests, and continued in the Canterbury school, was of little real influence. Until the introduction of the minuscule hand from the Continent in the tenth century, the Anglo-Saxons followed, with some modifications,

Irish models.[17] From this source, too, they learned
much of book illumination and adornment. The
example of the Irish can hardly have been confined to externals. The vivid Celtic imagination,
its peculiar treatment of the supernatural and of
the darker aspects of nature, may not have been
without influence upon Anglo-Saxon poetry. The
superb description of the haunt of the demons in
·Beowulf is often cited as an illustration of this.
Definite borrowings of incident are less probable.
The Celtic analogues to the Grendel story thus
far presented are not very striking; they must be
regarded as offshoots of the widespread "Bear's
Son" folk-tale, or as embodiments of common
popular themes of story-telling. Many attempts
have, however, been made in recent years to emphasize the importance of Irish elements in plot-
structure.[18]

If the composition of Beowulf is to be placed in
the half-century after the death of Oswy (671),
that period must be examined with especial care.
The old hostility between Northumbria and Mercia, reflections of which may be traceable in Beowulf in the feuds of Geatas and Swedes, flared up
again as soon as Oswy was in his grave, and the
Mercians under Æthelred finally gained a decisive
victory in 679. But at this point Theodore of
Tarsus, the great primate of all England, a personal friend of the sovereigns of both countries,

interposed, and a peace was made which lasted for thirty-five years. Conditions in both kingdoms during this period would appear to have been unusually favorable to literary composition. This is particularly true of the reign of Aldfrith (685–705), the son of Oswy by an Irish concubine. These twenty years were undisturbed by warfare, save for a certain amount of necessary defence against the Picts. Aldfrith was distinguished for piety and learning; he had studied in Ireland and learned to write Irish verse; he was a lover of books and a friend of literary men, chief of whom was Aldhelm. To his reign Professor Cook proposed to refer the composition of *Beowulf*.[19] After Aldfrith's death, the fortunes of Northumbria declined rapidly. His successor, Osred, who came of age in 714, was so vicious that he had to be put out of the way by a band of courageous conspirators. The line of incompetent and violent rulers following is a little relieved by the pious Ceolwulf (729–737), to whom Bede dedicated his *Ecclesiastical History*. Although its political fortunes declined, Northumbria maintained its supremacy in culture until the end of the eighth century, when the attacks of the Scandinavians, followed by their settlement in the ninth century, put an end to the activities of the monasteries, and made a continuation of the old traditions possible only in southern England.

In Mercia, too, the peace established by Theodore bore rich fruit. King Æthelred, who had conquered Northumbria, left it undisturbed. He was noted for his piety; in 704 he retired to a monastery, and became its abbot. His successor, Coenred, likewise ended his days in Christian humility, dying in Rome, where he had received holy orders from the Pope. Then, as in Northumbria, the crown fell into unworthy hands. Ceolred was a youth of much the same character as Osred of Northumbria; he died at a feast, raving from the effects of drink, in the very year in which Osred was murdered (716). The greatness of Mercia was firmly established by Offa (757–796), the most distinguished of all its sovereigns. He was a stout fighter and fond of show, but pious, a builder of monasteries, and liberal to men of letters. He founded the celebrated abbey of St. Albans, and enjoyed the friendship of Charlemagne.

There is, I think, little evidence for placing the composition of *Beowulf* in either kingdom definitely, or for establishing its date on the basis of historical conditions or family relationships. One thinks first of the reigns of such cultured men as Aldfrith of Northumbria or Æthelred or Coenred of Mercia. But it is always to be remembered that a period favorable to literary composition may continue after political conditions have changed, especially in an age when the labors of churchmen were respected by the most ruthless of warriors. It is perfectly conceivable that *Beowulf* might have been written in the troublous days of Osred of Northumbria or Ceolred of Mercia. Its references to the wicked and cruel Danish king, Heremod, who slew his companions in his drink, and had to be disposed of, might conceivably have been set down with one or the other of those degenerate youths in mind; and its constant emphasis upon virtue, courtliness, and piety may have been due to the lowering of the tone of a once-admirable court. This is, however, pure conjecture. Various similar attempts have been made to interpret events in the poem as allusions to contemporary affairs, such as have been often read into Shakespeare's plays. But there is no more validity in such conclusions than there is in perceiving an allegory of the relations of Elizabeth and Mary Queen of Scots in *A Midsummer Night's Dream*, or of the marriage of the daughter of James the First in *The Tempest*. Such ingenuities have been mostly expended upon the curious passage in the epic (1925-1962) in which Queen Hygd, the consort of Hygelac, is contrasted, by way of compliment, with the wild and shrewish Thryth, the wife of the old Anglian king, Offa. Thryth is generally held to have been confused, in later story-telling, with Cynethryth, the wife of the later Offa of Mercia, so the passage has sometimes been interpreted as a compliment to Offa, a warning to Cynethryth, and an indication of the Mercian origin of the poem. But Cynethryth was a lady noted for gentleness and piety; and to assign the composition of *Beowulf* to the reign of Offa conflicts with the best evidence, which points to an earlier date, just as in the case of the fancied allegory in *The Tempest*, which can hardly have been written as late as 1613. Quite as probable, if we must make conjectures, is the identification of Thryth with Osthryth, wife of King Æthelred of Mercia, of whom we know little, save that she was slain by her own people in 697. The whole point of the episode in *Beowulf* is surely the intolerable shrewishness of Queen Thryth; it is this that gives force to the compliment to Hygd. If the poet had any special contemporary lady in mind, he can hardly be said to have flattered her; it would seem quite as reasonable to suppose that he was, on the contrary, casting a poisoned dart at the queen of a neighboring and hostile kingdom. But why assume any personal reference at all? Both Mercians and Northumbrians were, of course, of Anglian stock; the earlier Offa was a well-known figure, as we learn from *Widsith*, and the poet was fond of introducing such contrasts, as he did (901–915) with Beowulf and Heremod. There could be no offence in referring to an old half-legendary queen of the Angles on the Continent. Moreover, there is some evidence that the passage is interpolated.[20]

It is of far greater importance to note the influence of the culture brought to England through the Roman church, which struck deeper roots than the Irish, chiefly on account of the foundation of the great monastic schools at Canterbury, York, and Jarrow. The mission of Augustine was of necessity first concerned with conversion rather than with culture. The beginning of the true glory of English learning dates from the arrival of Theodore of Tarsus. That distinguished scholar, born in Cilicia, and educated in the best that his age had to offer, landed in England in 669, and, as seventh Archbishop of Canterbury, carried out the arduous task of organizing the whole English church on the diocesan plan. He was followed shortly by the learned Hadrian from Africa, "equally skilled in the Greek and Latin tongues," who became abbot of St. Peter's in Canterbury. With these was associated the energetic Benedict Biscop, an Englishman who had been drinking at the springs of learning in Italy, and who came to England at the request of Pope Vitalian. He later became abbot of Wearmouth, where Bede got his early education. With the establishment of the schools at Canterbury, at Jarrow, the home of Bede, and at York, a new era dawned for English letters.

Close connection between England and Rome was maintained by frequent visits of English clerics to the Holy City, with sojourns in France along the way, where they came in touch with the best that the Frankish clergy had to offer. These visitors brought back not only spiritual refreshment but splendid vestments, church ornaments, pictures, relics, and, above all, books. Wilfrid, Bishop of Northumbria, was as much at home on the Continent — where he was, to be sure, generally on the way to air his grievances at Rome — as in his own see. The most energetic of travellers, however, seems to have been Benedict Biscop, who journeyed six times to Rome, bringing back, among other treasures, *magna copia . . . voluminum sacrorum*. He was cordially received by the Northumbrian monarchs, Ecgfrith and Aldfrith, and liberally recompensed. The book-loving Aldfrith estimated a volume of the Cosmographers as worth eight hides of land, and this, it will be observed, was not a devotional but an informational work. The finest flower of this learning appears in the later eighth century in Alcuin, whose reputation, even while he was still settled in England, was such that he was called to the most brilliant court in Europe, and became the friend and trusted supporter of Charlemagne. The range and variety of intellectual interests in England in his day is admirably illustrated by the books in the Cathedral

library at York, a collection that Alcuin missed
sorely abroad, as we know from an extant letter to
Charlemagne. It included not only the Church
Fathers, the grammarians and rhetoricians, but
Aristotle, Vergil, Cicero, Juvencus, Lactantius, Sta-
tius, Lucan, and Boethius.[21]

These familiar facts are of great importance for
an understanding of *Beowulf*. The half-century
from 675 to 725, within which it seems probable
that the poem was written, was just the period in
which the new religion and the new learning were
establishing themselves most firmly. It coincides
almost exactly with the lifetime of Bede (673–
735). Many of the ablest men in the country
turned their backs completely on the old dispensa-
tion, and set themselves to composition in Latin,
and to celebration of the new faith and of the
steps by which it had established itself in the
world. Bede himself, though he was skilled in
the vernacular poetry, as we know from the letter
of his pupil Cuthbert, describing his death, occupied himself with Latin hagiology, history, commentaries, and informational work. His activity,
though more distinguished, was not different in
kind from that of other churchmen. Not only was
such work esteemed far more worthy of attention
than the perpetuation of pagan tradition; it was
the surest of preservation in a day when written
literature was almost exclusively in the posses-

sion of the Church. Vernacular writing had little chance of survival unless it were in some way made to serve the new faith. But this is not to say that the churchmen had no sympathy with it. Enough purely heathen verse has survived from this period to show that the new learning and the new faith could not wholly destroy interest in it, and that those trained in the new arts of writing thought it worthy of preservation. The fragments of *Waldhere*, the *Fight at Finnsburg*, the Northumbrian lyrics, and many of the *Riddles* are, despite a modernizing touch or two, in the pure heathen style. The use of pagan poetic technique for religious themes, as in the eighth-century Biblical paraphrases and saints' lives, shows its vitality. Probably the men responsible for such work had been trained in pagan traditions, and continued them in modified form after their conversion. What, in a Christian era, were the court-poets, the *scops*, to do, except to fall in with the new ways? Probably many of them became minor clerics. Pious kings could not welcome unmodified heathendom, but they could enjoy good old stories with the curse removed. Such was the situation, apparently, that confronted the poet of *Beowulf*. Everything shows him to have been trained in the full technique of the professional poet. His heart was really in the pagan tales and traditions that had been celebrated for generations among his people by singers like himself. But, in the changed conditions of his time, he had to suppress all references to the old gods, save for reprobation, and make over his pagans into good Christians or else show the hollowness of their heathen faith. How deep and sincere his own religious convictions were we cannot fathom, but he fell into line, as he had of necessity to do.

The older idea, that the Christian elements in *Beowulf* are interpolations in an originally heathen poem, is now, as has already been suggested, generally abandoned. Careful study has shown no differences in style, metre, or dialect, such as would be likely to arise in the inserted sections. There is a possibility that some of the longer moralizing speeches are interpolated, but there is no direct proof of this, and they are very different in style from additions like those at the end of the *Seafarer*, for example, which betray clearly the clumsy hand of the reviser. Earlier scholars were loath to admit that the poet could attribute pious sentiments to his sixth-century heathen, but artistically this is no more of a blunder than to give to Biblical characters the customs and costumes of Teutonic warriors, as in *Genesis* or *Heliand* or *Andreas*. It was of course not the sort of blunder to which the Middle Ages were sensitive. The sources of the Christian elements in *Beowulf* are of just the sort that would have been accessible to a man in contact with the new religion, but not interested in theological subtleties. They suggest the convert rather than the cleric.

Christianity brought, too, a more fundamental change in the epic than the mere parade of passages of piety. It did not merely substitute the Christian God and His Divine Son for the heathen pantheon — it preached an entirely different attitude toward life and worship. The Germanic Valhalla was a paradise for warlike heroes; the chief requisite for admission was valor; it offered merely a more glorious continuation of the joys of eating, drinking, and fighting which had been pursued upon earth. Courage, loyalty to kin and friend and over-lord, hospitality, generosity — these were the finest qualities of its devotees. It promised nothing to the poor and lowly; it laid no value upon peace or forgiveness; it could tolerate the violation of oaths. A mysterious and cruel Fate was held to control both men and gods; the barbaric, splendid, and complicated mythology, a relic, in part, of more primitive times, held little hope for weary and storm-tossed human souls. Christianity, on the other hand, brought a gospel of humility, forgiveness, and charity. It apportioned the rewards of heaven and the torments of hell according to the merits of earthly life; it gave warning of the wiles of the devil and his cohorts, ready to ensnare the sinful, and it extended hope of

eternal blessedness to the pious and the just. Its
fundamental mildness was the complete antithesis
to the savagery of the worship of Woden and
Thor. Strange, indeed, were its effects among
some of its newly converted devotees: King Sige-
bert of East Anglia would not bear a sword in
battle, lest he should shed blood. The altered view
of life brought by Christianity is clearly observable in *Beowulf*. The lines in which the aged hero
reviews his life as it draws to a close emphasize
Christian virtues: the holding of peace with one's
neighbors, the keeping of oaths, the virtuous ordering of life in order to face death at the end with
composure. And the very words with which the
poem closes, after the long tale of adventure is
done, lay stress upon the good qualities that a
Christian king and hero might possess, if indeed
they are not directly in. .uenced by Scripture.[22]

It has frequently been suggested that the new
learning in Britain may be seen reflected in *Beowulf*
in the influence of the *Æneid*. This is supported
not so much by parallelisms of phraseology and
incident, which, though sometimes striking, are
not sufficiently close to be conclusive as evidences
of borrowing, as by the great popularity that
the *Æneid* enjoyed among those acquainted with
Latin letters. Both the Irish and the Roman
ecclesiastics in northern Britain knew it well;
indeed, of all the great works of classical antiquity

it was one of the best known and least misunderstood in the early Middle Ages. It would surely have appealed to a poet versed in Germanic traditions, on account of its plot, its heroic temper, and its detailed information in regard to a long-past age. The state of society and the ideals of the warrior class which it sets forth are very similar to those that existed among Germanic peoples at the time of the invasion of Britain. Many detailed resemblances between it and *Beowulf* which seem at first sight remarkable are really such as might easily have arisen both in classical antiquity and in the heroic age of Western Europe. The manners and customs of the days of the Trojan War — and this applies to the Homeric poems as well as to the *Æneid* — are often strikingly like those of Hrothgar and Hygelac and their cohorts. Descriptions of feasts, of seafaring, of warfare, of equipment, and the like, run in somewhat parallel lines. So, then, while the influence of Vergil may be regarded as entirely possible, it cannot be conclusively established.[23]

An extremely significant example of mediæval Vergilian influence may be studied in *Waltharius*, the Latin version of the old story of Walter of Aquitaine, composed about 930 by the monk Ekkehard of St. Gall, the famous religious settlement in eastern Switzerland, a little south of Lake Constance. Here is genuine old Germanic material transformed into a little Vergilian epic. "The assumption, which formerly enjoyed currency, that Ekkehard translated an Old High German epic, is untenable. His source was without doubt tradition in oral circulation in the form of a short lay." [24] The culture of the Swiss monastery in the tenth century was remarkable,—analogous to that of northern England two centuries earlier. The parallelism to the conditions under which *Beowulf* was composed, and to the sources from which the poet drew, is thus quite striking. The later author was so deeply affected by literary models that he cast his work in Latin, though his direct sources were vernacular; the earlier poet, if indeed he did have Vergil as a guide, preserved far more individuality and originality, in that he did not abandon the language and verse-technique of his own people.

How far the extension of epic lays into developed epic form was a genuine native development, and not suggested by classical models, is an unsolvable question. No other vernacular epic in the Germanic tongues, excepting the Old Saxon *Heliand*, written about a century later than *Beowulf*, has been preserved from the earlier Middle Ages. Old Norse never developed beyond the epic lay. But here again the story of Walter of Aquitaine presents valuable evidence. The two Anglo-Saxon *Waldhere* fragments recovered from the binding

of a volume of homilies in Copenhagen show, by
the presentation of the subject-matter, and by
stylistic adornments, that they are parts of a
somewhat extended and leisurely whole.[25] Had
we the original complete, it would probably belong
with *Beowulf*, in contrast to the more pregnant
epic lay, like the *Fight at Finnsburg*. The tracing
of the many differences between ballad and lay
(which are not the same thing) on the one hand,
and the developed epic on the other, is a long business, which cannot be attempted here. But the
tendency to greater length and elaboration seems
clearly indicated in the development of the ballad,
as in the *Little Gest of Robin Hood*,[26] and it would
appear strange if Germanic minstrels could have
learned only from the recovered classical authors
how to tell a story at ampler length.

In an earlier chapter it has been said: "It appears altogether probable that *Beowulf* was composed pen in hand, or written from the poet's dictation." After our review of the conditions under
which the poem was produced, and in view of the
extraordinary interest in foreign culture, of the
study of written texts, and of the supplanting of
Runic writing by the Roman script, this statement would seem to need little defence. Professor
Munro Chadwick has, however, attacked what
he calls "the chimæra of a literary *Beowulf*," and
challenged particularly Professor W. P. Ker's

statement that "*Beowulf* and *Waldhere* are the work of educated men, and they were intended, no doubt, as books to read." He has maintained that it is doubtful if English was commonly written before the late eighth or early ninth century, that a reading public for English was not to be looked for in the days of Bede, that the silence of Bede himself on the subject is a presumption that written vernacular poems did not exist, and that this is strengthened by the famous letter of Alcuin to Hycbald, with its scornful reference to the legends of Ingeld.[27] I think Professor Chadwick is wrong. The writing down of a poem in a scholarly age does not necessarily mean that this was done for the delectation of scholars. *Beowulf* appears to have been designed for a royal court — the same sort of entertainment, in more extended form, as the utterances of professional *scops* in the older days of purely heathen traditions. Its highly artistic form and the way in which its subject-matter is presented remove it immediately from work intended for the vulgar. We have little direct evidence as to the writing of English in the age of Bede, one way or the other, but there seems to me a strong presumption that this was far commoner, even for English verse, than Professor Chadwick thinks. What about the contemporary Cædmonian verse? Was that orally composed and transmitted? If professional scribes had written down the laws in the vernacular, far earlier than this, why should they not also have transcribed native poetry? A written version of *Beowulf* might conceivably have served as a guide for oral recitation, like the Oxford manuscript of the *Song of Roland*. But there seems to be no reason to doubt that cultivated Christian monarchs like Aldfrith, and his circle, including ecclesiastics, would have enjoyed a perusal of it on the written page. The new acquaintance with the classics did not stifle all interest in the older native stories, as plenty of evidences show. Are we to assume that ecclesiastics despised such stories, especially when they found them furbished up with pious Christian passages, as in *Beowulf*, merely because they themselves were concerned with composition of another sort? Bede and Aldhelm wrote native verse, as is well known, and Alfred the Great brought up his children on it, and he himself committed it to memory. Alcuin, in the letter referred to, was admonishing the clergy, *in sacerdotali convivio*, against welcoming the disorder of revellers in the streets, *ridentium turbam in plateis*, and mingling songs on sacred and profane subjects, Ingeld and Christ.[28] He was certainly right in his warning that debased popular lays, cheek by jowl with holy songs, were unsuited to a monastery; but does this mean that he would have disapproved of native traditions in a dignified and artistic form, like *Beowulf?*

Some three centuries elapsed before the poem attained the extant form in which we now read it. What were its fortunes in the meantime? How often was it recopied and revised, in other parts of Britain? Here evidence fails us; the varied dialectical forms are not, as they have sometimes been considered, trustworthy guides. By a series of fortunate chances, *Beowulf* was spared in the Viking pillagings and burnings, and was ultimately put into the West-Saxon dialect in southern England, where it was copied, not far from the year 1000, by two careless scribes, and made a part of one of the manuscript codices which were the treasured possessions of the learned. The general characteristics of this final written form have been traced in an earlier chapter. The copying took place at a time when the lamp of Anglo-Saxon letters was burning low, when the traditions of native verse were kept alive by little original production, and the English spirit of the older days was enfeebled and irresolute. The age of Æthelred the Redeless was a sorry contrast to the glory of the Anglian kingdoms. Is it fanciful to imagine that the man for whom the final transcript of *Beowulf* was made saw, in its tragic tale of the vanishing splendors of great kingdoms and the extinction of royal houses, a reflection of the misfortunes of the English crown and the dangers assailing his native land, and, in its story of courageous struggles against heavy odds, a faint hope that his countrymen might win through in the end? The fulfilment was long delayed; but if the heroism of Harold at Hastings came to naught, the indomitable Anglo-Saxon temper so strikingly illustrated in *Beowulf* ultimately prevailed in England over all invaders, and proved the foundation of the greatness of the English nation.

BIBLIOGRAPHY

BIBLIOGRAPHY

THE following bibliographical suggestions are intended chiefly for those who do not read the poem in the original, or are just beginning a study of the Anglo-Saxon text. Those who are obliged to rely upon translations will find that the editions will give much assistance. It must be remembered that no two translations follow precisely the same textual readings, and that considerable variations thus arise. Several renderings may be profitably examined, since no one of them reproduces the original exactly, although each contributes its share to a correct understanding of meaning, rhythm, and spirit. The oldest ones are better avoided. The prose versions are generally more faithful; those in verse of necessity sacrifice literalness to metrical form. The peculiar movement of Anglo-Saxon poetry is exceedingly difficult to reproduce in modern English. There is unfortunately at present (1928) no literal prose rendering which takes due account of the results of the latest researches.

The critical and illustrative literature is very extensive; much of the best of it is in foreign languages, and intended only for specialists. I have selected some twenty works which seem to me most generally helpful to the serious student. They will be referred to, in the notes following, only by brief titles, or the author's name.

The notes, as I have explained in the Preface, are added for more advanced readers who wish support for statements in the text, and references to special studies elsewhere. I have tried to make them as brief as possible, and only in rare cases have admitted discussion of technical questions.

EDITIONS

Especially to be recommended are those by A. J. Wyatt and R. W. Chambers, second revised edition, Cambridge, Eng., 1920, and by F. Klaeber, Boston, N. Y., and Chicago, 1922. The first of these should be supplemented by R. W. Chambers, *Beowulf, An Introduction to the Study of the Poem*, Cambridge, Eng., 1921. Klaeber's edition contains an extraordinary amount of concise information. The *Waldhere* fragments, *Deor*, and passages from *Widsith* are included. The edition by W. J. Sedgefield, second edition, Manchester, 1913, which contains text and comment in one volume, has an excellent glossary.

Of the German editions, the following deserve particular mention: Schücking (a revision of the older Heyne-Socin text), tenth edition, Paderborn, 1913, with many passages translated in the glossary; Holthausen, in two small volumes, third edition, Heidelberg, 1912–1913. *Waldhere, Deor, Widsith*, and the *Lay of Hildebrand* are included.

All the editions mentioned above contain the *Finnsburg Fragment*, with glossary and critical apparatus.

TRANSLATIONS

Chambers's review of the translations, *Introduction*, pp. 390 ff., including foreign languages as well as English, is especially detailed. See also Klaeber, pp. cxxvi ff. For earlier work, Chauncey B. Tinker, *Translations of Beowulf, a Critical Bibliography*, N. Y., 1903.

F. B. Gummere, *The Oldest English Epic*, N. Y., 1909 (verse), includes *Finnsburg, Waldhere, Deor, Widsith*, and the *Lay of Hildebrand*, with introduction and notes. The spirit and movement of the original are well suggested. J. R. C. Hall, *Beowulf in Modern English Prose*, second

edition, revised, London, 1911, brings out the structure
of the epic clearly, and adds some useful illustrative material. The metrical translation by the same author
(1914) is not so felicitous, and the illustrations and comment are almost wholly omitted. The prose version by
C. B. Tinker, second edition, N. Y., 1910, is simple in
style, and the episodes are printed, as in Clark Hall's
prose text, in smaller type. The translation by C. G.
Child, Riverside Literature Series, Boston, 1904 (prose),
is good and inexpensive. The metre of William Morris's
Sigurd the Volsung is used by Archibald Strong, *Beowulf
translated into Modern English Rhyming Verse*, London, 1925, in frank departure from the Anglo-Saxon
line. A foreword is provided by R. W. Chambers. The
German verse rendering by H. Gering, second edition,
Heidelberg, 1913, is excellent, with very good notes.

For illustrative reading in Anglo-Saxon literature
the following may be recommended: Cook and Tinker,
Select Translations from Old English Poetry, Boston,
1902; *Select Translations from Old English Prose*, Boston, 1908; J. D. Spaeth, *Old English Poetry*, Princeton,
1922.

Suggestions for reading in Old Norse literature will
be found in the notes to chapter II.

FACSIMILE AND CONCORDANCE

The poem was reproduced in facsimile by Zupitza,
*Beowulf: Autotypes of the Unique Cotton MS. Vitellius
A xv*, etc., Early English Text Society, no. 77, London,
1882. The description of the MS. by K. Sisam, *Modern
Language Review* (1916), xi, 335 ff., is very useful.

For ready reference to the Anglo-Saxon text, see A. S.
Cook, *A Concordance to Beowulf*, Halle, 1911.

SELECTED CRITICAL AND ILLUSTRATIVE WORKS

A. Brandl, "Englische Literatur: Angelsächsische Periode," in Paul's *Grundriss der germanischen Philologie* (Strassburg, 1908), ii, 941–1134. The best of all surveys of Anglo-Saxon literature; not adapted, however, to the elementary student. The section dealing with *Beowulf* contains much valuable material.

H. Bradley, article "Beowulf" in the *Encyclopædia Britannica,* eleventh edition, 1910, vol. iii. Reflects to a considerable extent earlier opinions; not in line with the most advanced research.

S. A. Brooke, *History of Early English Literature,* London and N. Y., 1892. Excellent for literary appreciation, but to be used with caution in scholarly matters.

Cambridge History of English Literature, 1907, etc. Vol. i contains various essays on early English literature, of unequal value. The treatment of *Beowulf* by Munro Chadwick embodies theories which are open to question.

H. Munro Chadwick, *Origin of the English Nation,* Cambridge, Eng., 1907. Best for more advanced workers, with discussions of controversial questions; extremely learned and suggestive.

H. Munro Chadwick, *The Heroic Age,* Cambridge, Eng., 1912. Interesting and illuminating comparison of the Germanic and the Greek epic.

R. W. Chambers, *Beowulf, an Introduction to the Study of the Poem, with a discussion of the Stories of Offa and Finn,* Cambridge, Eng., 1921. The most important of all commentaries on *Beowulf,* with full bibliographical and critical apparatus.

R. W. Chambers, *Widsith, A Study in Old English Heroic Legend,* Cambridge, Eng., 1912. A detailed review of the tribes and heroes mentioned in the poem, with discussion of disputed questions. The maps at the end are useful for the study of *Beowulf*.

R. W. Chambers, *England before the Norman Conquest*, London, 1926. "The object is to illustrate the way in which the history of the earliest England has to be constructed." The book consists largely of translations of sources.

Bruce Dickins, *Runic and Heroic Poems of the Old Teutonic Peoples*, Cambridge, Eng., 1915. The volume contains text, translation, and notes for *Waldhere*, the *Finnsburg Fragment*, *Deor*, and the *Lay of Hildebrand*, in addition to the runic poems.

Oliver Elton and F. York Powell, *The First Nine Books of the Danish History of Saxo Grammaticus translated*, London, 1894. A convenient English version of this very important text.

Max Förster, *Bēowulf-Materialien zum Gebrauch bei Vorlesungen*, Braunschweig, 1908. A convenient collection of important illustrative passages from various sources.

F. B. Gummere, *Germanic Origins*, N. Y., 1892. An account of the life and customs of the Germanic tribes on the Continent. An excellent survey, unfortunately out of print and hard to obtain.

J. Hoops (editor), *Reallexikon der germanischen Altertumskunde*, 4 vols., Strassburg, 1911–1919. Compact and suggestive essays by recognized authorities. Indispensable for the advanced worker.

W. M. Hart, *Ballad and Epic* (Harvard Studies and Notes, vol. xi), Boston, 1907. Elaborate discussion of the types of early narrative verse.

O. L. Jiriczek, *Die deutsche Heldensage* (Sammlung Göschen), fourth revised edition, Berlin and Leipzig,

1913; an earlier edition translated as *Northern Hero Legends* by M. G. Bentinck Smith for the Temple Classics, London, 1902. The later German editions are far superior.

W. P. Ker, *Epic and Romance*, London and N. Y., 1897. A delightful and highly suggestive discussion of the literary aspects of early mediæval literature. Particular attention is paid to Old Norse poetry.

W. W. Lawrence, *Medieval Story*, second edition, N. Y., 1926. Discussions of important pieces of mediæval literature, with special reference to the development of social ideals, designed rather for the general reader than the specialist.

R. M. Meyer, *Die altgermanische Poesie*, Berlin, 1889. An older book, with much that is suggestive for the advanced student.

A. Olrik, *Danmarks Heltedigtning*, 2 vols., Copenhagen, 1903, 1910. Very important for detailed study. Vol. i is translated into English as *The Heroic Legends of Denmark*, by L. M. Hollander, N. Y., 1919. Olrik contributed some notes to the translation which are not in the Danish volume.

A. Olrik, *Nordisches Geistesleben in heidnischer und frühchristlicher Zeit*. Translation from the Danish by W. Ranisch, Heidelberg, 1908.

C. Oman, *England before the Norman Conquest*, N. Y. and London, 1913. An excellent guide to the conditions in England during the development of the material in *Beowulf* into its finished epic form.

F. Panzer, *Studien zur germanischen Sagengeschichte*, I, *Beowulf*, Munich, 1910. An elaborate collection and discussion of folk-tale analogues. Extremely important.

K. Stjerna, *Essays on Questions connected with the Old English Poem of Beowulf*, translated and edited by

J. R. C. Hall, Coventry, 1912. The arguments advanced are often open to question, but there are valuable illustrations and discussions of armor, jewelry, dwellings, grave-mounds, etc.

Henry Osborn Taylor, *The Mediaeval Mind*, 2 vols., third (American) edition, N. Y., 1919. Admirable for suggesting the general development of thought and expression in mediæval Europe.

R. Wülker, *Grundriss zur Geschichte der angelsächsischen Litteratur*, Leipzig, 1885. A very useful review of earlier criticism. There is no book which performs this service from 1885 to the present time.

Studies by the present writer, containing more extended discussions of matters set forth in the preceding pages, are here listed together for convenience.

"Some Disputed Questions in Beowulf-Criticism," *Publications of the Modern Language Association of America* (1909), xxiv, 220–273.

"The Haunted Mere in Beowulf," *Ibid.* (1912), xxvii, 208–245.

"Beowulf and the Tragedy of Finnsburg," *Ibid.* (1915), xxx, 372–431.

"The Dragon and his Lair in Beowulf," *Ibid.* (1918), xxxiii, 547–583.

(The references above are to the Old Series of the Publications. The New Series subtracts seven from the numeral of the Old Series; thus, xxxiii, O. S., is xxvi, N. S.)

"The Breca Episode in Beowulf," *Anniversary Papers by Colleagues and Pupils of George Lyman Kittredge* (Boston and London, 1913), pp. 359–366.

NOTES

NOTES

CHAPTER I

1. For Sir William Temple's essay, see Spingarn, *Critical Essays of the Seventeenth Century* (Oxford, 1909), iii, 94, 95.

2. *The Little Clay Cart* (Cambridge, Mass., 1905), p. xvii.

3. See Brandl, p. 1001, who, however, puts the matter cautiously.

4. See below, pp. 284 ff.

5. A fuller discussion of much in the preceding paragraphs will be found in chapter VIII.

6. Henry Bradley, in "The Numbered Sections in Old English Poetical MSS" (*Proceedings of the British Academy*, London, 1915, vii, 90), suggested that "each section of *Beowulf* represents one of the sheets or leaves on which the poem was written by the man to whom it owes its present literary form . . . it may well have been written on scraps of parchment of various sizes, or on sheets already partially covered by writing. The inequality in the length of the various sections would thus be accounted for."

7. For a review of the principal studies in the "higher criticism" see especially Chambers, *Introduction*, pp. 112–120. The most important of the earlier studies are those of Müllenhoff (1869) and ten Brink (1888). The more recent works by Schücking, *Beowulfs Rückkehr*, 1905, and Berendsohn, 1913 (see Klaeber, p. cxxxix), are different in method, but open to many objections. The formal stylistic adornments of repetition and variation in Anglo-Saxon verse, which are so disturbing to modern feeling, appear to have been carried over into the larger units of narrative. Their importance for the critical reconstruction of *Beowulf* is discussed in an unpublished dissertation (1903) by the present writer, in the Harvard College Library.

8. For an illuminating comparison of historic fact with imaginative elaboration in the great stories of Germanic antiquity, see A. Heusler, "Geschichtliches und Mythisches in der germanischen Heldensage," *Sitzungsberichte der königlichen preussischen Akademie der Wissenschaften* (1909), xxxvii, 920 ff.

CHAPTER II

1. That the ancient Lethra and the hall of Hrothgar were located on the site of the modern village of Leire is generally accepted to-day. Dr. S. J. Herben, in a paper read at a meeting of the Modern Language Association of America, in December, 1924, presented a different view. I quote the summary of his paper. "The topographical passages in *Beowulf* do not constitute adequate evidence for assigning the location of Heorot to any definite spot. The identification with the present-day Leire is based upon inconclusive testimony. A combination of archæological, linguistic, and historical material points to a hill top in Viso parish, Smorum district, on the island of Sjælland as the site of Hrothgar's hall." For an early picture of Leire and general discussion, cf. Chambers, *Introduction*, pp. 16 ff.

2. Sarrazin, *Beowulf-Studien* (Berlin, 1888), p. 31.

3. See particularly the accounts in the *Poetic Edda* and the *Volsungasaga* (cf. notes 21, 22, below) and the discussions by Jiriczek (1913), pp. 40 ff., and Chambers, *Widsith*, pp. 15-20.

4. See the important study by Elias Wessén, *De Nordiska Folkstammarna i Beowulf*, Stockholm, 1927. It is of course impossible here to enter into a discussion of the difficult question of the relations between Danes, Heruli, and Heathobards.

5. H. G. Leach, *Angevin Britain and Scandinavia* (Cambridge, Mass., 1921), esp. pp. 6 ff.

6. Chambers, *Introduction*, pp. 333-345, gives a full and dispassionate review of this much-debated question. The time has arrived, it would appear, to consider the identification of the Geatas with the Jutes as definitely refuted.

"There is no good evidence that anybody identified the two tribes before the rise of modern scholarship" (Kemp Malone, *Modern Language Review* [1925], xx, 1–11).

7. W. A. Craigie, *Philologica* (ed. Baudis and Wharton for the Philological Society of London, 1923–1924), ii, 12–14. Cf. chapter VIII, note 20, below.

8. The fullest discussion is in Chambers's edition. See also W. W. Lawrence, "Structure and Interpretation of Widsith," *Modern Philology* (1906), iv, 329–374.

9. Chambers, *op. cit.*, pp. 164, 165.

10. Those who wish to follow further the sketch of early Germanic peoples may consult Bremer, "Ethnographie der germanischen Stämme," in Paul's *Grundriss der germanischen Philologie* (1900), iii, 735 ff., and Chambers, *Widsith*. There is much new and valuable material in Hoops's *Reallexicon*.

11. On this general subject, see H. Brunner, *Deutsche Rechtsgeschichte* (Leipzig, 1887), vol. i, and the various special articles in Hoops's *Reallexicon*. Klaeber's bibliography, pp. cxlix ff., may be used to advantage.

12. *Germanic Origins*, p. 17.

13. *Epic and Romance*, p. 7.

14. Text translated by Spaeth, *Old English Poetry* (Princeton, N. J., 1922), p. 140.

15. F. Seebohm, *Tribal Custom in Anglo-Saxon Law*, London and N. Y., 1902, has a chapter on "The Evidence of *Beowulf* on Tribal Custom Regulating Feuds," but he assumes that the father of Beowulf was a Swede (p. 57) and from this draws far-reaching conclusions.

16. Oman, p. 282.

17. Eleanor Hull, *The Cuchullin Saga in Irish Literature* (London, 1898), pp. 254 ff.

18. Leach, *op. cit.*, p. 336.

19. Ed. Foerster (Halle, 1891), pp. 46 ff., lines 1727 ff.; cf. translation by Comfort, *Eric and Enid*, pp. 202 ff. For an analysis of the interplay of passion and convention in chivalric tales, see S. F. Barrow, *The Medieval Society Romances*, N. Y., 1924.

20. See the excellent manual by A. Mawer, *The Vikings*, Cambridge (Eng.) and N. Y., 1913. A selection of the very extensive bibliography of the subject is given on p. 146. Particularly useful are W. A. Craigie, *The Religion of Ancient Scandinavia*, London, 1906; Axel Olrik, *Nordisches Geistesleben*, Heidelberg, 1908; and Valtýr Guðmundsson, *Island i Fristatstiden*, Copenhagen, 1924.

21. The *Poetic Edda* is accessible in English in a complete translation in verse, with notes and introduction, by H. A. Bellows, American-Scandinavian Foundation, N. Y., 1923. The best treatment of the mythology in English is the translation by S. B. Hustvedt of Munch's *Norröne Gude-og Heltesagn* revised by Olsen, under the title *Norse Mythology*, American-Scandinavian Foundation, N. Y., 1926. Very useful is R. M. Meyer's *Altgermanische Religionsgeschichte*, Leipzig, 1910. The bibliography of the subject is very extensive. For further discussion of mythology as affecting *Beowulf*, see chapter V, below. On Sigemund's dragon, see chapter VII, note 3.

22. Edition of the *Volsungasaga* by Magnus Olsen, Copenhagen, 1906–1908. The translation by Magnússon and Morris is accessible in the Scott Library, London, n.d. Cf. Morris's poetic paraphrase of the story, *Sigurd the Volsung*, London, 1904.

23. The *Prose Edda* has been rendered into English by A. G. Brodeur, American-Scandinavian Foundation, N. Y., 1916. Certain passages have been omitted. For the original, see edition by Finnur Jónsson, Copenhagen, 1900. For the skaldic verse, see Vigfusson and Powell, *Corpus Poeticum Boreale* (Oxford, 1883), vol. ii.

24. For a general discussion of the sagas, see W. A. Craigie, *The Icelandic Sagas*, Cambridge (Eng.), 1913. A special chapter is devoted to "English Translations and Other Aids," pp. 110 ff. The fullest criticism is in F. Jónsson's *Oldnorske og Oldislandske Litteraturs Historie*, 3 vols., Copenhagen, 1920–1924, unfortunately not accessible in English. See especially the treatment of the subject by Mogk in Paul's *Grundriss*, vol. ii.

25. On Danish traditions, consult especially Olrik, *Heltedigtning*, vol. i. The Lay of Bjarki is discussed in the English translation, pp. 66 ff. Excerpts from early documents are printed by Klaeber and by Chambers, *Introduction*. Further references will be given in the chapters following. For Saxo, see Bibliography, above.

CHAPTER III

1. It is impossible to indicate here the stages by which the history of the Danish royal house has been reconstructed. See especially the important discussion in Olrik, *Heroic Legends*, pp. 12 ff. I cannot accept his conclusions in all points. Klaeber gives a classified bibliography of historical legends (pp. cxxxiv ff.), and summarizes historical elements (xxix ff.). The reflections of early historical conditions in story are set forth by Kemp Malone, *The Literary History of Hamlet*, I, Heidelberg, 1923 (*Anglistische Forschungen*, lix). Professor Malone's reconstructions are ingenious, but seem to me largely hypothetical.

2. Sarrazin explains the name Heorot as arising from the worship of an ancient hart deity (*Anglia*, xix, 372 f.). Cf. G. Schütte, *Dänisches Heidenthum* (Heidelberg, 1923), p. 88.

3. The most recent discussion of the fall of the Scylding dynasty, published after the writing of the account in the text, is that by Kemp Malone, "Hrethric," *Publications of the Modern Language Association of America* (1927), xlii, 268–313.

4. The relations between *Beowulf* and the *Hrólfssaga* are discussed below, chapter VI.

5. A detailed argument to show that this is a prophecy, and not, as Olrik (*Heltedigtning*, ii, 37 ff.) argued, an account of events that had already occurred, will be found in my *Beowulf and the Tragedy of Finnsburg*, p. 380 n. Reconstruction of the whole tale is very difficult. Saxo and the *Hrólfssaga* must be taken with great care; their accounts are so much altered in points that are quite clear in Anglo-Saxon that they are not safe guides in the obscurer matters.

6. See below, chapter V. On Heremod, see Chambers, *Introduction*, pp. 89 ff.

7. On Swedish historical conditions in general, see Klaeber, p. xxxviii; for bibliography, p. cxxxvi. Also Weyhe, "König Ongentheows Fall," *Englische Studien*, xxxix, 14 ff., and Belden, *Modern Language Notes* (1913), xxviii, 149 ff., a suggestive if somewhat venturesome essay.

8. Klaeber, *Anglia*, l, 242 ff., reviews later discussions as to the date of Hygelac's death, and concludes that 516 may stand.

9. Antoine Thomas, "Un manuscrit inutilisé du Liber Monstrorum," *Archivum Latinitatis medii aevi* (Union Académique internationale: Bulletin DuCange; Paris, 1925), pp. 232–245.

10. See the detailed discussion in Chambers's *Introduction*, pp. 31 ff., with reproduction of early MS. drawings illustrative of the scenes of the story. For the theory that the passage is interpolated, see chapter II, note 7.

CHAPTER IV

1. The Anglo-Saxon text of the *Fragment* is to be found in all the editions mentioned above, and also in Bruce Dickins's *Runic and Heroic Poems*. It is also printed with notes and comment by W. S. Mackie, *Journal of English and Germanic Philology* (1917), xvi, 250–273. The most recent bibliography, with a list of the more important critical works, may be found in the edition by Klaeber, pp. 227 ff. See also Nellie S. Aurner, *An Analysis of the Interpretations of the Finnsburg Documents*, University of Iowa, 1917. For a detailed review of the earlier part of the story, and discussion of many points in this chapter, see W. W. Lawrence, "Beowulf and the Tragedy of Finnsburg." The best analysis of the later events is that by H. M. Ayres, "The Tragedy of Hengest in *Beowulf*," *Journal of English and Germanic Philology* (1917), xvi, 282–295.

2. For a discussion of the vexed question of the relationship of these tribes, and references, see Klaeber, pp. 220 ff.
The Ēotan — or Jutes, as they would appear to be — were
neighbors both of the Frisians and of the Danes, and may well
have been allied, now with one and now with the other people.
Klaeber asks: "Is it possible that the Ags. version embodies
two distinct strata of early legend reflecting different phases
of the history of the Jutes? . . . the sojourn of the Jutes in
proximity to the Frisians was apt to suggest an especially
close relation between these two tribes (hence *Ēotan = Frȳ-
san*)." There is no doubt on which side the sympathies of the
Eotens lie in the *Episode*. It seems to me, however, highly
probable that many of the difficulties in the interpretation of
the tale arise from the embodiment in it of contradictory
legendary elements, as in the dragon adventure.

3. The translation of this passage follows the text of Klaeber, not that of Chambers. I should prefer to put a period
after line 1065, and begin a new sentence: Þonne *healgamen*,
etc., but this is not of great importance. Klaeber rightly de-
cides that 1068–1159a should not be in quotation marks, as
Chambers prints it.

4. There has been much discussion as to whether the later
events take place in the same locality as the earlier ones. "An
unprejudiced reading gives the impression, I think, that
Hengest (with Finn) stayed where he was." Klaeber, *Anglia*,
l, 229.

5. Is the Hengest of Finnsburg to be identified with the
Hengest of the Conquest of Britain? The evidence is reviewed
by Nellie S. Aurner, *Hengest, a Study in Early English Hero
Legend* (Iowa City, 1921), pp. 56 ff., with conclusions in the
affirmative. Why should the leader of the Jutes in the Conquest be identified with the Danes in the Finnsburg story?
Wessén discusses this (see above, chapter II, note 4), p. 33. He
thinks Hengest was conceived as a Dane, Frisians and Jutes
identified, and Hengest therefore made an opponent of the
people to whom he really belonged.

6. Lines 1142 ff. are especially difficult and obscure. I
take them to mean: "So he [Hengest] did not prove recreant

to his duty [the duty of vengeance] when the son of Hunlaf presented him with a sword, the edges of which were well known among the Eotens [on account of the slaughter done with it in the earlier surprise attack on the Danes]." The passage is fully discussed in my article.

7. Jiriczek, 49.

8. Chambers's views are set forth briefly in his edition, p. 167, and very fully in his *Introduction*, pp. 245–289. The comments of Klaeber, *Anglia*, l, 224 ff., should be noted, in addition to those in his edition.

9. Chambers says, "That the Frisians are not to taunt the Danes with following the slayer of their lord is only one of two possible explanations of the ll. 1101–3" (*Introduction*, p. 271). But that the *Danes* were not to mention the fact that they were following the slayer of their lord, which I take to be the alternative reading, seems to me very forced. The simple and natural interpretation, especially in view of the fact that the whole lay is sung to a Danish audience, appears to me to be that all of lines 1098–1106 is a summary of Finn's promises.

10. R. A. Williams, *The Finn Episode in Beowulf*, Cambridge (Eng.), 1924. Professor Williams tells us that his study started in the conviction that the second part of the Nibelung story might serve to supply missing elements in the Finnsburg tale. His reconstruction of the latter, in briefest form, is as follows: Hnæf, prince of the Hocings, a tribe dependent upon the Danes, and also called Eotens, is invited by Finn, king of the Frisians, who covets his treasure, to become Finn's vassal. Hengest, Hnæf's chief retainer, does not like this proposal, but is overruled, and with Hnæf visits Finn's court, the treasure being carried along with them. One of Finn's sons plays a trick on the Danes, and in retaliation Hengest smites off the boy's head, and attacks the Frisians. Hnæf insists that peace be restored, but that night Hnæf is attacked by Finn and his men and killed. The treasure passes to Finn, who then schemes to bring also the Half-Danes in Denmark under his sway. He allows Guthlaf and Oslaf to return home, ostensibly with this proposal, but they return with Danish

troops, and take, with Hengest, a bloody vengeance on Finn.

Having worked this out, Professor Williams was "faced by the problem of reconciling this reconstruction with the text of the Episode in *Beowulf*." Disregarding, as far as possible, this reconstruction, he attacked the ambiguities of the text. "To my great pleasure," he continues, "the results gained harmonized fully with my reconstruction" (pp. v, vi). It seems to me, whether Professor Williams was conscious of it or not, that this harmony was gained by forcing the text of the *Episode* into the Procrustean bed of the Nibelung story. Simple and obvious readings are tortured to give new meanings. Great stress is laid upon logic as a guide, but logic takes queer turns. Although he puts analysis of the text first in his book, he later says, "The whole construction I give [that is, the reconstruction of the Finn story from the Burgundian saga] is . . . only a hypothesis, for which I claim no value except in so far as it allows us to deduce from it the text of the Finn Episode" (p. 113). He also states schematically the logical process for his whole reconstruction of the one story from the other. "If . . . in the incomplete saga, X, we find a part A which likewise exists in the complete saga, Y, compared with it, and if in the latter we find another part, B, organically related to A, but missing in X, there is a presumption that B was also present in X; and if this fills a gap and is not contradicted by anything else in X, the presence of B in the latter may be considered as established" (p. 111). This I flatly deny. Saga is not logical. Situations and motives recur again and again, but in bewildering complexity and with changing motivation.

Professor Williams's book is reviewed by Kemp Malone, *Journal of English and Germanic Philology* (1926), xxv, 114–117, who gives a reconstruction of the story in a later article (*Ibid.*, pp. 157–172), which differs in some respects from that which I have outlined above.

CHAPTER V

1. For useful discussions of Germanic mythology, see references to Munch and Meyer in chapter II, note 21, above. Meyer gives a review of the principal authorities and a general history of the subject (pp. 569 ff.). P. D. Chantepie de la Saussaye, *The Religion of the Teutons*, Boston and London, 1902, is readable, but not up to date. W. A. Craigie, *The Religion of Ancient Scandinavia*, London, 1906, gives a good brief survey. Many of the more significant later studies must be sought in special articles in periodicals. The contributions to Hoops's *Reallexicon* are important; see iv, 602, index under "Mythus und Aberglaube." S. Bugge's *Home of the Eddic Poems*, translated from the Norwegian by W. H. Schofield, London, 1889, stresses Christian influences.

2. On the Scyld story the following may be consulted: Chambers, *Introduction*, pp. 68–86, one of the clearest and most recent statements of the problem; Axel Olrik, *Heroic Legends*, pp. 436 ff., which should be supplemented by the second (untranslated) volume of the *Heltedigtning*, pp. 249–254; Klaeber, pp. 121 ff., an excellent brief review; Chadwick, *Origin*, pp. 274 ff. Many references to further discussions will be found in connection with the foregoing.

3. A convenient review of the subjects discussed in greater detail in the many volumes of the large edition is the one-volume edition of *The Golden Bough*, N. Y., 1922. "The Corn-Mother in Many Lands" is the title of chap. 46, pp. 412–420.

4. Chadwick, *Origin*, p. 278.

5. Bruce Dickins, *Runic and Heroic Poems*, p. 21.

6. Kaarle Krohn, *Finnisch-Ugrische Forschungen* (1904), iv, 231–248. I expressed the view in 1909 (*Some Disputed Questions*, p. 259) that the boat-story belonged first to Scyld and was later transferred to Sceaf. Later discussions, and particularly this evidence from the Finnish, with which I was not then acquainted, have convinced me that the contrary is the case. Axel Olrik, who in the first volume of his *Heltedigtning* regarded Scyld as the original hero of the boat-story, altered his views in his second volume.

7. K. Müllenhoff, *Beovulf: Untersuchungen* (Berlin, 1889), pp. 1 ff. Müllenhoff had expressed himself in regard to the mythical elements in *Beowulf* as early as 1844; this (posthumous) volume represents his final statement.

8. *Sitzungsberichte der Gesellschaft der Wissenschaften zu Leipzig*, xlvii, 181.

9. A more elaborate review and discussion, with references, will be found in *Some Disputed Questions*, pp. 247 ff.

10. A. Lang, *Custom and Myth* (London, 1893), p. 62. See also Lang's *Myth, Ritual and Religion*, 2 vols., London, 1906, and his article, "Mythology," in the *Encyclopædia Britannica*.

11. I am indebted here for suggestions to Professor Kittredge.

12. For the Breca story in general, consult Klaeber, pp. 144 ff., and Chambers, *Widsith*, pp. 110 ff. The current misunderstandings of the whole episode were, I believe, first pointed out in my article in the *Kittredge Anniversary Papers*, pp. 359–366. References to details of the present discussion may be found in that article. For Sarrazin's remark about Beowulf as a sun-god see his *Beowulf-Studien* (Berlin, 1888), p. 66. Oddly enough, Chambers nowhere examines the Breca story in his *Introduction*.

CHAPTER VI

1. *Egotism in German Philosophy* (N. Y., 1917), p. 144.

2. Some interesting light is thrown on the human qualities of the bear by A. Irving Hallowell, "Bear Ceremonialism in the Northern Hemisphere," *American Anthropologist* (January–March, 1926), xxviii, 149 ff. Skeat, *Journal of Philology*, xv, 120 ff., proposed to trace the Grendel combat to a fight between a man and a powerful bear. This element in the story is well worth considering if it is remembered that it is only one of many, that the monsters of *Beowulf* have a complex origin. The etymology of the name "Beowulf" is fully discussed by Chambers, *Introduction*, pp. 365 ff.

3. For the connection of Grendel with Cain and with devils, see the monograph by O. F. Emerson, "Legends of Cain . . .

in Old and Middle English," *Publications of the Modern Language Association of America*, xxi, 831–929. The derivations of the name Grendel are reviewed by Chambers, *Introduction*, pp. 304 ff., where the passages from the charters are given. On etymologies of "Beowulf" and "Grendel," see Klaeber, pp. xxvii f.

4. The charming edition of *Perrault's Popular Tales* by Andrew Lang, Oxford, 1888, has elaborate introductory material. Grimm's *Household Tales* are conveniently read in English in the translation by M. Hunt, with the notes, and with an introduction by Andrew Lang, 2 vols., London, 1913–1915.

5. See M. R. Cox, *Cinderella*, published for the Folk-Lore Society, London, 1892; G. L. Kittredge, *A Study of Gawain and the Green Knight*, Cambridge (Mass.), 1916, and "Arthur and Gorlagon," *Harvard Studies and Notes* (1903), viii, 149–275; A. C. L. Brown, "Iwain: A Study in the Origins of Arthurian Romance," in the same volume of the *Harvard Studies and Notes;* G. H. Maynadier, *The Wife of Bath's Tale*, London, 1901. For studies in Shakespeare by the present writer, see *Shakesperian Studies* (N. Y., 1916), pp. 187–211; *Publications of the Modern Language Association of America*, xxvii, 391–431 (New Series), xxxvii, 418–469.

6. F. Panzer, *Studien zur germanischen Sagengeschichte, I: Beowulf*, Munich, 1910. The conclusions in regard to literary relationships in the latter part of this work are sometimes open to question.

7. *þā wæs hwīl dæges, ær hē þone grund-wong ongytan mehte* (1495, 1496). Klaeber refers to line 1600, where the blood appears in the water at *nōn dæges*, the ninth hour, about 3 P.M., and consequently favors translating "a good part of the day." So Chambers, following Earle. But the epic is not consistent in such details, and I prefer the simpler and more vigorous figure.

8. The best edition of the saga is that by P.. C. Boer, Halle, 1900. There is an inexpensive translation in the Everyman's Library. Boer's *Altenglische Heldendichtung, I: Beowulf*, Halle, 1912, may be consulted also. While much of the book

should be taken with reserve, the remarks on the literary relationships of the saga are valuable. The distance in fathoms from the top of the cliff to the water, in the passage just quoted, differs in different MSS.

9. What follows is discussed in much fuller form in my article, "The Haunted Mere in Beowulf." See Bibliography above. On the meaning of words used in Anglo-Saxon descriptions of nature, see L. L. Schücking, *Untersuchungen zur Bedeutungslehre der angelsächsischen Dichtersprache*, Heidelberg, 1915.

10. On the *nøkken* and his music, see the Munch–Olsen *Norse Mythology*, p. 311 of the English translation.

11. The following passage from Sir W. T. Grenfell's *Labrador: the Country and the People* (N. Y., 1922), p. 434, is worth noting. "On one occasion a trapper on his fur path found a convenient hole into a cave under a cliff. He crept in, lighted a small lantern which he carried, and, after having his supper, lay down to sleep. In the night a noise, as of some visitor, awakened him, and he turned up his lantern to find a large bear, standing as high as the roof. He promptly shot the bear and got outside, where, by waiting, he got two others." In connection with the commonly accepted etymology of Beowulf as "bee-wolf," the following also is of interest. "Their fondness for sweets, and especially molasses, occasionally gets them into trouble. One time a trapper hauled over two hundred dollars' worth of food to one of the huts on his fur path. When he came back he found a big hole through the roof and most of his food spoilt. He nailed up the hole twice as strong and headed up the barrel of molasses. On his next visit he found that bears had again got in, broken the top of his barrel, and eaten all his molasses."

12. The saga is accessible in print, so far as my knowledge extends, only in two forms: the *Nordiska Kämpa Dater* of Erik Julius Björner, a folio printed in Stockholm in 1737, in which the text is accompanied by paraphrases in Latin and in Swedish; and *Samson Fríði og Kvintalin Kvennaþjófur, Riddarasaga*, Reikjavik, 1905, a small and cheap print, with no indications of MS. or editor, which looks as if it had been

struck off to meet a local demand for good old native stories. An outline of the saga is given by Jónsson, *Den Oldnorske og Oldislandske Litteraturs Historie* (Copenhagen, 1902, etc.), iii, 108. The saga has never been translated into German or English to my knowledge. I am publishing elsewhere a more detailed examination of the significant passages for *Beowulf*, with the text and translation of those passages. Since the saga is very little known, I am here reprinting from the Icelandic the account of the fight between Samson and the she-troll (pp. 14, 15, of the Reikjavik text).

"Meðan þeir ræða þetta, stóð Samson á fossbrúninni; veit hann ei fyr en tekið er um báða fætur hans og honum kipt ofan í fossinn. Er það tröllkona afarmikil, er hann brestur karlsmensku á við; sviftast þau um fast og lengi og berast niður að grunni — verður honum það til lífs að hann verður ofan á henni er þau kenna botns, og nær því fljótt til hnífs er hann bar í belti sínu og Valentina hafði gefið honum, rekkur hann hnífinn í kvið henni svo út fara öll inníflin. Hann kafar undir fossinn, er hann er laus úr faðmlögum skessunnar, og finnur brátt hellismunna, en svo er hann þrotinn að kröftum að hann verður að láta þar fyrir berast góða stund. Er hann var kominn svo til sjálfs sín eftir volk þetta, vindur hann klæði sín og gengur í hellirinn, og hugði að hann mundi aldrei þaðan komast. Hann gengur lengi eptir hellinum, og undrast stærð hans og lögun, en um síðir kemur hann að afhelli nokkrum, og finnur þar allskonar varnað, dýra gripi, gull og silfur. Sæng var þar með forkunnarfögru fortjaldi fyrir, að sama skapi voru rekkuklæði öll, þar í hellinum finnur hann kyrtil og möttul Valentínu kóngsdóttur, einnig hennar djásn og mittisband. Tekur hann af þessum hlutum það sem hann girnist og gengur því næst hellirinn á enda, finna hann loks stóra hurð, er hnigin var á klofa, en ólæst, og er hann hefur fengið opnað hana með erfiði miklu, því hún var afarþung, sjer hann framundan sér skóg mikinn og fagran."

13. *English and Scottish Popular Ballads* (Boston and N. Y., 1882–1898), i, 50. Professor Child's discussion of "Lady Isabel and the Elf-Knight" and its analogues is important for the story of Samson the Fair.

14. The Icelandic text of the *Þáttr Orms Stórólfssonar* is printed by Chambers, *Introduction*, p. 186, with translation (brief comments, pp. 53 ff.). See also H. Gering, *Anglia*, iii, 74–87, and Boer's study of *Beowulf* (cf. note 8 to this chapter), pp. 175 ff. Boer had earlier shown the dependence of the *þáttr* on the *Grettissaga*, and here reviews the matter.

15. Icelandic text of the *Hrólfssaga* (ed. Jónsson, Copenhagen, 1904), chap. 23, pp. 65 ff.; reprinted by Chambers, *Introduction*, pp. 138 ff., with translation; also selections from the *rímur*, which are printed in Jónsson's edition, with translation into English, Chambers, pp. 182 ff. (discussion, pp. 54–61). Relationship between the saga and *Beowulf* was denied by Olrik, *Heltedigtning*, i, 134–137, *Heroic Legends*, pp. 247–251. He was followed in this by O. L. Olson, "The Relation of the Hrólfs Saga Kraka and the Bjarkarímur to Beowulf," *Publications of the Society for the Advancement of Scandinavian Study*, Urbana, 1916. Olrik, in a note to the English translation of the *Heltedigtning*, says, "I am not convinced that he [Olson] has found the final solution of this problem." I do not think that it is possible to reach results as definite as Olson's; too little evidence has been preserved. Most scholars take the view that some connection with the *Beowulf* story (and this does not necessarily mean the Anglo-Saxon epic) exists; see Chambers, *Introduction*, p. 61. Panzer discusses the question from the point of view of folk-tales, pp. 364–386. See also Klaeber, p. xviii note. I have reviewed the matter at length in "Some Disputed Questions," pp. 237 ff. I was then inclined to assume influence of the Beowulf legends upon the saga alone. I now feel, however, that one can see their effect also upon Saxo, particularly in the name "Bjarke" and the setting at the court of King Rolf, and upon the *rímur*, which preserve the recollection of Bjarki's assistance to Athils on the ice of Lake Wener. The exact relationships are probably not to be traced with any certainty.

16. The Latin text of Saxo is printed by Chambers, *Introduction*, pp. 132 ff. I quote from the translation by Elton and Powell (see Bibliography), pp. 69, 80.

CHAPTER VII

1. *The Historie of Serpents, or the Seconde Booke of Living Creatures*, London, 1608. Topsell had published his *Historie of Foure-footed Beastes* in 1607. In 1658 the two books were reissued in two volumes, with the addition of the *Theatre of Insects* by Thomas Moffett. The quotation is on page 701 of the edition of 1658.

2. Panzer tried to arrange the dragon material schematically, but admits that it shows a mixture of types (p. 309), with features not found elsewhere. His conclusions in regard to the deposition of the treasure seem to me to need correction; the discussion in the present chapter will make this clear.

3. Panzer thinks that the addition of the dragon-story to the Bear's Son tale was suggested by the combats of the hero, in certain versions, with a dragon or dragons, while in the underworld (p. 293). But the *Beowulf* dragon-fight shows no resemblances to those versions, as he acknowledges, and the whole adventure falls in Beowulf's old age, long years after the Grendel-fights. An attempt was made by Sievers, whose opinion is always of great weight, to connect the *Beowulf* dragon-contest with that of Frotho, in the second book of Saxo Grammaticus. (See chapter V, note 8.) He regarded the exploits of Beowulf the Geat as originally told of Beowulf the Dane, the son of Scyld, whom he identified with the Frotho of Saxo. Danish tradition makes Frotho the son of Sciold (Scyld) and gives him a son, Haldanus (Healfdene). The weakness of the underlying hypothesis has already been pointed out in chapter V. And when we consider that the resemblances between the two fights are really slight, the commonplaces of such tales, the whole theory of Sievers appears highly questionable. Olrik has shown the fundamental differences; one tale presents a victorious young hero, the other an aged champion defending his people. He is supported by Chambers, who argues against the parallel at length, and with convincing logic (*Introduction*, pp. 92–97,

with references). Klaeber seems to think there is something in Sievers's position, although he frankly admits that "in some respects the other dragon-fight told in the *Beowulf*, that of Sigemund (884 ff.), exhibits a closer affinity to Saxo's Frotho parallel." The Beowulf and Sigemund contests are alike in that the dragon is killed in a stone lair, by a blow from a sword, that treasure is gained, and that the monster is burned in his own fires. They are unlike in that Sigemund was alone, that the sword stuck in the wall as he pierced the beast, and that he loaded the treasure in a boat. Sigemund's contest may again be compared with the well-known accounts of his son Sigurd or Siegfried, the slayer of Fafnir. The theory that the exploit of the son was transferred to the father appears unlikely; see Neckel, "Sigmund's Drachenkampf," *Edda*, xiii, 122–140, 204–229. It is stated in the *Poetic Edda* that Sigmund was invulnerable to poison, which was probably the result of his encounter with a dragon spewing venom. It would appear that the exploit of the father was in course of time transferred to the son, a conclusion reached by von Sydow, *Lund Univ. Årsskrift*, N. F. Avd. I, xiv, "Sigurds Strid med Fåvne" (1918). When all is said and done, however, definite conclusions in regard to the literary relationships of dragon-fights must be regarded as very difficult of attainment. See further, Klaeber, *Anglia*, l, 238 ff.

4. See chapter VI, note 3, and cf. p. 882 of Professor Emerson's monograph.

5. B. C. Williams, *Gnomic Poetry in Anglo-Saxon* (N. Y., 1914), pp. 127, 128.

6. For discussion of the dragon's barrow, the deposition of the gold in the earth, and the plundering of the hoard, see my article on "The Dragon and his Lair in *Beowulf*." Further references to this will not be given here, except in special cases.

7. O. Montelius, *Civilization of Sweden in Heathen Times*, transl. by F. H. Woods (London, 1888), p. 32.

8. For detailed discussion of this passage, see the article referred to in note 6, pp. 561 ff.; Klaeber, edition, p. 214,

where further bibliography is given, also *Anglia*, l, 221 f.; Hubbard, cf. note 12, below.

9. Most critics prefer to translate the second member of *gold-hwæt*, "greedy for," "eager for," which I adopt, though I do not feel sure that this is the exact meaning.

10. *Dania*, i, 558.

11. Especially Bugge and Panzer; see references in my article (cf. note 6, above), p. 558.

12. F. G. Hubbard, "The Plundering of the Hoard in Beowulf," *University of Wisconsin Studies in Language and Literature*, xi (1921), esp. 8 ff. For some methods of argument employed in this article, and the conclusions reached, see *Journal of English and Germanic Philology* (1924), xxiii, 299 note. Whether the slave stole a cup alone, or rings as well, it is difficult to determine. As I noted in my article, "there is not enough direct evidence to furnish details." The poet is not always consistent in small matters, in this episode or elsewhere. Klaeber, who adopts the conjectural reading *þ(ēow)*, "slave," l. 2223, in his edition, says (*Anglia*, l, 214): "It is true, as Lawrence observes, that his own reading of the story is more in harmony with the general standard of life pictured in the poem. But it is also true that the man in question is a very peculiar person, who seems to stand apart from the noble society of courtiers." Why is he a peculiar person? Of course he stands apart from the noble society of courtiers, since he has committed a grave crime, in stealing from the hoard of the dragon, which has brought great distress upon the land, and since he is a prisoner.

13. See the critical translation of the *Mabinogion* into French by J. Loth, 2 vols., Paris, 1913, and the edition of Lady Guest's translation into English by Alfred Nutt, London, 1902. The latter rearranges the material according to literary types, and provides a suggestive commentary.

14. Panzer, p. 298.

15. The characteristic understatement in the Anglo-Saxon text must not be misunderstood.

16. *Jordanis*, ed. Alfred Holder (Freiburg and Tübingen, 1882), xlix, 57–59.

17. The whole matter is reviewed by Klaeber, *Publications of the Modern Language Association of America* (1927), xlii, 255 ff. He thinks that funeral games, taking the form of remarkable feats and equestrian exhibitions, are to be inferred, if I understand him, from the sentence: "Nam de tota gente Hunorum lectissimi equites in eum locum, quo erat positus, *in modum circensium cursibus ambientes,* facta eius canto funereo tali ordine referebant." But surely all that the italicized words mean is that the men moved about the body in the fashion of riders at the circus, that is, in repeated circles. It will be noticed that the *strava* described farther on in the text appears to have been a joyous celebration, contrasting with the lamentations of the riders. Most writers have seen in the descriptions of Jordanes a reflection of Gothic customs; Schröder, *Zeitschrift für deutsches Althertum,* lix, 240 ff., thinks them almost purely Hunnish.

18. On the significance of the funeral in *Beowulf,* and analogous descriptions elsewhere, see Chadwick, *Heroic Age* (references *sub* "cremation"); Chambers, *Introduction,* pp. 121–128; Klaeber, *Anglia,* xxxvi; Schücking, *Englische Studien,* xxxix, 1 ff. On the subject of early burials in general, see article, "Totenbestattung," in Hoops's *Reallexicon.*

19. Translations from the version by Butcher and Lang (N. Y., 1893), pp. 192, 390. Cf. the note on Burial, p. 424.

20. R. Koegel, *Geschichte der deutschen Litteratur* (Strassburg, 1894), p. 48.

21. Lines 1322–1329. I have not indicated the restorations in the text.

22. See the article by Schücking (note 18, above), p. 13.

23. Klaeber, edition, p. 217. The references on this page will be noted.

CHAPTER VIII

1. See Heusler in Hoops's *Reallexikon,* ii, 490.

2. Chambers, *Introduction,* pp. 102 f. Chambers was referring specifically to the proper names mentioned by Sarrazin in his arguments for the Scandinavian origin of the poem, but his statement need not be so limited; see Brandl

(cf. introductory bibliography in this volume), pp. 1000 f., who, in speaking of the fortunes of the story on English soil, observes: "In any case the assumption must be given up that the recollection of the affairs of the Danes and the Geatas of the early sixth century had always been lacking, or had been forgotten [*verloren*], before the composition of the epic, and then had reached the epic poet through a foreign source, as, for example, a Scandinavian minstrel. For the proper names in this connection have passed regularly through all the linguistic changes of Anglo-Saxon in the sixth and seventh centuries." This is a point that is not sufficiently considered by those who would set the transplantation of the Beowulf story to England late, as Schück (*Studier i Beowulfsagan* [Upsala, 1909], pp. 41 ff.), Wessén (*De Nordiska Folkstammarna i Beowulf*, p. 82). Schück lays stress on Beowulf's long reign of fifty years, which, added to the date of Hygelac's death in 516, and the short reign of Heardred, and with allowance for the development of the legends on Scandinavian soil, would set the date of the possible transference to England of the completed story about A.D. 600, "a hundred years after the end of the Saxon invasion." This is not at all convincing to me. The fifty-year reign of Beowulf is not historic fact, but fiction (which Schück recognizes, but minimizes); the tendency in story-telling would be to exaggerate the length of a glorious and peaceful reign; the fifty years may be a purely arbitrary number, due to the Anglo-Saxon poet, like the fifty feet of the dragon's length. The Saxon invasion of Britain cannot have ceased by A.D. 500 (Wessén puts this fifty years later), and there certainly must have been sufficient intercourse with the Continent to have made it possible for a singer to bring over the material even after colonizing had ceased.

3. See Leach, *Angevin Britain*, p. 3.
4. Oman, p. 218.
5. *Das Altenglische Volksepos* (Kiel, 1883), vol. i.
6. Chambers, *Introduction*, pp. 98–104.
7. Edition, p. cxviii.
8. Klaeber, *ibid.*

9. *Beowulf. Untersuchungen (Quellen und Forschungen*, vol. lxii), Strassburg, 1888.

10. Brandl (*loc. cit.*, p. 991) suggests as date "um 700"; Schücking, (ed. 1910), p. 95, following Morsbach, 700-730; Chambers (*Introduction*, pp. 104-112, 329), after discussion of tests, does not commit himself further than to say, "The age of Bede"; cf. also his foreword to Strong's translation, p. viii); Sedgefield (second edition), p. xliii: "The poem may have been composed as early as the middle of the seventh century, but was written down perhaps some fifty years later, with some few interpolations and alterations"—a statement certainly open to challenge; Holthausen, ii, xviii: "probably in the first half of the eighth century"; Klaeber, edition, p. cxvi: "the first half of the eighth century, perhaps not far from the middle of it."

11. *Introduction*, pp. 121 ff, 322 ff.

12. Neilson and Thorndike, *Facts about Shakespeare* (N. Y., 1913), p. 70.

13. Klaeber, edition, pp. cx ff., esp. cxv, cxvi; cp. the remarks of Blackburn, *Exodus and Daniel* (Boston, 1907), p. xxiii.

14. By Chadwick, whose position is stated and fully discussed by Hoops, in his *Reallexikon*, article "Angelsachsen," pp. 91 ff.   Hoops disagrees.

15. Hoops, *Ibid.*

16. C. J. B. Gaskoin, *Alcuin* (London, 1904), pp. 6 ff.

17. E. Maunde Thompson, *Handbook of Greek and Latin Palæography* (London, 1906), pp. 244 ff.

18. See in general, Klaeber, edition, xx, and especially von Sydow, *Anzeiger für deutsches Altertum*, xxxv, 129. Dr. von Sydow writes me that he has conclusive evidence, not yet published, of the derivation of the plot of *Beowulf* from Celtic.

19. "The Possible Begetter of the Old English *Beowulf* and *Widsith*," in *Transactions of the Connecticut Academy of Arts and Sciences* (April, 1922), xxv, 281-346.

20. See chapter II, note 7. The Offa-episode has been repeatedly discussed; see, for references and comment, Klaeber,

edition, pp. 187 ff., and Chambers, *Introduction*, pp. 31–40; also Cook, *loc. cit.*, pp. 312 ff.

21. See A. F. West, *Alcuin* (N. Y., 1912), p. 34.

22. See chapter VII, note 23.

23. The best discussions of this whole subject are by Chambers, *Introduction*, pp. 121–128, and Klaeber, *Anglia*, xxxv, (1911), 111–136, 249–270, 453–482; xxxvi (1912), 169–199. Further references in Klaeber, edition, p. cxl. Earlier writers generally underestimated the depth of Christian influence; see the excellent study by Hart, *Ballad and Epic*, pp. 174, 175.

24. Jiriczek, *Deutsche Heldensage* (1913), p. 123.

25. Brandl, *loc. cit.*, pp. 987, 988.

26. See the analysis by Hart, *Ballad and Epic*.

27. *Heroic Age*, pp. 73–76. Professor Chadwick's argument should be read in full; it is difficult to do it full justice in a brief summary.

28. "Verba dei legantur in sacerdotali convivio. Ibi decet lectorem audiri, non citharistam; sermones patrum, non carmina gentilium. Quid Hinieldus cum Christo? Angusta est domus: utrosque tenere non poterit. Non vult rex caelestis cum paganis et perditis nominetenus regibus communionem habere; quia rex ille aeternus regnat in caelis, ille paganus perditus plangit in inferno. Voces legentium audire in domibus tuis, non ridentium turbam in plateis." (Letter to Hygbald, Bishop of Lindisfarne, 797, reprinted by Förster, *Materialien.*)

APPENDICES

A

ANALYSIS OF THE EPIC

THE following outline aims to show the main events of
the action, and the chief episodes and digressions, in the
order in which they appear in the epic. A connected
account, in chronological sequence, of the histories of
the Geat and Danish and Swedish royal houses will be
found in chapter III; an analysis of the Tale of Finnsburg, as found in the *Episode* in the epic and in the
Finnsburg Fragment, in chapter IV. The proportion of
the principal episodic material, here printed in smaller
type, to the main narrative, may be readily observed;
the greater extent of the digressions in the Dragon Adventure will be noted. The account of the swimming
feat with Breca has not been arranged as episodic, since
it is a part of the main narrative of Beowulf's reception
by Hrothgar, and not a pure digression, like the tales of
the Swedish wars or the Finnsburg feud.

It should be understood that the ordering of the material as Prologue, First and Second Adventures, Interlude, and Third Adventure is purely arbitrary, for convenience in analysis. There is no evidence that such
divisions were felt by the poet. The Prologue may be
held to end with line 52 (instead of line 63), the next
sentence introducing Hrothgar and the line of historic
kings. This is borne out by the Roman numeral marking the first section of the MS. The story proper really
begins, however, with the reign of Hrothgar, and the
building of the mead-hall, lines 64 ff.

The remarks in parentheses are intended as guidance
to an understanding of the story, though they are not in
the text, or not at the point where the remark occurs.

Prologue

The glory of the Danish kings, and especially of Scyld Scefing, founder of the Scylding dynasty. His sea-burial. His descendants: Beowulf the Dane (not the hero of the poem); Healfdene and his children.

First Adventure: The Fight with Grendel

Hrothgar, son of Healfdene, builds the mead-hall Heorot. The joy and revelry therein anger Grendel, a demon, of the brood of Cain, who attacks the hall at night, kills thirty thanes, and escapes to his lair. He makes a second onslaught on the following night. In consequence of his continued depredations, the hall stands empty for twelve years. Nothing avails; the best of counsels, even desperate prayers to heathen gods, are in vain. (Lines 64–193.)

Beowulf, nephew of Hygelac, king of the Geatas, determines to slay the monster, and sails with fourteen companions to the court of Hrothgar. After a parley with the coast guard, in which the purpose of the visit is explained, the Geatas arrive at Heorot, and Beowulf asks of Wulfgar, chief of the Wendlas, an audience with the king. Hrothgar recalls Beowulf's father Ecgtheow, and foresees that the hero has come to offer aid against Grendel. The Geatas are immediately admitted. Beowulf, mentioning his past exploits against sea-monsters, asks permission to purify the hall. Hrothgar recalls a feud which he composed in which Beowulf's father was concerned, and describes the ravages of Grendel. (Lines 194–490.)

A ceremonial banquet is held. An unfortunate incident interrupts the feasting: Unferth, Hrothgar's chief counsellor, insults Beowulf, asserting that he showed less endurance in a swimming-match than Breca of the Brondingas, and prophesies a disastrous outcome in the approaching encounter with Grendel. Beowulf gives the true facts of the case: it was not a swimming-match, but the mutual fulfilment of a boast, to venture in swimming upon the icy sea of winter. He had no wish to outstrip Breca; stormy weather parted them; Beowulf himself displayed unmatched heroism and endurance in contests with sea-monsters. The hero reiterates his resolve to meet Grendel without delay. Wealhtheow, queen of Hrothgar, offers the mead-cup to Beowulf, who again promises to slay the monster or die in the attempt. (Lines 491–641.)

Hrothgar and his court retire for the night; Beowulf and his thanes remain in the hall. The hero watches, while the rest sleep. Grendel approaches over the moors, bursts into the hall, seizes a sleeping thane (Hondscio), and devours him on the spot. He then clutches Beowulf, who grapples with him. A long struggle ensues; the swords of the Geatas are powerless, but at length Beowulf (who has the strength of thirty men in his grasp) tears off the demon's arm. Wounded to death, Grendel flees to his lair in the forest. (Lines 642–836.)

In the morning, the warriors follow Grendel's footprints to the Haunted Mere, all stained with blood, into which he has escaped.

On the way back to Heorot, a thane improvises a lay in honor of Beowulf, comparing him with Sigemund the dragon-slayer, and contrasting him with Heremod, an early Danish king distinguished for violence and cruelty.

The king, queen, and court visit the hall. Hrothgar formally thanks Beowulf, who makes a fitting reply. The arm of Grendel is affixed to the gable; the hall is decorated, and a banquet is held, at which rich gifts are bestowed upon Beowulf and his warriors. (Lines 837–1062.)

Hrothgar's minstrel entertains the company with a story of Danish valor, the Tale of Finnsburg. A paraphrase of his lay, or of the situation on which his lay was based, is given by the poet.

Hnæf, prince of the [Half-]Danes, was doomed to fall in a bloody contest in Friesland. (This contest is described in the *Finnsburg Fragment*, which relates how Hnæf and his Danes, quartered by themselves in a hall, were treacherously attacked at Finnsburg [by followers of King Finn]. The struggle lasted five days; the Danes successfully defended the hall.) Hildeburg, sister of Hnæf, and queen of Finn, was thus forced to mourn the loss of kin by blood and by marriage. After both parties had fought to a standstill, Finn made a truce with Hengest, leader of the Danes after the death of Hnæf: the Danes were to become Finn's men, but were to enjoy equal privileges with the Frisians, a hall of their own, an equal share in gifts, and were never to be taunted as followers of the man responsible for the death of their lord. The dead of both parties were burnt on a huge funeral pyre. Hengest stayed quietly with Finn through the winter, but in the spring was roused to vengeance; Finn and his men were attacked, Finn was slain, his treasures plundered, and his queen carried back in triumph to the land of the Danes. (Lines 1063–1159.)

More presents are bestowed. Queen Wealhtheow asks Beowulf to aid her sons, Hrethric and Hrothmund, should need arise, and emphasizes the friendship of Hrothulf, their cousin. The court retires for the night. The Danes occupy the hall; Beowulf is quartered elsewhere. (Lines 1159–1250.)

Second Adventure: The Fight with Grendel's Dam

During the night Grendel's mother comes to Heorot to avenge his death. She seizes a Danish warrior (Æschere) and, amid the confusion in the hall, escapes to her lair, carrying with her Grendel's arm. At dawn Beowulf is summoned, and told by Hrothgar of the death of Æschere. Hrothgar describes the Haunted Mere where the monsters dwell: a pool surrounded by trees, into which a waterfall breaks, in high and rocky land — an uncanny spot. He looks to Beowulf for deliverance from this new enemy and promises him rich rewards. Beowulf accepts the task, and proposes an immediate start. With a band of warriors, both Danes and Geatas, they make their way to the Haunted Mere. Here they find the head of Æschere. Beowulf kills one of the water-monsters in the pool. Unferth loans Beowulf the sword Hrunting. Beowulf commends his thanes to Hrothgar's care, and directs that the gifts received be sent to Hygelac in case he perishes in the undertaking, as he will if need be. (Lines 1251–1491.)

Beowulf dives into the mere; is seized by the she-demon, and borne to her cave (under the waterfall). Beowulf cannot wound her with a sword; he trusts to the strength of his grip; she throws him down and is about to stab him, when he regains his feet. Seeing an old sword of giant workmanship, he grasps it and slays the demon with it. He then cuts off the head of Grendel, who lies dead in the cavern. The warriors watching above see blood in the water, and conclude that Beowulf has been slain. The Danes return home; the companions of Beowulf remain. The giant sword melts in the demon's blood; Beowulf carries the golden hilt and the head of Grendel through the water to the surface of the pool. (Lines 1492–1625.)

The Geatas, bearing Grendel's head, return to Heorot. Beowulf tells Hrothgar briefly of his adventure, assures him that he may now enjoy tranquillity, and presents him with the hilt of the giant sword. Hrothgar, in a long speech of congratulation, contrasts the renown of Beowulf with the evil reputation of Heremod (see lines 901 ff.), and warns Beowulf of the dangers of pride and worldly success. On the following morning, the Geatas prepare to return to their own land. Beowulf pledges assistance to Hrothgar in future, should he need it, and promises Hrethric a cordial welcome, if he should visit the Geatas. Hrothgar, in reply, emphasizes the friendly relations between the two peoples. Presents are bestowed, and the Geatas leave Heorot. (Lines 1626–1887.)

INTERLUDE: THE RETURN AND NARRATIVE TO HYGELAC

Beowulf and his companions set sail, and in due time arrive in the domains of Hygelac. (Lines 1888–1924.)

The queen, Hygd, is complimented by contrasting her with Thryth, queen of Offa, king of the Angles.

Thryth was of so violent a temper that she became unbearable to live with. But when she was given in marriage to Offa, her shrewishness was completely subdued. (Lines 1925–1962.)

Beowulf is immediately introduced into the presence of Hygelac, and tells of his adventures in the land of the Danes. He recalls the princess Freawaru, the daughter of Hrothgar, betrothed to Ingeld, prince of the Heathobards, forecasting the probable course of events following their union.

Hrothgar hopes by this match to end the ancient feud between Danes and Heathobards. But such hopes are seldom realized. After Freawaru is married, and living at the Heathobard court, one of her retainers will wear a sword taken from a Heathobard chieftain in the late wars. Then an old Heathobard warrior will incite to vengeance the son of the former owner of the sword, who will slay the bride's thane who has had the imprudence to wear it, yet escape, since he knows the land well. Then the love of Ingeld for his bride will cool, and strife between the two peoples break out afresh. (Lines 1963–2069.)

Beowulf then narrates his contests with Grendel and Grendel's dam, and gives to Hygelac the presents received from Hrothgar, in particular the war-gear of Hrothgar's elder brother, Heorogar. To Queen Hygd he gives a necklace bestowed upon him by Queen Wealhtheow, and three horses. The poet recalls that Beowulf was little esteemed in his boyhood. Hygelac presents Beowulf with a precious sword, seven thousand (hides of land), and a hall and high-seat of his own. (Lines 2070–2199.)

THIRD ADVENTURE: THE FIGHT WITH THE DRAGON; BEOWULF'S DEATH

After the death of Hygelac, and of Heardred his son, Beowulf becomes king of the Geatas. He rules over them for fifty years, when a dragon, which has guarded treasure in a grave-mound on a height (for three hundred years), attacks his people, to avenge the plundering of the hoard. For a man, a fugitive from the court, stole a precious cup. An account of the early history of the treasure is given; it had been placed in the earth by a solitary man, the sole survivor of a noble race. His lyrical lament is given by the poet. (Lines 2200–2270.)

The dragon, whose nature it is to guard treasure, had found the hoard, and thenceforth had brooded over it as guardian. The thief bore the precious cup to his lord (probably Beowulf), and obtained with it the boon which he desired. When evening came, the dragon rained down fire upon the countryside, returning to his lair before daybreak. Beowulf now prepares to do battle against the monster, and provides himself with an iron shield. His end is foreshadowed. (Lines 2270–2349.)

The poet digresses to mention the cleansing of Hrothgar's hall, and events in the history of the Geatas in which Beowulf has figured; he escaped by swimming after the disastrous expedition in which Hygelac lost his life. Queen Hygd then offered him the crown, but he preferred to act as regent for Heardred. The sons of Ohthere, who had rebelled against their uncle, the Swedish king (Onela), took refuge at the court of Heardred; Onela invaded the land of the Geatas and slew Heardred, but allowed Beowulf to succeed to the throne. Later Beowulf aided Eadgils in an expedition against Onela, in which the latter was slain. (Lines 2349–2400.)

With eleven warriors, Beowulf sets out to meet the dragon. He has learned the cause of the dragon's ravages. The thief acts as guide to the dragon's barrow, — much against his will! (Lines 2401–2424.)

Beowulf, addressing his companions, recalls his youthful days at the court of King Hrethel. Herebeald, the elder of Hrethel's sons, was acccidentally slain by his brother Hæthcyn. The tragic grief of Hrethel ultimately brought about his death. The wars with the Swedes are mentioned. The sons of (the Swedish king) Ongentheow, (Onela and Ohthere), invaded the land of the Geatas and slew Hæthcyn, but Ongentheow himself was killed by Eofor (a Geat warrior). (Cf. lines 2922–2998.) Beowulf recalls his own services to Hygelac; he slew

Dæghrefn (apparently the man who killed Hygelac). (Lines 2425-2509.)

Beowulf says farewell to his companions, and announces his resolve to win the dragon gold, or to die in the attempt. (Lines 2510-2537.)

Beowulf advances to the mound; the dragon comes forth. The hero strikes with his sword, but without effect; the dragon belches forth fire and flame. Beowulf's companions have withdrawn to a wood near by. But his young kinsman Wiglaf comes to his assistance, after reproaching the warriors for their cowardice. Wiglaf's wooden shield is consumed; he takes refuge behind Beowulf's iron shield. Beowulf strikes at the monster again, but his sword Nægling breaks. The dragon buries his fangs in Beowulf's neck. Wiglaf then inflicts a mortal wound, and Beowulf, drawing his short sword, cuts the dragon in two. The poison in the wound is taking effect, however, and realizing that death is not far distant, Beowulf asks to look at the treasure. Wiglaf enters the mound, and returns with an armful of the gold. Revived with water, Beowulf gives directions that a barrow be erected on the Whale's Ness after his body has been burned, bestows his neck-ornament, helmet, and corselet upon Wiglaf, and dies. (Lines 2538-2820.)

Wiglaf bitterly reproaches the cowardly thanes, and prophesies their disgrace when their conduct becomes known. A messenger is sent to bear the news of Beowulf's death to his people. (Lines 2821-2899.)

The messenger prophesies hostilities on the part of the Franks and Frisians, and also of the Swedes. He recalls incidents of the wars with the Swedes: Ongentheow slew Hæthcyn, son of Hrethel, and rescued his queen, whom Hæthcyn had captured, pursuing the Geatas into Ravenswood, where Hygelac came to their rescue. Ongentheow was attacked by Wulf, and slain by Wulf's brother Eofor. The latter was in reward given Hygelac's daughter in marriage. With all this in mind, the Swedes will not be slow in attacking, when they hear of Beowulf's death. The messenger advises immediate preparations for the funeral; the dragon's gold is to be placed on the pyre; no fair maid or warrior shall wear it, but exile and sorrow shall be their portion in days to come. (Lines 2900–3027.)

The Geat warriors go to the spot where Beowulf and the dragon lie in death, with the treasure beside them. A second version of the deposition of the gold in the earth is given (cf. lines 2231–2270); illustrious chieftains placed it there in days of yore, protecting it by a curse upon the man who should disturb it. Wiglaf describes how he brought out the gold for Beowulf to look upon in his last hour, and how the hero gave commands for the building of his funeral pyre. With seven thanes, Wiglaf penetrates again into the dragon's mound, and carries out the treasure. This is laden on a wain, and brought, with the body of Beowulf, to the Whale's Ness. The dragon is shoved off the cliff into the sea. (Lines 3028–3136.)

The Geatas build a huge funeral pyre, adorned with armor, and lay the hero upon it. The flames arise amid the lamentations of the people, and the weeping of Beowulf's widow (?). The embers are surrounded by a high mound, in which is deposited the (dragon's) treasure. Twelve noble warriors ride solemnly about the mound, extolling Beowulf's virtues and mourning his death. (Lines 3137–3182.)

B

GENEALOGICAL TABLES

THE DANISH ROYAL HOUSE

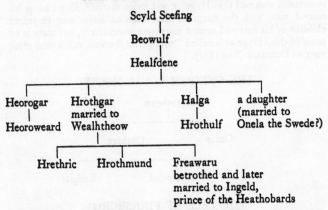

Scyld Scefing

Beowulf

Healfdene

| Heorogar | Hrothgar married to Wealhtheow | | Halga | a daughter (married to Onela the Swede?) |

Heoroweard

Hrothulf

Hrethric   Hrothmund   Freawaru
betrothed and later
married to Ingeld,
prince of the Heathobards

Scyld Scefing and Beowulf are mythical progenitors; Beowulf is probably an error for Beowa or a similar name, by confusion with Beowulf the Geat, the hero of the poem. The historical line begins with Healfdene or with his sons; he himself, as his name suggests, is perhaps an imaginary figure.

THE GEAT ROYAL HOUSE

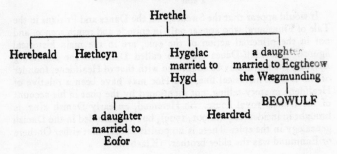

Hrethel

Herebeald   Hæthcyn   Hygelac
married to
Hygd

a daughter
married to Ecgtheow
the Wægmunding

BEOWULF

a daughter
married to
Eofor

Heardred

No mythical progenitors of Hrethel are given. A certain Swerting is mentioned (line 1203), who may be regarded as Hrethel's uncle or grandfather. The table probably reflects historic tradition, with the exception of Beowulf, and possibly of his parents. It will be noted that both the Geat and Danish lines include, in the principal generation, an unnamed daughter, who does not appear in the action. It is sometimes assumed that Hygelac was twice married, Hygd being his second wife, and the daughter who married Eofor and Heardred children of his first and second marriages respectively, but there is no proof of this. Hygelac is called "young" by Beowulf at the time of his visit to Denmark (line 1831).

THE SWEDISH ROYAL HOUSE

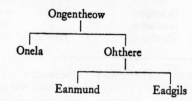

THE TALE OF FINNSBURG

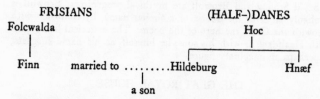

It would appear that the Swedes, and the Danes and Frisians in the Tale of Finnsburg, who appear only in episode and reminiscence, and not in the principal action of the epic, are in the main historical figures. The Half-Danes are also called Danes in the *Finnsburg Episode;* the name may be connected with that of Healfdene, founder of the Danish historical line; and Hoc may have been a relative of Healfdene in story-telling, not mentioned by the poet in his account of the Danish royal house. So Heremod, an early Danish king, is brought in incidentally (ll. 901, 1709), but not included in the Danish genealogy in the epic. There is no positive proof that either Ohthere or Eanmund was the elder brother. (Klaeber.)

INDEX

INDEX

References are here given to personages and incidents in the epic, and to the more important illustrative material and authorities in the text and notes preceding. The principal topics discussed are grouped under *Beowulf, epic*. All the occurrences of important and frequently recurring names, such as *Danes, Hygelac, Chambers, Klaeber*, etc., are not listed.